Social Problems

Recent Sociology Titles from W. W. Norton

The Contexts Reader, Third Edition, edited by Syed Ali and
Philip N. Cohen

In the Trenches: Teaching and Learning Sociology by Maxine P.
Atkinson and Kathleen S. Lowney

The Art and Science of Social Research by Deborah Carr, Elizabeth
Heger Boyle, Benjamin Cornwell, Shelley Correll, Robert
Crosnoe, Jeremy Freese, and Mary Waters

The Family: Diversity, Inequality, and Social Change, Third Edition,
by Philip N. Cohen

You May Ask Yourself: An Introduction to Thinking like a Sociologist,
Sixth Edition, by Dalton Conley

Race in America, Second Edition, by Matthew Desmond
and Mustafa Emirbayer

The Real World: An Introduction to Sociology, Seventh Edition,
by Kerry Ferris and Jill Stein

Essentials of Sociology, Seventh Edition, by Anthony Giddens,
Mitchell Duneier, Richard P. Appelbaum, and Deborah Carr

Introduction to Sociology, Eleventh Edition, by Anthony Giddens,
Mitchell Duneier, Richard P. Appelbaum, and Deborah Carr

Mix It Up: Popular Culture, Mass Media, and Society, Second Edition,
by David Grazian

Readings for Sociology, Ninth Edition, edited by Garth Massey
and Timothy L. O'Brien

Families as They Really Are, Second Edition, edited by Barbara J.
Risman and Virginia E. Rutter

Sex Matters: The Sexuality and Society Reader, Fifth Edition, edited
by Mindy Stombler, Dawn M. Baunach, Wendy O. Simonds,
Elroi J. Windsor, and Elisabeth O. Burgess

Gender: Ideas, Interactions, Institutions, Second Edition,
by Lisa Wade and Myra Marx Ferree

American Society: How It Really Works, Second Edition, by Erik Olin
Wright and Joel Rogers

**To learn more about Norton Sociology, please visit
wwnorton.com/soc**

Social Problems

Fourth Edition

JOEL BEST

W. W. NORTON & COMPANY, INC.

INDEPENDENT PUBLISHERS
SINCE 1923

W. W. Norton & Company has been independent since its founding in 1923, when William Warder Norton and Mary D. Herter Norton first published lectures delivered at the People's Institute, the adult education division of New York City's Cooper Union. The firm soon expanded its program beyond the Institute, publishing books by celebrated academics from America and abroad. By midcentury, the two major pillars of Norton's publishing program—trade books and college texts—were firmly established. In the 1950s, the Norton family transferred control of the company to its employees, and today—with a staff of five hundred and hundreds of trade, college, and professional titles published each year—W. W. Norton & Company stands as the largest and oldest publishing house owned wholly by its employees.

Editor: Sasha Levitt
Project Editor: Jennifer Barnhardt
Assistant Editor: Erika Nakagawa
Managing Editor, College: Marian Johnson
Managing Editor, College Digital Media: Kim Yi
Production Managers: Ashley Horna and Stephen Sajdak
Media Editor: Eileen Connell
Media Project Editor: Danielle Belfiore
Associate Media Editor: Ariel Eaton
Media Editorial Assistant: Samuel Tang
Marketing Manager, Sociology: Julia Hall
Designer: Margaret M. Wagner
Director of College Permissions: Megan Schindel
Composition: Achorn International, Inc.
Manufacturing: LSC Crawfordsville

Library of Congress Cataloging-in-Publication Data

Name: Best, Joel, author.
Title: Social problems / Joel Best.
Description: Fourth Edition. | New York : W. W. Norton & Company, 2020. |
    Revised edition of the author's Social problems, [2017]
Identifiers: LCCN 2020010662 | ISBN 9780393533040 (paperback)
Subjects: LCSH: Social problems.
Classification: LCC HN28 .B45 2020 | DDC 306—dc23
LC record available at https://lccn.loc.gov/2020010662

W. W. Norton & Company, Inc., 500 Fifth Avenue, New York, NY 10110-0017
wwnorton.com

W. W. Norton & Company Ltd., 15 Carlisle Street, London W1D 3BS

1 2 3 4 5 6 7 8 9 0

Contents

Figures

Boxes

A Note to the Reader

Many, many books titled *Social Problems* have been published in the past hundred years. Their tables of contents look a lot alike: they begin with a brief discussion of the nature of social problems, then consider a list of different problems. Each chapter presents more or less up-to-date information about a particular social problem: there is a chapter about crime, another about racism, and so on. If your parents, grandparents, or even great-grandparents read a social problems textbook, that book almost certainly fit this pattern.

This is not your parents' social problems textbook.

The chapters in this book do not deal with different problems. Instead, each chapter deals with a different stage in the *social problems process*—the process by which particular problems become a focus of concern. Why do we worry about, say, the risks of fracking in one year, opioid addiction in another, and fake news in still another? This book seeks to explain how and why attention to different issues rises and falls.

If you're a student who's been assigned to read this book, it probably already seems long. All I can say is that it could have been a lot longer. Lots of people have written about the rise and fall of social problems; hundreds of studies have been published on the topic, particularly since the 1970s. But I have decided to cite relatively few sources. Often where I've cited one source, I could have cited dozens. In general, I have chosen to cite sources that appeared relatively recently. In addition, because this book is intended as an introduction to thinking about social problems, I have tried to hold jargon to a minimum. If you go on to read more of what sociologists have written on the topic—and I hope that this book will get you interested enough to do just that—you will find that other authors have explored the ins and outs of studying social problems in far more detail, and that they have developed many specialized terms and concepts to help us think about the social problems process. However, my goal is not to summarize everything that has been written about what I call the constructionist approach to social problems. Rather, I want to give you a basic framework for understanding this approach. This book is intended to help you become a more critical thinker; it provides some tools that can help you better analyze what you read and hear about social problems.

Acknowledgments

I particularly want to thank Karl Bakeman, Norton's editor for sociology at the time I started this book. Over the years, I had been approached by several publishers who said they wanted me to write a book about social problems. I had a standard response: "You don't want to publish the book I want to write, and I don't want to write the book you want to publish." That was enough to discourage everyone—except Karl. I appreciate his willingness to take a chance on the book I wanted to write.

Years before I began working on this fourth edition, Karl had taken on new responsibilities, and Sasha Levitt became the sociology editor for the third and now the fourth revisions. Like Karl, she was committed to the project, and I really appreciate her help.

Over the years, a lot of people gave me a lot of useful feedback, and the earlier editions listed all their names. I remain grateful to them, but the list started to seem unwieldy. So, this time I am only going to mention people who made comments or suggestions for this fourth edition: Manabu Akagawa, Jun Ayukawa, Eric Best, Katie

Bogle, Brian Monahan, Larry Nichols, Dan O'Connell, and Dave Schweingruber. Thank you all.

Finally, I want to thank the other folks at Norton who helped me pull the book together. In particular, Laura Sewell did the copyediting on the fourth edition.

Social Problems

1

The Social Problems Process

The title of this book identifies its subject: social problems. But what are *social problems*? If asked, most people have no difficulty listing some examples: crime, suicide, racism, sexism, terrorism, climate change. Most people have a commonsense notion of what the term covers, but actually defining the concept turns out to be much trickier.

Suppose we agree that suicide and climate change are both social problems. What, exactly, do the two have in common? They seem very different: we usually think of suicide as an extremely personal act, committed by individuals who feel isolated and in despair, whereas climate change involves physical warming across a whole planet. What sort of definition can cover both individual acts and global transformations?

TWO WAYS TO DEFINE SOCIAL PROBLEMS

Social Problems as Harmful Conditions: The Objectivist Outlook

The usual answer is to define social problems as conditions that somehow harm society. For example, another recent book that shares the title of this book, *Social Problems*, offers this definition:

"A social problem is a social condition or pattern of behavior that has negative consequences for individuals, our social world, or our physical world" (Leon-Guerrero, 2019, p. 4). In other words, some conditions have the characteristic of "negative consequences" that makes them social problems. Although the precise wording of their definitions varies, most books on the topic characterize social problems as harmful conditions.

This approach to defining social problems is sometimes called **objectivist** because it tries to couch the definition in terms of objectively measurable characteristics of conditions. Once we define social problems as having negative consequences, we can look around until we spot a condition with negative consequences and then identify it as a social problem. Most books titled *Social Problems* have chapters devoted to crime, racism, and other conditions that presumably have been objectively determined to be harmful.

Objectivist definitions seem fine—until we start to think about them. Then some problems with the objectivist approach become obvious. The first difficulty is that conditions that might be deemed harmful aren't always identified as social problems. Take sexism. Virtually all the books titled *Social Problems* and published in the United States in recent decades discuss sexism; it is widely understood to be a social problem. And yet, although social arrangements that discriminate against females have had a very long history, often they have been taken for granted, viewed as normal and natural—not at all a problem. Even today, many people around the world believe that their religions or traditions justify—even require—such discriminatory social arrangements. In fact, even American books about social problems published before 1970 rarely mentioned sexual discrimination. Only in recent decades has the term *sexism* emerged to refer to a form of discrimination seen as analogous to racism (which already was widely understood to be a social problem).

If we ask people to explain why racism is a social problem, they are likely to emphasize justice or fairness. It is, they will explain, unjust to discriminate against people simply because they belong to a particular race. Some may add that racism also harms society in that victims of racial discrimination are blocked from making all of the contributions they might make to the larger society, so that not only are those victims harmed, but the larger society is damaged because it misses out on what the victims could contribute; moreover, society is harmed further because racial tensions create conflict that makes the society less productive and harmonious. In other words, it is easy to argue that racism is a harmful condition and should be recognized as a social problem.

Obviously it is possible to make analogous arguments about sexism—that it is unfair, blocks women from fulfilling their potential, fosters conflict, and therefore harms the larger society. Thus, by objective standards, we might assume that racism and sexism should both be seen as social problems, although we know that—at other times or in other places—people have treated both racist and sexist practices as normal, even as the way things ought to be.

Note, however, that we might make essentially the same arguments about discrimination based on height. Studies show that taller people have various advantages; for example, they are more likely to be hired and more likely to be promoted. Thus, short people can be seen as victims of height discrimination (Rosenberg, 2009). Such discriminatory treatment also might be considered unfair, and ultimately harmful to society in much the same ways that racism and sexism are harmful. By objective standards, then, shouldn't "heightism" also be considered a social problem?

The first difficulty with objectivism becomes apparent: although we might argue that racism, sexism, and heightism all have analogous effects on society, as social problems these three forms of discrimination have not received anything like the same degree of attention. Racial discrimination has long been understood to be a serious social problem; sexism has only recently been added to the list of significant social problems; and heightism rarely receives mention as a social problem. As far as I know, no book about social problems includes a chapter about height discrimination. The different treatment of these three forms of discrimination makes it difficult to argue that there is an evenly applied objective standard for identifying what is or is not a social problem.

A second challenge to objectivism is that the same condition may be identified as a social problem for very different reasons; that is, people may disagree about why a certain condition is harmful. For example, some commentators argue that contemporary society discriminates against people who are overweight; heavier people find it more difficult to get jobs, are the objects of scorn, and so on. In this view, weight discrimination, like racial, gender, or—yes—height discrimination, should be considered a social problem because it is unjust and blocks some individuals from opportunities. More recently, however, attention has focused on obesity itself as a social problem. Here the argument is that heavier people are less healthy, and that obesity costs society many millions of dollars in additional health care expenditures. Critics taking this view consider obesity a social problem not because it leads to discrimination, but because it harms individuals and is a drain on societal resources (see Box 1.1).

Note that, although both arguments suggest that there is a social problem related to weight, they make very different claims: the former suggests that discrimination against overweight people is unfair (presumably, this position might lead to suggestions that society ought to become more tolerant of weight differences and that such discrimination should be discouraged); the latter views obesity itself as a source of harm (and would presumably lead to calls to reduce obesity). This example reveals a second problem with the objectivist view of social problems: very different—even contradictory—objective standards may be used in identifying a condition as a social problem.

A third problem with objectivism has already been suggested: our lists of social problems include wildly diverse phenomena. They

Box 1.1 A Weighty Disagreement

Many Americans are heavy. Is this a social problem? If so, what exactly is the nature of this problem? Is it a discrimination/civil rights problem? Or is it a medical/public health problem?

The fat acceptance movement (led by the National Association to Advance Fat Acceptance) argues that weight is a form of diversity. In its view, fat people (to use the term the movement favors) are stigmatized; they are ridiculed and face discrimination in the workplace and elsewhere. Fat acceptance activists argue that this is a civil rights issue, that discrimination based on weight is no more justified than racial or gender bias. They point to research suggesting that people cannot control—and therefore should not be blamed for—their weight.

In contrast, many medical authorities and government officials warn that increases in Americans' average weight constitute an "obesity epidemic." They note that higher weight increases one's risks of heart disease and other medical problems, and that this has consequences, not only for the affected individuals who suffer more health problems, but for the larger society, which must bear the increased costs of medical treatment. In this view, obesity is a public health issue, analogous to smoking, and policies are needed to encourage citizens to maintain healthy weight.

These different views on obesity illustrate that even people who agree that a particular condition is a social problem may disagree about the sort of social problem it is.

Source: Saguy, 2013.

usually range from problems affecting particular individuals, such as suicide or mental illness, to global trends, such as overpopulation, globalization, or climate change. Any objective definition that tries to cover such a broad range of topics must be fairly vague, and speak in only the most general terms about harm, negative consequences, or anything else. Although objectivists argue that social problems are harmful conditions, they don't specify what constitutes harm. Instead, harmfulness becomes a big conceptual umbrella, covering a huge array of phenomena, ranging from, say, the pain experienced by those who knew someone who committed suicide, through all of the economic and ecological costs that might be incurred as global temperatures rise. In practice, then, objective definitions of social problems turn out to be so vague as to be almost meaningless.

For all of these reasons, it is quite difficult to devise an objective definition of social problems that can distinguish between the things that people consider social problems and the things that they don't. So let's ask the question again: what, exactly, do suicide and climate change have in common? Once we think about it, we realize that there is really only one quality that all of the diverse phenomena considered social problems share: they are all considered social problems. The point is not so much that some conditions cause harm, but that people think of some conditions as being harmful.

Social Problems as Topics of Concern: The Subjectivist Outlook

Imagine two societies with arrangements that discriminate against women: in one, people consider these arrangements normal and natural; in the other, some people consider these arrangements wrong. From the point of view of the first society's members, sexism is not a social problem; some members of the second society, though, do regard sexism as a social problem. Of course, people's views may change. In recent decades, most Americans have come to view social arrangements that treat men and women differently as problematic, so even though sexism was formerly not considered a social problem, it has become one.

We might think of this as a subjectivist approach, in that it defines social problems in terms of people's subjective sense that something is or isn't a problem. If people don't think that heightism is a social problem, then it isn't one; but if height discrimination began receiving a lot of concerned attention, heightism could become a social problem. If people consider both suicide and climate change to be social problems, then both are.

Once we start thinking about social problems in terms of subjective judgments, we realize that people often disagree about what should be considered social problems. We might expect people of above-average height to dismiss arguments that height discrimination should be considered a social problem, and those of below-average height to be more receptive to those claims. Similarly, the views of individuals outside a society may differ from those of its members. When Americans criticize sexism in other countries, they are identifying a social problem, even if most of the occupants of those countries disagree. Remember, there is no objective standard that lets us declare, "X is a social problem, but Y is not." Rather, whether a condition is a social problem depends on different people's points of view—and they won't always agree.

In this view, social problems will come and go as people's subjective judgments change. Announcements of discoveries of a new disease or a new environmental threat can vault previously overlooked conditions onto people's lists of social problems. Other social problems fade away. For example, during the 1950s many commentators worried that young Americans were apathetic, but apathy stopped being considered a social problem during the 1960s, when campus demonstrations led critics to charge that students had become too concerned, too involved in political activity.

From the subjectivist outlook, it is not an objective quality of a social condition, but rather the subjective reactions to that condition, that make something a social problem. Therefore, social problems should not be viewed as a type of social condition, but as a *process* of responding to social conditions. Thus, we can define social problems as efforts to arouse concern about conditions within society. Or, to quote one influential definition, social problems are "the activities of individuals or groups making assertions of grievance and claims with respect to some putative conditions" (Spector & Kitsuse, 1977, p. 75). In other words, the study of social problems should focus not on conditions, but on claims about conditions.

At first glance, this approach may seem wrongheaded. If we're interested in, say, poverty, then shouldn't we be studying poverty as a condition? We might try to measure the number of poor people, determine the causes of poverty, and so on. In other words, shouldn't we adopt a more objectivist approach and focus on the condition of poverty, rather than on claims about poverty? Of course, it is possible to study poverty and other social conditions, and there is nothing wrong with doing so. But that has nothing to do with studying poverty *as a social problem*.

Studying poverty as a social problem requires asking how and why people came to consider poverty problematic. After all, poverty has been around for a long time; throughout history, many people in many societies have taken poverty for granted, seeing it as necessary, normal, even just. Some societies with very large populations of poor people have not viewed poverty as a social problem. In contrast, in the United States and many other modern societies, the widespread view is that poverty should be considered a social problem, and that we ought to do something about it. Studying poverty *as a social problem* requires studying how that view emerged and spread.

In other words, efforts to find a workable definition of social problems based on the objective characteristics of social conditions have proved futile. Thinking systematically about social problems requires adopting a subjectivist approach that focuses on the process by which people identify social problems. That process involves what sociologists call *social construction*.

SOCIAL CONSTRUCTION

By **social construction**, we mean the way people assign meaning to the world. People use language; language is essential to our understanding of the world that surrounds us (just try thinking without using words). One of the principal accomplishments of infancy and early childhood is learning to recognize, understand, and use words. Through language, we learn to categorize the world, to understand that some things are edible (*food*) while others are dangerous and must not be eaten (*poison*), and so on. This is obviously a social process: we do not invent our language; rather, we learn to use the language of our parents and the other people around us. The meanings of their words—their categories for classifying the world—are the ones that we learn. Children grow up speaking English, or Spanish, or whatever language the people in the group around them speak, and they learn to assign that group's meanings to the world.

Language is flexible: as people learn new things about the world, they devise words with new meanings. In this way, people continually create—or construct—fresh understandings about the world around them. Because this is a social process, sociologists refer to it as *social construction* (Berger & Luckmann, 1966).

Sociologists do not view social construction as a completely arbitrary process; it is constrained by the physical world within which people find themselves. We can imagine all sorts of ridiculous meanings that people might, in theory, construct. For instance, an imaginary society might, in theory, teach its young that rocks are edible, or that people can fly by flapping their arms, but this is hardly likely. Although this could happen, it probably wouldn't, because those lessons would prove worthless, even dangerous. In general, the meanings people construct need to make sense of the world they inhabit.

The point is not that people could assign ridiculous meanings to the world, but rather that they must assign some meanings to at least some of their surroundings. Probably every human society throughout history has categorized people as either male or female. The distinction is relatively clear-cut: we can look at virtually any newborn infant and confidently declare that it falls into one category or the other. If this doesn't seem to be a social process, remember that a tiny fraction of infants (about one in every thousand) are born with anomalous sexual organs that do challenge the simple male/female classification, and societies have to decide how to deal with those cases (Feder, 2014). These individuals, once called her-maphrodites but now termed *intersex*, pose challenges to simplistic male/female categories. There are various solutions: Many Native American societies defined these individuals as having a special status as *two-spirits*—a sort of third sex outside the standard male/female divide. By contrast, in contemporary America surgeons often "correct" the anomalies, to give the infant either a male or a female appearance, and foster an unambiguous gender identity, while some critics oppose this practice as depriving individuals of their right to be intersex.

Similarly, Americans are increasingly acknowledging that some people—often beginning in childhood—are not comfortable with the gender they have been assigned, and they may reject it in favor of various non-binary identities, including becoming transgender—a member of the other gender (Stein, 2018). The assumption that everyone is simply born male or female overlooks the diversity of ways people think of themselves.

This example reminds us that even something as apparently straightforward as sorting people into males and females is a social process of constructing meanings. Note, too, that the precise mean-ings assigned to these categories—the qualities attributed to males or females—vary from one society to another. Both the two-category male/female classification and the specific qualities associated with each category are instances of social construction. All meanings, including how we designate planets in the solar system and all other elements in the physical world, are socially constructed (see Box 1.2).

Box 1.2 Pluto: A Planetary Problem?

For decades, schoolchildren learned that there were nine planets, but that changed in 2006, when astronomers demoted Pluto from the list, reclassifying it as a *dwarf planet*. Pluto is unlike the other planets in several ways: (1) It is much smaller. (2) It has a different composition; the four inner planets (Mercury, Venus, Earth, and Mars) are basically rocks, and the four giant planets (Jupiter, Saturn, Uranus, and Neptune) are composed of gas, but Pluto is basically a big lump of ice. (3) It has a less circular, more elliptical orbit than the other planets, so sometimes it is closer to the Sun than Neptune is. And (4), unlike the other eight planets, whose orbits fall more or less along the same plane, Pluto has an orbit that is at an angle to that plane.

No one denies that Pluto exists; the question is whether it makes more sense to classify it as a planet or as belonging to a differ-ent category. When Ceres—the largest asteroid—was discovered in 1801, it was initially considered a planet, but astronomers dropped that classification once they realized that there were many asteroids. Now Ceres joins Pluto in the new category of dwarf planet. These examples remind us that *planet* is a social construction, a category that people use to assign meaning to the world. Our words are social products: we create them and teach them to one another. Because we understand our world through language, sociologists view all knowledge as socially constructed.

Source: Tyson, 2009.

Sociologists sometimes illustrate social construction by pointing to problems that seem ridiculous. These examples offer a sort of analytic leverage: they lay bare the process of social construction. Witch hunts are a favorite historical example; UFO abductions and satanic ritual abuse offer more contemporary cases. Critics might argue that there is no convincing evidence that witches, UFOs, or child-abusing satanists exist (ignore, for the moment, those people who remain convinced that these are real phenomena). Therefore, the sociologists declare, witchcraft, UFOs, and satanic blood cults are clearly social constructions.

This conclusion is true, but its implication is quite false. UFO abductions are a social construction, in the sense that this term was created and disseminated by people. But the implication—that only unprovable claims are socially constructed—is wrong. Poverty is just as much a social construction as UFO abductions are. The term *poverty* is another category that people have created to make sense of the world. Just as some people have drawn attention to UFO abductions, others have campaigned to raise concern about poverty (during the 1960s, for example, President Lyndon Johnson declared "war on poverty"). Saying that poverty is a social construction does not mean that poverty doesn't exist, that it somehow doesn't occur in the real world; obviously some people have much less money than others. But the words we choose to describe those people (*impoverished*, for instance, rather than *wretched* or *depraved*—terms that were once used to describe the poor), how we explain their condition, and what we recommend doing about it are meanings that people create and use. In that sense, poverty—like everything else we know about—is a social construction.

Once we recognize that social problems are social constructions, and that what the conditions constructed as social problems have in common is precisely that construction, then it becomes apparent that social problems should be understood in terms of a **social problems process**. That is, the study of social problems should focus on how and why particular conditions come to be constructed as social problems. How and why did poverty—or UFO abductions—emerge as topics of interest and concern at particular moments, and in particular places? Why do people decide that something needs to be done about some conditions, and how do they decide exactly what should be done? This approach to studying social problems is called **constructionist**, and it is the perspective adopted in this book.

THE BASIC FRAMEWORK

The constructionist approach requires understanding a few basic terms. These will reappear throughout the chapters that follow. The first is **claim**. Constructing a social problem involves a process of **claimsmaking**: someone must bring the topic to the attention of others by making a claim that there is a condition that should be recognized as troubling, that needs to be addressed. For constructionist sociologists, social problems are defined in terms of this claimsmaking process, because it is claimsmaking—and only claimsmaking—that all social problems have in common.

Note that claims may be supported by very different sorts of evidence: someone making claims about poverty might present poverty statistics, photographs of poor people, or all manner of other evidence; claims about UFO abductions tend to rely on first-person accounts by people who say they recall having been abducted. Whether other people find a claim convincing is a separate issue. At one extreme, we can imagine a claim that no one finds convincing: picture a man standing on a street corner warning passersby that invisible, undetectable aliens from planet Zorax have infested the very air that they're breathing. This may be a claim, but if everyone who hears it dismisses or ignores it, it will have no impact. The social problems process requires not only that someone make a claim, but that others react to it.

The people who make claims are, of course, **claimsmakers**. They are the ones who seek to convince others that something is wrong, and that something should be done about it. Obviously not all claimsmakers are equal: we tend to treat some claims more seriously, simply because they seem more plausible, or because they are promoted by people we respect—experts, officials, and so on. Successful claims spread, so that they become the subject of media coverage and debates over public policy.

These few concepts—claim, claimsmaking, and claimsmaker—provide a foundation on which we can build a more elaborate analysis of the social problems process. Throughout this book, we will distinguish between claims and the conditions about which claims are being made. We will refer to **troubling conditions**— that is, the conditions that become subjects of claims. The word *troubling* focuses our attention on people's subjective reactions: a condition is troubling if it bothers someone. Note that it isn't necessary for everyone to accept the claim; some people may consider UFO abductions troubling, even though others regard such claims as fantastic. We can consider both poverty and UFO abductions troubling conditions, regardless of whether we agree that they both exist.

Adopting a subjectivist stance can seem confusing at first. In particular, two sorts of confusion arise. We have already discussed the first: people sometimes wrongly imagine that *social construction* refers only to imaginary, nonexistent phenomena. Again, this is wrong—all human knowledge is socially constructed through our language, which means that all social problems are socially constructed.

The second source of confusion is that we must acknowledge that sociologists are themselves engaged in social construction. Like all other people, sociologists must use language to make the world meaningful; they devise their own categories—such as *claims* and *claimsmakers*—that they use to classify the world. This book, for instance, can be understood as a set of sociological claims about the social problems process.

Some people worry that, if sociology is one more social construction, we can't really have confidence in sociological knowledge. The response, of course, is that we can have exactly the same sort of confidence in sociology that we have in our other sorts of knowledge. When we encounter claims in everyday life—when someone gives us a compliment, politicians ask for our votes, or advertisers try to sell us their products—we neither accept everything we hear at face value nor assume that it is all meaningless. Rather, we learn to evaluate claims, to look for evidence, and so on. Similarly, sociologists can offer support for their arguments, and this book will try to suggest the nature of that support. (For more detailed discussions of various theoretical and methodological aspects of the constructionist approach, see Harris, 2010; Holstein & Gubrium, 2008; Loseke, 2003; D. Weinberg, 2014).

THE PLAN OF THE BOOK: THE NATURAL HISTORY OF SOCIAL PROBLEMS

To understand the approach that this book takes toward social problems, it may help to begin with a familiar example from U.S. history: the 1960s civil rights movement against segregation. After World War II, the southern states retained customs and laws maintaining racial segregation: African Americans were blocked from voting; intermarriage was illegal; whites and blacks attended different schools; and other institutions were segregated so that the races ate in different restaurants, sat in different sections on buses, and used racially separate restrooms and drinking fountains. Organized protests against this system of segregation became more common; in particular, the 1955–56 bus boycott in Montgomery, Alabama, brought national attention to the leadership of the Reverend Martin Luther King Jr.

By the early 1960s, there were numerous civil rights organizations— including King's Southern Christian Leadership Conference (SCLC), the Congress of Racial Equality (CORE), and the Student Nonviolent Coordinating Committee (SNCC, pronounced "snick")—leading marches, boycotts, freedom rides, voter registration campaigns, and other sorts of protests. Television news programs showed dramatic scenes of police beating and arresting protesters, and public opinion— particularly outside the South—increasingly sympathized with the civil rights campaign. In 1963, the great March on Washington called for congressional action, and Congress eventually passed the Civil Rights Act of 1964 and the Voting Rights Act of 1965. By the end of the 1960s, segregation in the South had generally lost its legal standing, although of course other forms of racial inequality remained.

We can use the story of the civil rights movement's campaign against segregation to illustrate a more general phenomenon: the natural history of a social problem. The term **natural history** refers to a sequence of stages that tends to appear in lots of different cases. While the term originally referred to observational studies of the lives of plants and animals, it has been adopted by sociologists who study social processes. Figure 1.1 diagrams the natural history of the social problems process.

This natural history identifies six stages: claimsmaking, media coverage, public reaction, policymaking, social problems work, and policy outcomes. The figure sketches a general framework. Describing a natural history helps us organize our thinking about a typical social problems process, although not every instance of social problems construction will fit this model. In fact, other sociologists have offered different natural histories of the social problems process (see Blumer, 1971; Spector & Kitsuse, 1977). Figure 1.1 is a simplified diagram intended to give an overview of what is actually a much more complicated process. In later chapters, we will expand this diagram to consider some of those complexities, but this version gives us a starting point.

Stage One: Claimsmaking

The first stage in Figure 1.1 concerns claimsmaking. During this stage, claimsmakers make claims; that is, they argue that a particular troubling condition ought to be recognized as a social problem, and that someone ought to do something about that problem. In the case of the civil rights movement, the claimsmakers were the social movement activists and demonstrators who protested against the system of racial segregation. We can distinguish between claimsmakers and their claims. *Claims* are arguments, efforts to persuade others that something is wrong, that there is a problem that needs to be solved. For example, the civil rights movement

Figure 1.1 Basic Natural History Model of the Social Problems Process

Claimsmaking	→	Media Coverage	→	Public Reaction	→	Policymaking	→	Social Problems Work	→	Policy Outcomes
People make claims that there is a social problem, with certain characteristics, causes, and solutions.		Media report on claimsmakers so that news of the claims reaches a broader audience.		Public opinion focuses on the social problem identified by the claimsmakers.		Lawmakers and others with the power to set policies create new ways to address the problem.		Agencies implement the new policies, including calls for further changes.		There are various responses to the new arrangements.
Example: Civil rights activists, such as Martin Luther King Jr., call for an end to racial segregation in the South, hold marches and demonstrations.		**Example:** Reporters from newspapers and television describe the conflict over the civil rights campaign.		**Example:** People become more concerned about racial segregation and more supportive of the campaign against it.		**Example:** Congress passes the Civil Rights Act of 1964 and the Voting Rights Act of 1965.		**Example:** Under the new federal laws, states and localities are forced to end formal policies of racial segregation.		**Example:** People call for additional changes to reduce racism, as well as campaigns to promote the rights of women and other groups.

claimed that racial segregation was wrong, that it was unjust, and violated the basic American belief in equality. The social problems process always begins with claims, so we will begin this book by exploring various aspects of claims in Chapter 2.

Typically we think of claimsmakers as **activists**, members of social movement organizations such as the civil rights movement's SCLC, CORE, or SNCC. Lots of people want to make claims, but it is often hard to get others to pay attention. Activists must devise ways of drawing attention to their cause; civil rights demonstrators conducted sit-ins, boycotts, freedom rides, and marches as ways of attracting notice. Activists also need to recruit people to join their movement, manage the movement's operations, and maintain interest in their cause. Chapter 3 examines the role of activists as claimsmakers, as well as some of the challenges that social movements confront.

Not all claimsmakers are social movement activists. Claims also come from various sorts of **experts**, such as physicians, scientists, lawyers, and officials. These people claim to speak with special authority because they have special knowledge; for example, scientists may have done research that shows the nature or extent of a particular troubling social condition, or lawyers may argue that the law related to the condition needs to be reinterpreted. During the civil rights movement, for example, social scientists and psychiatrists claimed that segregation had harmful consequences, while lawyers devised strategies to challenge segregation in the courts. Many societies grant authority to those seen as having special, expert knowledge; Chapter 4 considers how experts can use their authority as claimsmakers.

Stage Two: Media Coverage

The second stage shown in Figure 1.1 is media coverage. Claimsmakers often seek such coverage to bring their claims to the attention of a wider audience. The nature of the media may change—from stories and photographs printed in newspapers and magazines, or reports broadcast on radio and television news programs, to social media and the endless array of sites on the Internet—but they all offer forums that can make both the public and policymakers more aware of claims. Civil rights demonstrators depended on this reporting; traditionally it had been easy for Americans outside the South to ignore segregation, but dramatic clashes between protesters and police created major news stories that focused national attention on civil rights. The media face practical considerations that affect how they address social problems, and media coverage inevitably reshapes claims. This is the topic of Chapter 5.

Stage Three: Public Reaction

The general public, then, learns about claims either directly from claimsmakers or indirectly through media reports. The public's response to these claims forms the third stage in Figure 1.1. Usually efforts to understand the public's reactions involve public opinion polls that seek to measure people's attitudes. In some cases, claimsmaking can have dramatic effects on public opinion; during the civil rights movement, for instance, polls indicated an increase in the proportion of Americans who considered civil rights a major problem, and who disapproved of the South's segregation policies. Such shifts are considered important in a democracy because voters may elect officials who reflect their changed views. Chapter 6 looks at polling, as well as other, less traditional ways of understanding the public's reactions.

Stage Four: Policymaking

The fourth stage in Figure 1.1's natural history is **policymaking**. Social policies are the means that society adopts to address troubling conditions, and such policies can be made in various ways. Most obviously, laws can be changed, as when Congress passed and President Johnson signed the Civil Rights Act of 1964 and the Voting Rights Act of 1965—the principal federal responses to the civil rights movement (over time, state legislatures and local city councils also had to modify their laws regarding segregation). But legislation is not the only form of policymaking; all sorts of bodies set social policies: government agencies establish standards for, say, clean water; schools create dress codes for their students; and so on. Policymakers respond to claimsmakers, media coverage, and public opinion, but their own considerations also shape the policies they create. Policymaking is the focus of Chapter 7.

Stage Five: Social Problems Work

Declaring that there will be a new social policy is not the end of the matter; policies have to be implemented, carried out by police officers, social workers, teachers—whoever is responsible for enforcing the particular policy. This is **social problems work**—the fifth stage in Figure 1.1. Often claimsmakers, the media, the public, and policymakers discuss social issues in fairly abstract, theoretical terms: here's what's wrong, and this is what ought to be done. In contrast, social problems workers confront these issues as practical matters. They must deal with particular cases and address a messy real world that often seems quite complicated. For example, civil rights laws had to be translated into specific enforcement practices. It is one thing to say, for instance, that an all-white police force should be integrated, but even if everyone agrees on that principle, people may disagree about practical details regarding how officers should be selected. Chapter 8 tackles the complexities of social problems work.

Stage Six: Policy Outcomes

The sixth and final stage in Figure 1.1 is **policy outcomes**, reactions to the social problems process. Several sorts of outcomes are possible. Some relate directly to the ways in which social policies are implemented. Critics may argue that the new policies are ineffective—that they don't do enough to address the troubling condition, or that the policies actually cause new problems, even making things worse. For instance, the federal civil rights laws passed in the 1960s have been criticized for not going far enough; even though the formal system of legal segregation was dismantled, all sorts of racial inequality remained (thus, blacks continue to have lower incomes, shorter life expectancies, and so on). Other critics may argue that a policy goes too far, as with charges that the affirmative action policies that emerged from the civil rights movement themselves create unequal arrangements. There may be efforts to measure the policy's impact, to evaluate its effectiveness, but how should effectiveness be judged? Often such complaints and questions lead to new claims, and the social problems process begins anew. Such reactions to social policies are the topic of Chapter 9.

In contrast, Chapter 10 explores a broader set of outcomes that often extend over time and space. Consider the impact of the civil rights movement. The dramatic, heavily publicized campaign against segregation inspired other claimsmakers, both within the United States and around the world. Civil rights activists learned valuable practical lessons about how to organize a social movement, attract media coverage for their cause, and so on. Veterans of civil rights protests began to apply their new skills in other social movements, becoming involved in protests over the war in Vietnam or campaigns to advance women's rights or gay and lesbian rights. Claimsmakers in other nations also tried to duplicate the success of the American civil rights movement by organizing protests over troubling conditions in their own countries. In addition to examining how claims spread, Chapter 10 considers cycles in claimsmaking—a pattern in which claims rise to attract a good deal of attention, then recede, before rising again years later.

Finally, Chapter 11 uses the discussion of Chapters 2 through 10 to revisit Figure 1.1 and develop a more elaborate natural history of the social problems process. Chapter 11 also discusses the uses and future of the constructionist approach.

ADDITIONAL THEMES

Chapters 2 through 11 are organized according to the natural history model illustrated in Figure 1.1. In general, we will discuss topics in the order in which they occur in the social problems process; this is the book's central organizing principle. In addition, two other themes will run through every chapter: resources and rhetoric. As Figure 1.2 suggests, these themes influence each stage in the social problems process.

Resources

The first theme concerns the **resources** that people bring to the social problems process. A society's members are not equal; some have more money than others, or more power, more status, more education, more social contacts, and so on. These are resources that

Figure 1.2 RESOURCES AND RHETORIC AFFECT EACH STAGE OF THE
SOCIAL PROBLEMS PROCESS

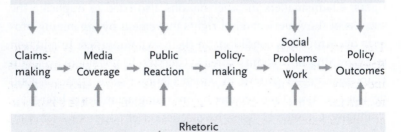

Resources
Actors are not equal. Some have more power, status, contacts, education, and money than others. These resources can make it easier to influence every stage in the social problems process.

Claims-making → Media Coverage → Public Reaction → Policy-making → Social Problems Work → Policy Outcomes

Rhetoric
Any troubling condition can be understood in various ways. At each stage in the social problems process, a troubling condition can be reconstructed to fit the concerns of the actors involved in that stage.

people can draw on in the social problems process. We will discover that each stage in Figure 1.1 involves competition: claimsmakers compete to attract attention to their claims, claims compete for media coverage and attention from the public and policymakers, and so on. At each stage in the social problems process, some claims succeed in moving to the next stage, while others fail to attract much notice. History is filled with claims that never attracted many adherents, and were ignored, dismissed, or discredited.

Resources affect this competition. In general, people with more money, power, and other resources find it easier to have their claims heard. The resources available to major corporate leaders give them considerable influence over social policy; they have money to spend on political contributions that allow them and their lobbyists access to policymakers. In contrast, the story of the civil rights movement is inspiring precisely because most African Americans living under segregation had such limited resources; they had relatively little in the way of money or political influence, yet they mounted a campaign that successfully changed social policy. At every stage in the social problems process, inequality—whether based on race, class, gender, or something else—means that people bring different resources to the process. It is much easier for those with ample resources to make claims and get them heard, than it is for those with fewer resources.

Rhetoric

The second theme that runs through each chapter is rhetoric. **Rhetoric** is the study of persuasion. Social problems construction is inevitably rhetorical. Whenever people make claims, they are trying to convince others that something is a problem, that it is a problem of a particular sort, and that specific action needs to be taken to deal with this problem. These arguments evolve with each stage in the social problems process; that is, every problem is constructed and reconstructed. Even people who are allied in a claimsmaking campaign may adopt different rhetoric; the claims of activists and experts often emphasize different elements. The media, when they cover claimsmaking campaigns, reshape claims to fit their needs, just as the public's awareness of social problems tends to emphasize some aspects and downplay others. Similarly, when policymakers try to devise means of addressing troubling conditions, they, too, offer their own constructions of what is at issue. And when social problems workers try to implement policies, the practical requirements of their tasks lead them to focus on particular aspects—yet another reconstruction. Finally, at the stage of policy outcomes, there are likely to be all sorts of reinterpretations of previous claims and the policies they inspired.

Rhetoric involves appeals to emotions, as well as appeals to reason. Claimsmakers try to elicit emotional reactions, such as horror or sympathy, to get people to share their concerns, and of course much media coverage encourages the audience to feel outrage or compassion. Throughout the social problems process, people invoke feelings, as well as ideas, to convince others to share their views. Thus, rhetoric is a central theme in the chapters that follow because social problems claims are not static; rather they shift and morph at each stage in the larger social problems process as the rhetoric changes.

The themes of resources and rhetoric remind us that the social problems process occurs within a broader structural and cultural context. Existing social structural arrangements—resources—give some actors advantages in claimsmaking; having more money or more power makes it easier to promote particular constructions. At the same time, the larger culture makes particular claims—rhetoric— more or less compelling. At each stage in the social problems process, then, actors compete to devise claims that others will find persuasive.

Feedback

Finally, there is a third theme that both Figure 1.1 and Figure 1.2 overlook. These diagrams oversimplify the social problems process. In both, the arrows between stages of the social problems process point in only one direction; that is, claimsmaking is shown as affecting media coverage, media coverage in turn shapes public reaction, and so on. In fact, the social problems process is more complicated, involving a great deal of **feedback**. That is, claimsmaking does affect media coverage, but claimsmakers are also affected by that coverage (for example, if the press ignored a civil rights demonstration in the 1950s and '60s, activists knew that they needed to adjust what they were doing, in order to attract better coverage for future demonstrations). Similar feedback processes can occur at every stage in the social problems process because the actors at the various stages—the claimsmakers, people who work in the media, and so on—don't just act, but also pay attention to how others react to what they have done, and then respond to those reactions by adjusting what they're doing.

At several points in the book we will consider more elaborate diagrams that illustrate some of these feedback processes; in addition, Chapter 11 will discuss feedback processes in more detail. Remember, Figure 1.1 is designed to help us start thinking about the social problems process; it is by no means the last word.

SUMMARY

This book explores the constructionist approach to social problems. Rather than assuming that social problems are conditions that share some objectively defined characteristic, it defines social problems as a process of raising subjective concerns. This process follows a typical course, a natural history that provides a framework for the rest of the book.

The chapters that follow will focus on specific stages in the social problems process. Taken together, these chapters develop a general framework for thinking about the construction of social problems. The chapters contain many brief mentions of examples that illustrate whatever principle is being discussed. In addition, each chapter features several boxes (somewhat more detailed discussions of how a specific theme in the text is related to a particular social problem), and each chapter ends with a longer case study that explores how the ideas developed in that chapter can be applied to a particular case. Of course, all of these examples are merely illustrative. The goal of this book is to give you a better way of thinking about whatever social problems strike you as interesting.

MAKING CONNECTIONS

- *A social constructionist approach to social problems focuses on the process by which people identify social problems.*

- *As you read the upcoming chapters on claims and claimsmaking, keep in mind how claimsmakers use rhetoric to convince others that a troubling condition is a social problem.*

- *In Chapter 10 you will learn how claims about troubling conditions change depending on the time period and geographic location.*

2

Claims

Anyone who follows the news cannot help but hear claims about new social problems. Stories on news websites announce that doctors have identified a new disease, or that scientists have discovered a new environmental threat. Television commentators warn that a dangerous new drug is spreading, or that law enforcement is battling a new crime. Bloggers discuss new problems brought on by technological developments or changing lifestyles.

Often the new problem has a catchy name, such as *road rage*, *the digital divide*, *human trafficking*, or *racial profiling*. Suddenly, the brand-new term seems to be on everyone's lips. In many cases, interest in the new problem will prove to be short-lived; people will worry about it for a time, but then their attention will wander. But other terms—think of *sexism*, which first entered the language around 1970—seem to take up permanent residence in our society's vocabulary and consciousness, and the problems they identify remain topics of concern.

Constructing a new social problem involves making claims— that is, calling attention to a troubling condition. Claims are the first element in the social problems process, and they are this chapter's focus. After examining the basic structure of claims, we will consider how audiences respond to them, how they evolve, and where they fit in the larger culture.

THE RHETORIC OF CLAIMS

Every social problems claim makes a persuasive argument; it is an effort to persuade others, to convince them that a particular troubling condition ought to be recognized as a social problem, that that problem has certain characteristics, that the problem demands attention, and that it should be addressed in a specific way. When we analyze claims as arguments or statements, it matters less whether the claims are true or false than whether the people who make the claims and the audiences for those claims find the reasoning convincing.

One of the lessons of this chapter is that claims tend to take standard forms, because people who share a culture are likely to find the same sorts of arguments persuasive. Claims need to be tailored to their audiences, but of course the people who make claims usually belong to the same society as their audience, so when they devise claims that they themselves find sensible, those claims are likely to persuade their audiences. For example, members of a highly religious society may find claims based on theological reasoning compelling, whereas members of another society may be more likely to be swayed by scientific evidence. As a result, within a given society, even claims about very different problems tend to be structured in similar ways. This means that a claim you find utterly convincing will probably contain persuasive elements that resemble those in a claim you consider completely unreasonable. Keep in mind that our topic is how claims work, and understanding this does not require knowing whether the claims are, in fact, true.

The study of persuasion is called *rhetoric*, and we can analyze the rhetoric of claims. Persuasive arguments share a rhetorical structure with three fundamental components: grounds, warrants, and

Figure 2.1 THE STRUCTURE OF SOCIAL PROBLEMS CLAIMS

Grounds ─────────────────────────────────▶	Conclusions
Information and evidence about the troubling condition— typifying examples, statistics, etc. (Also called the *diagnostic frame*.)	Recommended changes, new policies, etc. to address the problem. (Also called the *prognostic frame*.)

Warrants

Justifications, appeals to values—reasons why something must be done about the troubling condition. (Also called the *motivational frame*.)

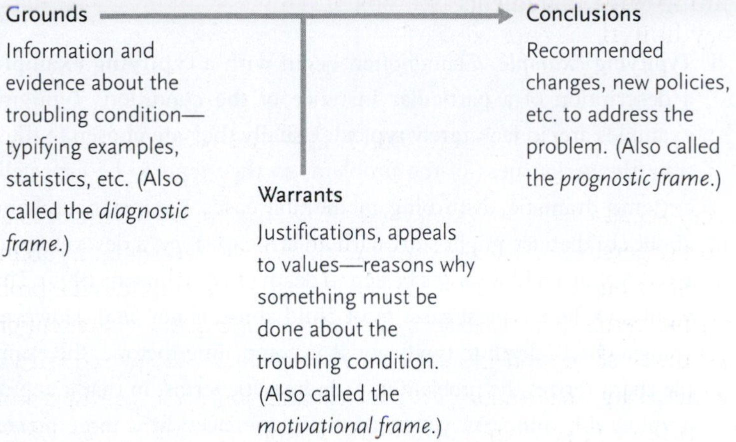

Sources: J. Best, 1990; Snow & Benford, 1988; Toulmin, 1958.

conclusions (J. Best, 1990; Toulmin, 1958). In social problems claims, *grounds* are statements about the nature of the problem, *warrants* justify taking action, and *conclusions* explain what that action should be. Figure 2.1 illustrates the connections among grounds, warrants, and conclusions. We will consider each in turn.

Grounds

Every social problems claim begins by identifying a troubling condition. Two sorts of statements are involved: those describing the condition and those explaining why it should be considered troublesome. The former are the grounds; the latter are the warrants (discussed in the next section).

The Basic Rhetorical Recipe. A claim's **grounds** usually are assertions of fact; that is, they argue that the condition exists and offer supporting evidence. Claims in the contemporary United States often establish their grounds by following a rhetorical recipe containing three ingredients (see Box 2.1).

1. *Typifying example.* Claims often begin with a **typifying example**, a description of a particular instance of the condition. Typifying examples are, in fact, rarely typical. Usually they are chosen to illustrate the seriousness of the problem, so they tend to be especially extreme, dramatic, disturbing, memorable cases. For instance, claims about child abuse might start with an atrocity story, a description of a very young child who was beaten to death (J. M. Johnson, 1995). This would not be a typical case; most child abuse is not fatal. However, using a child's death to typify abuse is compelling rhetoric; the example characterizes the problem in melodramatic terms, in that it depicts a vulnerable, innocent youngster being menaced by a more powerful, villainous adult. This example suggests that child abuse is a very serious problem, because it can involve real, terrible harm. Because the example is so disturbing, people are likely to pay attention, to start worrying about innocent children being threatened by this evil.

2. *Name.* Next the claim **names** the problem. The fatal beating in our example will be transformed from a horrific *incident* to an *instance* of the larger problem of child abuse (J. Best, 1999). Sometimes a new name is attached to an old behavior: bad driving has long been a familiar problem, but calling it *road rage* is a relatively recent development. In other cases, both the name and the troubling condition are new; *sexting* could not exist before technology made it possible. Note that naming a problem is not the same as defining it. Many claims-makers avoid defining a problem by instead focusing on typifying examples. In spite of all the attention that *child abuse* and *road rage* have received in the media, it can be very difficult to find precise definitions of either term in that coverage. Rather, the people who make up the audience for these claims probably assume that they understand the nature of these problems because they are familiar with one or more typifying examples.

3. *Statistic.* A third ingredient in the basic recipe that establishes the grounds for many claims is some sort of **statistic**, a number that

Box 2.1 The Basic Recipe: Constructing the Burmese Python as a Social Problem

Burmese pythons are snakes that have been imported from Southeast Asia as pets. Some escape or are released by their owners; in South Florida, they can survive in the wild, and ecologists had long warned that pythons were becoming an invasive species because the Everglades offered them a favorable climate where there were few predators to control their numbers. However, pythons only attracted public attention after a 2009 incident in which a pet python that had not been properly fed or contained killed a two-year-old child. Politicians used this extremely atypical typifying example to campaign for banning pythons.

The python was now characterized not just as an invasive species, but as a "deadly predator" and a danger to people. There were claims that there was no safe way to keep them (although the vast majority of owners successfully kept their pythons where they could not escape or harm people). One member of Congress envisioned them "killing and consuming just about anything in their path."

This frightening portrait was coupled with statistical estimates that South Florida was now inhabited by 150,000 invasive pythons. This figure was vastly larger than the estimate produced by researchers studying the area (who thought there might be about 5,000 pythons in the wild).

In short, claims about the python problem characterized it in a particular way that both severely exaggerated the threat to people and downplayed ecologists' concerns about pythons' invasive role in South Florida's ecosystem.

Source: Moloney & Unnithan, 2019.

suggests the scope of the problem. In our child abuse example, we might be told that authorities receive nearly three million reports of suspected child abuse annually. In contemporary American culture, statistics imply accuracy and precision—that someone must have counted something. In practice, this is not necessarily true. When claimsmakers are first trying to draw attention to a social problem, they often argue that this problem has been neglected or overlooked. But if people have been ignoring a particular social condition, they probably haven't been carefully measuring its extent, which means no one has been keeping accurate statistics. As a result, early claims often feature figures that are ballpark estimates or educated guesses (J. Best, 2013). And just as claimsmakers favor dramatic typifying examples, they usually prefer big numbers, statistics that suggest that the problem is widespread, because a big number implies there is a big problem. Particularly at the beginning of the social problems process, claims often feature big numbers that are really little more than rough estimates (see Box 2.2).

The three ingredients in the basic rhetorical recipe—a disturbing typifying example, a name, and a big number—combine to create a troubling impression. For example, a description of a small child being beaten to death, coupled with both an explanation that this death is just one instance of the larger problem of child abuse and a statement that three million cases of suspected abuse are reported each year, conveys a sense that millions of children are in danger—possibly of losing their lives. This basic recipe offers a quick, compelling case for recognizing a new social problem. It is an effective rhetorical formula, one that can be spotted in many social problems claims.

Additional Grounds. Claims often feature grounds beyond the basic recipe's three ingredients. Many different rhetorical devices can appear as grounds in social problems claims; what follows is just a sampling.

• *Worsening situation.* Very often, claims insist that the problem is getting worse. Words like *epidemic* and *crime wave* convey a sense of urgency: the problem is spreading, and—unless something is done—it may soon spiral out of control.

Box 2.2 Straw Figures

In 2011, a nine-year-old boy contacted three American manufacturers of drinking straws, asked them to estimate the number of drinking straws produced each year, averaged their responses, and announced that Americans consume 500 million straws per day. This figure found its way into media coverage (often coupled with a video of a sea turtle having a straw removed from its nostril) as evidence of the problem of plastic pollution in the ocean.

There is good reason to question the 500 million figure. In 2011, the U.S. population was about 312 million, which would require every man, woman, and child to use 1.6 straws per day—which seems like a lot. Moreover, a firm that tracks trends in the food-service industry by surveying more than 1,000 restaurant operators, estimated that restaurants used 172 million straws per day in 2016. That's still a lot of straws, but it works out to about one straw per person every other day, which seems more reasonable, and of course the firm's methods seem more likely to produce an accurate number. Some media sources have argued that this lower figure seems more credible, but the larger number lives on in media coverage.

Why does the less accurate number survive? It is a big, round number (half a billion straws each day), so it seems impressive and is easier to remember. But also note that reporters tend to treat numbers as facts, as true, so they often feel free to repeat numbers. Careful wording, such as "By some estimates, Americans throw away 500 million plastic straws each day" makes the statement true—after all, it is true that someone has made that estimate, even if there is good reason to doubt the number's accuracy. Watch for other suspiciously big, round numbers in social problems claims.

Source: Britschgi, 2018.

● *Familiar type of problem.* Claims often categorize a problem as being of a recognizable type, such as a crime or a disease. These types are characterized by familiar patterns: we think of crime as being perpetrated by a criminal who intentionally preys on an innocent victim, and diseases as striking vulnerable individuals who should not be considered responsible for getting sick. When a claim classifies the new problem as belonging to a particular type, the claim's audience immediately has a sense of how to think about the problem.

- *Kinds of people involved.* Most claims identify categories of people involved in the troubling condition, and explain how their involvement should be understood (Loseke, 2003). Among the most common person categories are *victims* (those harmed by the problem, who may be characterized as bearing no responsibility for their plight, and therefore meriting society's support and sympathy) and *villains* (those responsible for the problem, usually depicted as deserving blame and punishment). Typifying examples often illustrate the principal categories of people involved in the troubling condition (such as an innocent, abused child and an abusive parent).

- *Range of people affected.* Another popular ground for claims is the suggestion that the problem affects a broad range of people— rich and poor, white and black, and so on. Sometimes it is argued that the problem strikes "randomly" (J. Best, 1999). Of course, if a problem strikes at random, then it might affect anyone, including anyone listening to the claim. Such randomness suggests that each person who hears the claim has a personal interest in doing something to deal with the problem—before it affects him or her.

- *Challenge to older interpretations.* Claims also may challenge existing or alternative interpretations of the social problem. For instance, students who don't do well in school traditionally were held responsible for their poor performance, which was attributed to their inattention, lack of discipline or effort, and so on. But recent decades have featured claims that many students should not be blamed because their poor performance is due to biologically based learning disabilities that deserve accommodation (Conrad, 2007). Such claims challenge older, more familiar constructions. These challenges may be quite explicit; claims may list—and debunk—what they describe as "myths," widely held beliefs about the problem that the claim dismisses as wrong. For example, claims that seek to reconstruct the problem of rape criticize "rape myths" for distorting people's thinking about that crime (Suarez & Gadalla, 2010).

Again, these are just a few of the many kinds of grounds statements found in claims. Taken together, a claim's grounds give a sense of the problem—its nature, scope, and future prospects. Effective grounds convince listeners that the condition is real, thereby setting the stage for the claim's warrants.

Warrants

A claim's **warrants** justify doing something about the troubling condition; they explain why something *ought* to be done. Warrants invoke values and emotions. That is, warrants argue that the condition identified in the grounds is inconsistent with what we value, and therefore we need to do something about it. Thus, claims suggest that the troubling condition violates our sense of justice, fairness, equality, or other values; in turn, we may experience anger, pity, or other emotional reactions.

Values tend to be expressed as vague principles that most—if not all—people can endorse. Most Americans can be expected to hold freedom, justice, equality, protecting the vulnerable, and humanitarianism as cherished values. But what does this mean in practice? It is not always clear how abstract values apply in real-world situations. It is not unusual for opponents in debates over social issues to endorse the same values, even as they support opposing policies. Thus, both those who favor and those who oppose restricting access to abortion tend to invoke *rights*: pro-life abortion opponents speak of the "unborn child's right to life," while pro-choice abortion advocates speak of a "woman's right to choose." Similarly, those who favor affirmative action argue that affirmative action programs foster equality by giving advantages to those who have been disadvantaged, yet affirmative action opponents insist that the programs subvert equality because they don't treat everyone evenhandedly. Although virtually all Americans can be expected to affirm their beliefs in rights or equality, obviously they can disagree over how those abstract values should be translated into practical policies.

Warrants rise and fall in popularity. Sometimes new warrants—new ways of justifying claims—emerge, and change how social problems are characterized. For example, in recent years the rising costs of medical care have inspired a new warrant: arguments that some troubling conditions need to be addressed because they create costly health care burdens for the larger society. For instance, laws requiring motorcycle riders to wear protective helmets have been justified by the high costs of providing long-term medical care to head injury patients, just as campaigns to restrict smoking and reduce obesity have emphasized how those conditions add many millions of dollars to the nation's medical costs.

Warrants based on medical costs seem to have emerged to counter arguments that defended motorcycle riding and other risky activities using another, older warrant: personal freedom. That is, motorcycle riders, smokers, and overweight individuals have long argued that they ought to have the freedom to make their own choices, even if those choices involve risks. American culture generally considers freedom an important warrant, particularly if the person taking the risks is not harming others. Using medical costs as a warrant tries to counter this older defense based on individual liberty by arguing that helmetless motorcycle riders and other risk takers are not just endangering themselves, but are also harming everyone else, in that their risky behavior raises health care costs across the board, and society has a right to try to discourage people from taking such costly risks.

Because people can be strongly attached to particular values, and because claims need to be compelling, claims' warrants often inspire powerful emotional reactions, such as outrage, shock, sadness, or guilt. Effective claims move people to take action. While it may be possible to assemble a claim that relies on bloodless cost–benefit reasoning to convince people that it is in their best interest to respond to a social problem, it is often more effective to arouse emotional reactions, to make them feel that something must be done right away. This is why claims favor melodramatic typifying examples: it is harder to ignore the plight of innocent victims or of those who are especially deserving. Claims can make use of a wide range of emotional appeals (see Box 2.3).

Because claims can invoke many different values and emotions, and because those values are abstract and subject to conflicting interpretations, claims often feature multiple warrants so differ- ent people may agree that something needs to be done about a troubling condition even though they disagree on the reasons for taking action.

Conclusions

Every claim, then, offers a justification for taking action: the grounds identify a troubling condition, and the warrants explain why some- thing should be done about it. Thus, all claims lead to **conclusions**, statements that specify what should be done, what action should be taken to address this social problem. The nature of the conclu- sions is shaped by the grounds and warrants. If a claim's grounds have depicted a condition that causes terrible suffering, and the warrants speak to humanitarian concerns about the need to alleviate suffering, then the conclusions are likely to focus on ways to help the afflicted. On the other hand, if the grounds emphasize the terrible nature of a particular crime, and if the warrants focus on society's need to protect its members from such evils, then the conclusions will probably advocate cracking down on this crime.

Claims → Conclusions
grounds ID problem
Why something should be done – warrant

Box 2.3 The Meth Lab Formula

Once a social problem has been effectively constructed, people can use the construction to interpret events. Revier (2017) examined local and regional press coverage of the response to a meth lab explosion in which a woman in the building died from severe burns. Two men who had been cooking meth in the house were convicted of manslaughter.

Press coverage and the testimony at the trial revealed that this incident was interpreted as an instance of a standard, formula story about meth labs. This story featured villains (those who callously choose to break the law by manufacturing a drug that can lead to explosions if important precautions are ignored, which not only endangers those in the vicinity of the lab but also spreads a harmful drug in the community); victims (those who can be harmed by explosions or drug use, as well as relatives and other community members who suffer collateral damage from the drug's effects); and heroes (law enforcers seeking to bring villains to justice).

Such formula stories seem to make sense because they use the heroes/villains/victims elements found in much of our thinking. But notice what gets lost in these apparently straightforward accounts. There is no sense of how larger social conditions might provide a context for such tales; of how, for instance, better understanding of rural unemployment, the decline in family farming, or the effects of welfare reform might help explain why meth labs began cropping up in rural America. Constructing a problem in terms of villains who make evil choices allows us to bypass asking why such villainy seems to crop up at particular times and in particular places. Formula stories help us see some things, but they also encourage us to ignore others.

Often conclusions include both short-range and long-range goals. Within the short term, claimsmakers may be trying to arouse concern—to make others aware of the problem, to get people to join their campaign, or to encourage the media to cover the issue.

Longer-range goals typically seek policy changes by arguing that policymakers need to pass a new law, fund a program, or otherwise deal with the troubling condition in a new, more effective way. Usually the short-range goals are seen as steps toward making these long-range changes possible.

Conclusions range from vague endorsements of change to extensive, detailed agendas for action. Early in the social problems process, when claimsmakers' primary aim is to raise awareness of the troubling condition, grounds and warrants tend to receive more emphasis. At later stages in the process, when concern about the problem has become widespread, policy choices become a more central focus, and conclusions are likely to receive greater, more detailed attention.

Summary

Grounds, warrants, and conclusions, then, are standard elements in most arguments (Toulmin, 1958). In the case of social problems claims, this rhetorical structure explains what is wrong, why it is wrong, and what should be done about it. But who hears these claims? Which audiences are these claims meant to persuade, and how do they respond?

CLAIMS, THEIR AUDIENCES, AND THE SOCIAL PROBLEMS MARKETPLACE

Every claim involves communication between at least two parties: those who make the claim (*claimants* or *claimsmakers*), and an **audience** whom the claim is meant to persuade. The audience for claims can include all of the other participants in the social problems process: people who might be enlisted in the cause, other claimsmakers, members of the media who might publicize

people to persuade

the claims, the general public, policymakers, and so on. Audiences differ in what they find persuasive, so effective claims need to be tailored to fit their audiences' concerns. How claimsmakers understand those concerns should affect their rhetorical choices. Because there is little point in presenting claims that an audience will not find convincing, claimsmakers must devise arguments that they believe will persuade their audience.

Some claims face little resistance, quickly gaining widespread acceptance among those who hear them. For example, claims about child abuse, child pornography, and other similar threats to children tend to be well received (J. Best, 1990). American culture views children as vulnerable innocents who deserve societal protection. Therefore, claims that children are being menaced by adults can arouse widespread concern. The arguments seem so compelling that it is difficult to imagine anyone opposing such claims; how could child abuse possibly be defended? Political scientists sometimes refer to claims that inspire this sort of general agreement as **valence issues** (Nelson, 1984), although what seems at first glance to be consensus may encompass different views.

At the other extreme are claims related to entrenched controversies that will probably never lead to consensus. The debate over abortion remains intense because it features people who have taken intractable, opposing positions: some pro-life advocates argue that abortion is murder and should never be tolerated, while some pro-choice proponents insist that women must be able to control their own bodies and therefore must be free to choose to have abortions. It is very unlikely that a new pro-life claim will persuade those who hold hard-core pro-choice beliefs to change their minds, and equally unlikely that pro-choice arguments can be devised that will change the opinion of those firmly committed to a hard-core pro-life position. When addressing such contested issues, or **position issues**, claimsmakers know that they cannot persuade everyone; they can expect their claims to encounter opposition from at least some people who hear them (Nelson, 1984).

The audience for claims is not an undifferentiated mass. Rather, it can be subdivided—or **segmented**—by race, age, social class, gender, region, and so on. Different segments of the audience tend to have different interests and ideologies. People may respond to a claim by recognizing that they stand to gain or lose if the claims succeed: claims probably seem more compelling to segments of the audience who perceive themselves as directly threatened by the troubling condition, while other segments may resist claims that might adversely affect them by, for example, restricting their freedom or raising their taxes.

Such perceptions of interest are often linked to ideologies or systems of beliefs; different segments of the population are likely to view the world differently, to place different emphasis on particular values, explanations, justifications, and so on. As a general rule, those who benefit from existing social arrangements are more likely to view those arrangements as just, fair, and reasonable, and they are less likely to be sympathetic to claims arguing that those arrangements need to be overturned. Thus, both their interests and their ideologies make them a tough audience, while those disadvantaged by the troubling condition are more likely to be receptive to such claims. Different segments of society, then, view the world differently, and persuasive claims need to match the various worldviews of the segments of the audience toward which they are directed.

Claimsmakers devise various methods to deal with audience segmentation. One tactic is to preach to the choir—that is, to direct claims toward those segments of the audience most likely to respond favorably. For example, abortion activists often direct their claims toward those who they believe already share their beliefs—as when they speak to sympathizers at pro-choice or pro-life rallies. Directing claims to those most likely to be supportive can be a particularly important tactic at the beginning of the social problems process, when claims are first being made: addressing a presumably sympathetic audience first can make more people aware of an issue, rally supporters to the cause, give claimsmakers a chance to hone their claims to make them as persuasive as possible, and create some momentum for carrying the claim to a broader, more diverse audience (such tactics for mobilizing supporters into a social movement are discussed further in Chapter 3).

An alternative approach is to craft claims so as to maximize their appeal to the broadest possible audience. Claims can incorporate multiple grounds, warrants, and conclusions that appeal to different people, thereby seeming to offer something for, if not everyone, at least lots of people. For instance, many advocates of vegetarianism see ethical issues as central to their cause, and they oppose meat eating as morally wrong. However, they also know that these ethical claims encounter widespread resistance; most Americans enjoy eating meat and don't consider it wrong, so moral arguments alone are unlikely to persuade a large audience (Maurer, 2002). However, other grounds and warrants are available: vegetarians can argue that eating meat is unhealthy, in that it fosters heart disease and other ailments; or they can claim that raising animals for food damages the environment. Such arguments add additional grounds and warrants to vegetarians' claims that might appeal to people who are worried about their health or the environment, even if they don't have moral qualms about eating meat. Expanding claims in this way offers vegetarians a chance to persuade people who could be expected to resist narrower ethical arguments that eating meat is wrong.

Well-crafted claims sometimes create surprising alliances among people who usually don't agree, inspiring consensus and converting potential conflict into a valence issue. For instance, political liberals and conservatives often disagree about educational policies. Yet, during the 1990s, many liberals and conservatives joined forces to promote policies requiring public school students to wear uniforms (Brunsma, 2004). Liberals argued that uniforms would make social class differences among students less visible, reduce pressure on parents to purchase expensive clothes for children, and enhance students' self-esteem; conservatives claimed that uniforms would encourage discipline and orderly behavior among students. Both sides insisted that school uniforms could reduce violence and improve learning. In this case, people who usually disagree found themselves promoting the same solution, even though they disagreed about the precise nature of the problem.

Similarly, advocates representing a wide range of ideologies support efforts to exclude troubling material from elementary and secondary school textbooks: liberals call for excluding material that might reinforce gender or racial stereotypes, fundamentalist Christians want to block content mentioning witches or other supernatural elements, and so on (Ravitch, 2003). Mandating school uniforms and regulating textbook content are just two examples of claims constructed in ways that build broad-based consensus among people who often disagree on other educational issues.

It is important to recognize that the audiences for claims are not passive. People who hear claims react, and claimsmakers must take those reactions into account, by adjusting, revising, and fine-tuning their claims to make them more effective, more persuasive. Claims should not be viewed as one-way messages, transmitted from claimsmakers/senders to their audiences/receivers. Rather, claimsmakers need to be sensitive to their audiences' reactions, to figure out which parts of their claims are working and which are not persuasive and need to be revised. In other words, claimsmakers and their audiences engage in a **dialog** in which the audience's feedback leads claimsmakers to modify their claims (Nichols, 2003).

If a particular ground or warrant fails to elicit a good reaction, claimsmakers may strike it from their claims and substitute something that they hope will evoke a more favorable response from their audience. For instance, activists campaigning to halt impending cuts in programs that had provided support to immigrants began with general claims ("immigrant rights are human rights") that proved ineffective. However, they soon found that the media and politicians responded more favorably to claims about the vulnerability of elderly, disabled immigrants, so they refocused their campaign on these more sympathetic cases (Fujiwara, 2005).

Claimsmaking is usually not a one-shot effort; it takes time to develop effective claims. Most claimsmakers have to try again and again to achieve widespread attention for their claims; they must try out claims, assess the audience's response, revise the claims, and so on, until they develop a persuasive argument. After all, claims compete within a **social problems marketplace** (J. Best, 1990; Hilgartner & Bosk, 1988). At any given moment, countless claimsmakers are struggling to get their particular claims heard—far more than can hope to capture the audience's limited attention. For example, at the beginning of September 2001, President George W. Bush's top priority was passing a comprehensive immigration reform program (Gonzales, 2016). In a related effort, an event had been scheduled in Washington, D.C., on September 12 to mobilize support for the DREAM Act (which would allow individuals who had entered the country illegally as children to eventually qualify for citizenship). Of course, the 9/11 terrorist attacks derailed all of these plans: the focus of policymakers, the media, and the public concentrated on addressing terrorism, and immigration issues effectively dropped from view for months. Claims do not exist in a vacuum.

The best-known claims are those that achieve widespread recognition—what has been called **societalization** (Alexander, 2018). That is, they attract attention to what becomes understood as a national issue, engaging a nation's policymakers (such as Congress or federal agencies) and major media (such as the most prestigious newspapers or major television news channels). Often the troubling condition that these claims highlight may not be all that new, but it may have been concealed by the practices of particular institutions. For example, the Catholic Church had long recognized that some priests had sexual contact with youths, but it had handled these cases by quietly transferring the priests to other assignments, just as in the run-up to the 2008 financial crisis, major investment banks had been selling—and financial rating agencies had been approving these sales—high-risk investments as safe. In these cases, events (news that the Church had not told law enforcement about priests with long records of criminal misbehavior, the collapse of major investment banks) generated intense media scrutiny that made the institutions' questionable practices public. In the face of this attention, the institutions lose the ability to retain control of their own activities, and there are calls for policies that will end both the troubling condition and the institutional practices that tolerated it. As these issues develop, it may become apparent that there has been a long history of claimsmakers trying—and generally failing—to draw attention to the troubling condition that now seems to be a focus for general concern. Of course, not all claims achieve societalization; some issues play out in smaller local or regional arenas, and, of course, at any time there are other current claims that are being ignored, as they await a societalizing spotlight.

The competition to capture the audience's attention helps explain some of the features of social problems rhetoric that we noted earlier. Why do claimsmakers so often begin claims with disturbing typifying examples? Why do claims usually settle for naming the problem—often with a catchy label like *road rage*—and avoid giving detailed (and therefore boring) definitions of the problem? Why do claimsmakers favor statistics that suggest the problem is surprisingly large? Why do they favor prominent targets? Each of these rhetorical devices is arresting, eye-catching; each can draw people's attention to this claim (and away from those other claims competing for the audience's attention). The goal is to grab and hold the audience. This competition in the social problems marketplace means that claimsmakers are encouraged to devise dramatic, disturbing, easily grasped claims that will command attention over competing claims. Simpler, stronger arguments work better (see Box 2.4).

In sum, claimsmakers present what they hope will be persuasive arguments, but they must then attend to the audience's responses, and those responses and their own sense of how they need to revise

Box 2.4 Stories as Resources

We use stories to make sense of our world in general, and of social problems in particular. Claimsmakers' arguments often incorporate elements of particular stories, such as vulnerable innocents imperiled by more powerful villains; this very juxtaposition of good and evil allows us to cast some troubling condition—perhaps some unfamiliar topic that we knew nothing about until a claimsmaker brought it to our attention—into a familiar framework, a type of story that we may know well, a plotline that we first heard as children and have since consumed in countless movies, TV shows, comic books, and novels.

Consider, for example, stories about underdogs, such as David facing off against Goliath. We tell ourselves that underdogs deserve our sympathy and support because they face stiff odds but bravely stand up anyway. Claimsmakers often portray themselves as underdogs, taking up a righteous cause against formidable opposition. Invoking this imagery gives people an emotional investment in the claims; it gives them someone with whom they can identify and support. The underdog plot is yet another cultural resource that can make claims easier to understand and more persuasive.

Notice that invoking a story or some other cultural resource may or may not be warranted. It should not surprise us that claimsmakers see themselves as on the side of righteousness and justice; after all, their claims are meant to persuade and they probably find their own claims convincing. But, of course, critics may dispute any of the elements in a claim; they may, for instance, question whether the underdogs in the claimmaker's story deserve to be cast in such emotionally sympathetic terms.

Source: Presser, 2018.

their rhetoric in turn may be affected by all the other claims and events that are competing for the audience's attention in the social problems marketplace.

EVOLUTION AND OPPOSITION

Social problems claims are not static; rather, they keep evolving. This process continues even after the audience becomes concerned about the problem. Once a claim has attracted recognition and acceptance, we can consider it *well established*; that is, there is widespread agreement that this troubling condition ought to be considered a social problem. Yet this is not the end of the matter; even well-established claims need to change. However compelling claims may seem when they first gain acceptance, they tend to become familiar, stale, boring (Downs, 1972). Audiences find it easier to forget about or ignore claims that can be dismissed as old news, particularly because other, newer claims are always competing for their attention. Audiences also may become frustrated by problems that aren't easily solved—where efforts to address the problem don't seem to make much progress. Each time a claim is repeated, it seems more familiar, less interesting—and less persuasive.

Therefore, claimsmakers often find it necessary to revise and repackage their claims, just to make them seem fresh and interesting. They may add additional grounds, more warrants, or fresh conclusions to give their claims a new look. For instance, instead of simply criticizing the general problem of sexism, the women's movement has been successful at calling attention to a long series of women's issues, each revealing a different aspect of sexist practices, through claims about sexual harassment, date rape, the glass ceiling (which blocks female executives from rising to the top of corporations), and so on. Continually identifying additional forms of sexism keeps the women's movement's claims fresh.

Once a claim has gained acceptance, it is often possible to build additional claims on that foundation. One possibility is **domain expansion** (J. Best, 1990, 2015). As we have seen, initial claims often emphasize disturbing typifying examples. In the 1960s, for example, claimsmakers described the *battered child syndrome*, the problem of brutal beatings of infants or very young children. Terrible examples tend to make claims more interesting and effective; they help raise concern about an issue. In turn, once this concern has been established, it becomes possible to argue that other conditions are just as bad as—really just another form of, or the moral equivalent of—the initial problem. (Think of domain expansion as like opening an umbrella, so that more topics are covered by a social problem.)

In the case of child beating, battered child syndrome was soon renamed *child abuse*, and then the boundaries of what was considered abusive began to expand: Abuse also could affect older children and even adolescents. People began to recognize new types of abuse; beatings were now termed *physical abuse*, as distinguished from emotional abuse, sexual abuse, and so on. And advocates began applying the now widely accepted *child abuse* label to a range of other phenomena, so smoking around children, failing to strap kids into protective car seats, and circumcision, among other things, were claimed to be forms of child abuse. In other words, over time, the domain of child abuse expanded to include more and more phenomena. This sort of domain expansion can occur whenever initial claims become well established.

In a related process, claimsmakers choose to **piggyback** a new troubling condition on a well-established problem (Loseke, 2003; J. Best, 2015). Again, child abuse is a good example. The popularity of the label *child abuse* inspired other claimsmakers to characterize their troubling conditions as varieties of *abuse*—so people began speaking of wife abuse, sibling abuse, elder abuse, and so on. Similarly, the successes of the civil rights movement led, in turn, to other campaigns promoting the *rights* of various groups—such as women's rights, gay rights, children's rights, prisoners' rights, and animal rights. And mid-1990s claims about road rage (typified as drivers becoming frustrated and violently attacking others) led journalists to begin identifying all sorts of other *rages*: air rage (among airline passengers), desk rage (office workers), even shopping cart rage (J. Best & Furedi, 2001). In each of these cases, a well-established social problem created opportunities to construct

claims about other troubling conditions as being somehow analogous to the familiar original—in effect arguing that there was a sort
of family resemblance among types of abuse, rights, or rages—that
if the familiar case deserved to be considered a social problem, then
so, too, did these other troubling conditions. (Claimsmakers can,
in effect, borrow someone else's umbrella, using an existing term
to cover an additional problem.)

Claims do not have to use the same terms—*abuse, rights, rage,*
and so on—to piggyback on successful constructions. In some cases
the rhetorical formula used to construct one social problem can be
applied to other problems of the same general sort. There is, for
example, a fairly standard recipe for identifying new drug problems:
claims are made that a drug is particularly harmful, that its use
is rapidly spreading, and so on (Reinarman, 1994). This familiar, well-established formula means that contemporary arguments
about the dangers of Ecstasy or crystal meth do not look a great deal
different from nineteenth-century warnings about opium smoking.
Similarly, claims about new forms of victimization often use a well-
established rhetorical formula arguing that victimization is widespread and serious yet remains hidden, so extraordinary measures
are needed to identify it, and so on (J. Best, 1999). In other words,
the structure of successful claims—combinations of grounds, warrants, and conclusions that have proved effective in bringing attention to one drug problem or one form of victimization—can be
copied and brought to bear on other, analogous issues (see Box 2.5).

Claims often inspire **counterclaims**, arguments in direct opposition to the original claims. Again, think of the pro-life and pro-
choice movements' struggle over abortion; or the claims that climate
change is a serious problem exacerbated by humans' activities, and
the counterclaims that global warming may be neither as serious
as has been feared nor caused primarily by people's actions. Or
the disputes may be much narrower, focused on the meaning of
a particular individual's life. In all of these cases, advocates with

Box 2.5 Canadian Cannabis Claims and Counterclaims

In 2015, Justin Trudeau became prime minister of Canada; one of his campaign pledges was to legalize recreational marijuana use. While legalization did not occur until 2018, a number of cannabis shops opened soon after the election, often calling themselves dispensaries. Medical cannabis was already legal in Canada, but selling the drug—whether for medical or recreational use—through shops was not at the time legal. However, police tended to treat the shops as low priority, and when operators were arrested, courts tended to dismiss the charges. Change seemed in the air.

However, in May 2016, Toronto police raided forty-three dispensaries and arrested operators on various criminal charges. Police spokespersons justified these raids using factual, neutral language. Outside the formal press conferences, however, they tended to dramatize the issues, warning that Toronto could become the "Wild West" and that children were endangered by marijuana sales.

The police claims led to counterclaims, which adopted similar rhetorical styles. On the one hand, they adopted a factual, neutral tone to argue that cannabis shops did not deserve to receive so much police attention, and that this was an inefficient use of police resources. On the other, they also used more dramatic rhetoric by emphasizing that the shops promoted public health by serving individuals who depended on marijuana for medical purposes, and who might find it difficult to acquire the drugs they needed if they had to order them legally through the mail. In other words, the rhetoric of the anti-shop claimsmakers and the counterclaimsmakers who defended the shops drew upon similar cultural resources to mirror the rhetorical styles favored by their opponents.

Source: Müller, 2019.

opposing views develop full-fledged arguments—each with its own set of grounds, warrants, and conclusions, and each trying to make the most persuasive case.

Such debates often revolve around confrontations over grounds or warrants. Each side may challenge the evidence—the grounds—presented by its opponents, charging that those opponents have misunderstood or misrepresented the nature of the troubling condition. "Stat wars" may arise in which each side denounces its opponents' statistics and argues that its own numbers are more accurate (J. Best, 2013). Similarly, opponents may insist that some warrants ought to be more compelling than others; in the abortion debate, for example, there are sharp disagreements about whether the rights of the fetus or those of the pregnant woman ought to be considered more important.

Many claims emerge within and are promoted as linked to particular **ideologies**—that is, more or less coherent sets of beliefs, such as libertarianism, feminism, liberalism, conservatism, or specific religious doctrines. Ideologies usually emphasize particular warrants; for example, libertarianism views liberty as a central value, and feminism opposes social arrangements that block opportunities for women. Often, too, those familiar with an ideology favor particular grounds; feminists, of course, look for evidence of sexism, and so on. In addition, ideologies often recognize competing belief systems, so liberals and conservatives anticipate disagreeing over many issues. These ideological disputes make it very easy to mount counterclaims; the news that someone associated with a rival ideology is making a claim invites counterclaims.

Claims often have to be modified in response to counterclaims. Opposition means that one's arguments will be subjected to sharper scrutiny and criticism, and those elements that prove easiest to challenge may need to be changed or reinforced. A statistic that has been debunked by one's opponents may be dropped and a more defensible number added to fill the gap, and so on. At the same time, the fact that there is opposition can be incorporated into one's claims. It may be possible to characterize one's opponents as part of the problem, turning the fact of opposition into a new ground for the claims. At least for those who share our ideology, news that the opposition is making counterclaims can reassure us that we're correct.

Opposition is often predictable. There are **social problems clusters**—sets of claimsmakers who take similar positions regarding related social problems (J. Best, 2015; Griffiths & Best, 2016). When new issues emerge, many of the same people are likely to find themselves making claims that resemble those they've made in the past. For instance, claims about a new drug problem are likely to resemble those made about older drugs, with drug control advocates calling for new laws and tougher enforcement, even as advocates of drug abuse prevention and drug treatment warn that cracking down will only make things worse. There are lots of familiar social problems clusters: if you imagine some new issue related to guns, women, the environment, or race, you can probably predict some of the people likely to make claims, the sorts of rhetoric they are likely to adopt, and the interplay between claims and counterclaims.

In sum, claims are constantly in play. They evolve, and they can inspire both other claims and opposition, so new claims are almost always shaped by those that preceded them.

CULTURAL RESOURCES

Theoretically, claimsmakers are free to assemble claims in any form they choose. In practice, however, claims have to make sense—both to the claimsmakers who choose to make them, and to the audiences whom the claimsmakers hope to persuade. This means that claims must draw on the larger culture; they must be consistent with people's understandings of how the world works. In some societies, attributing misfortune to the acts of witches has been seen as a perfectly sensible explanation. In contemporary American society, however, claims about witchcraft are likely to be rejected out of hand by most people—although not by all. Most would-be claimsmakers recognize that this is the prevailing view, so they tend to avoid blaming witches or, more generally, constructing problems along lines that they and their audiences will find unconvincing.

Every culture, then, can be seen as a large repository of evolving, more or less familiar ideas about how the world works—and how it should work. These **cultural resources** are available to be exploited whenever claims are created. Our culture, for example, tends to idealize children as vulnerable innocents, and claims that warn about threats to children often elicit sympathetic reactions. This is such a widely shared view that we have trouble imagining people thinking any other way. However, New England's Puritans had a much darker view of children: they worried that children were born in a state of sinful willfulness, and they believed that children needed to have their wills broken to become properly God-fearing (Fischer, 1989, pp. 97–101).

Such different assumptions lead to quite different visions of, say, discipline. For some modern Americans, spanking is seen as harmful, even as a form of child abuse—one more way that adults inflict injuries on innocent children (P. W. Davis, 1994). Although the Puritans considered spanking a last resort, they used a variety of physical restraints and shaming devices, such as forcing a child who talked during church services to wear a wooden bit; such practices, which seem quite shocking to us, were standard ways of disciplining children, designed to teach them to be submissive and to understand God's wrath. It's easy to imagine that some claims about endangered children that might seem very powerful to us would have fallen on deaf ears among the Puritans (see Box 2.6).

Claims, then, draw on a society's cultural resources—the fund of words, ideas, images, and emotional reactions that most people understand to be reasonable. It is easier to arouse contemporary Americans' concern about threats to children or violence against women—two groups that are widely understood to be relatively vulnerable to victimization and therefore in need of protection—than to promote claims about endangered adult males. Nevertheless, although culture does limit the range of possible claims to

Box 2.6   Problem Children

The array of available cultural resources invites many ways of constructing claims, but it also places constraints on would-be claims-makers when claims seem to contradict cultural expectations.

Consider children. Americans think of children as innocent, vulnerable, in need of protection. When a child misbehaves, there is a strong tendency to blame this on the failure of adults to properly raise that child. Constructions of child sexual abuse routinely invoke images of innocents victimized by exploitative adults.

And yet children sometimes behave in sexual ways; becoming sexual is a process that individuals experience in different ways, not something that occurs on everyone's eighteenth birthday. Popular culture simultaneously uses sexualized images of children, while insisting that children are innocent, and that anyone who has sexual contact with a child is committing a seriously deviant act. Think about the difficulties adult authorities had trying to devise policies toward sexting: in a world of ubiquitous smartphones, there was shock that some children were using—and encouraging other children to use—phones to produce and distribute sexually provocative images. Are they best understood as misguided innocents or despised child pornographers?

The point is that we take our cultural assumptions for granted; we assume that the way we categorize and interpret the world is the correct—really, the only possible—way to understand it. This makes it difficult for us to think critically about our assumptions, so that while it is easy to construct children as being "at risk," it is much harder to talk about children "as risks" in their own right.

Source: McAlinden, 2018.

some degree, it still offers a broad array of choices. For example, various segments of the U.S. population attribute different social problems to quite diverse causes—causes such as acts of God (for instance, to explain natural disasters), germs, conspiracies, belief systems (for example, particular religious or political ideologies), people's upbringing, and so on. Of course, part of being familiar with a culture is having the ability to predict which audiences will find which explanations appropriate for which problems (see Box 2.7).

Note that the fund of cultural resources is large, diverse, and not necessarily logically consistent. The point is not that all social problems have to be constructed in the same way, but that any culture offers various ideas and images that might be incorporated into successful claims. Just as American culture supports values that can sometimes conflict with one another, so, too, it encompasses other competing, conflicting notions.

This cultural diversity means that most social problems might be constructed in very different ways. For example, debates over poverty often feature dramatically different interpretations: Some commentators argue that the poor bear much of the responsibility for their plight, that they make bad choices (such as dropping out of school) that make poverty a likely outcome. Other critics insist that poverty is largely a product of a social structure that blocks too many opportunities, creating obstacles (such as a shortage of high-paying jobs) that make it hard for people to overcome poverty. Both the idea that individuals must bear responsibility for their own decisions, and the idea that a fair society should offer opportunities for advancement are familiar; both belong to the stock of cultural resources from which claims can be assembled. Such competing accounts of poverty's causes—although derived from the same culture—can reveal bitter differences within the culture. Claimsmakers may charge that rival claims are morally irresponsible because they apply inappropriate explanations, that they ignore God's laws, blame victims who should not be blamed, or err in some other way. Not everyone subscribes to every element in the larger culture—certainly not all of the time.

Moreover, the cultural context for claims is continually shifting. Ideas, values, imagery, explanations—all the elements of culture—can go in and out of fashion. In part, this fluctuation reflects people's ongoing quest for novelty: both claimsmakers and their audiences

Box 2.7 Expanding the Domain of Stockholm Syndrome

Claims can have convoluted histories. For instance, Stockholm syndrome was a label originally applied to former hostages who expressed sympathy for their kidnappers. It was understood as a narrowly defined psychiatric problem, an apparently irrational response to having experienced great stress as a crime victim, for which psychological counseling was recommended.

Over time, Stockholm syndrome's domain expanded. In cases where women who had experienced domestic violence—or children who had been abused—continued to express emotional ties to their abusers, claimsmakers argued that these victims were displaying the syndrome. Later, claimsmakers applied the label to cult members, prostitutes, suicidal terrorists, and others as a way of dismissing the victims' emotional bonds to cult leaders, pimps, the leaders of terrorist movements, and so on. Eventually, Stockholm syndrome became a cultural resource for all sorts of claimsmakers seeking to criticize what they defined as inappropriate attitudes or alliances (for instance, arguing that those who do not join some popular cause are victims of the syndrome).

Notice that the claimsmakers who originally constructed Stockholm syndrome sympathized with and sought to understand and help various sorts of victims. As its domain expanded, however, the term became a resource that could be used to criticize as irrational the feelings of all sorts of people with whom the claimsmakers disagreed.

Source: Adorjan, Christensen, Kelly, & Pawluch, 2012.

can become bored when claims seem stale—too familiar—so claims must be continually repackaged to make them appear fresh and interesting. In addition, genuinely new elements are added to the stock of cultural resources; a scientific discovery, the spread of a new disease, a new invention, or a dramatic event can have far-reaching consequences. Such novelties can reverberate through society generally, and through the social problems marketplace in particular, in complex ways.

Consider the identification of AIDS as a new disease in the early 1980s. No sociologist could have predicted all of the consequences that derived from that development: shifts in funding priorities for medical research and reforms in the methods used to test new treatments, the promotion of AIDS prevention policies (including condom distribution and needle exchange programs), all manner of art portraying aspects of the epidemic, and on and on. Or consider how the spread of cell phones has spawned new social problems claims—about the risks when drivers are distracted while talking on their phones, about the propriety of carrying on phone conversations where they can be overheard by others, and about allegations of health hazards from cell phones.

Cultural shifts are reflected in social problems claims. Many social problems—for instance, gangs, cults, racism, and poverty—have been the subject of claims going back many decades, even centuries, but the particular constructions of these problems in different periods reflect current cultural developments during those periods. This means that cultural conditions during particular historical periods affect how social problems are constructed during those times. For example, the theme of expanding individual rights during the 1960s (as reflected in the civil rights movement and the sexual revolution), or the shift toward more conservative values that began in the late 1970s (as reflected in growing concerns about sex and drugs), can be seen as having influenced claims about many different social problems (Jenkins, 2006). (Chapter 10 will have more to say about the historical context of claims.)

Cultural resources, then, both constrain and enrich claims. Claims almost always use familiar language, imagery, forms of explanations, and other cultural elements. After all, the claimsmakers are themselves members of the culture, and they are almost forced to construct claims that they themselves view as sensible, claims that they also believe will receive a receptive hearing from their audiences.

Thus, cultures constrain the sorts of claims that are likely to emerge. However, cultures are complex enough, multifaceted enough, that claimsmakers still have considerable leeway in choosing and shaping the arguments they present. Although we can note similarities among claims, such as cases in which new claims seem modeled on others, and we can imagine claims (about, say, witchcraft) that seem too far-fetched to succeed in our society, it is still true that claimsmakers have a lot of flexibility in devising their arguments.

UNDERSTANDING CLAIMS

This chapter has explored various aspects of social problems claims. It began by considering claims as rhetorical arguments—the ways in which grounds, warrants, and conclusions structure claims. To be effective, though, claims have to persuade audiences, so claimsmakers must understand who their audiences are and shape their arguments to fit those audiences' concerns. As a result, claimsmakers and audiences find themselves in a dialog as they respond to one another's ideas. Claims also are influenced by other claims. They evolve over time; claims need to be periodically revised to make them seem fresh. They are also shaped by the successes and failures of earlier claims: successful claims invite domain expansion or other efforts to piggyback on their success, just as claimsmakers try to avoid the mistakes of failed claims. And for highly contentious issues, claims face counterclaims, and opponents must respond to one another's constructions within the larger social problems marketplace. Finally, the broader culture provides a context for claims: language, imagery, and other cultural resources offer raw material from which claims can be built. Figure 2.2 illustrates all these various processes.

Of course, claims are social products; they do not exist independently of people. People assemble—construct—claims in hopes of persuading others. Although this chapter has focused on the

Figure 2.2 DYNAMICS SHAPING CLAIMS

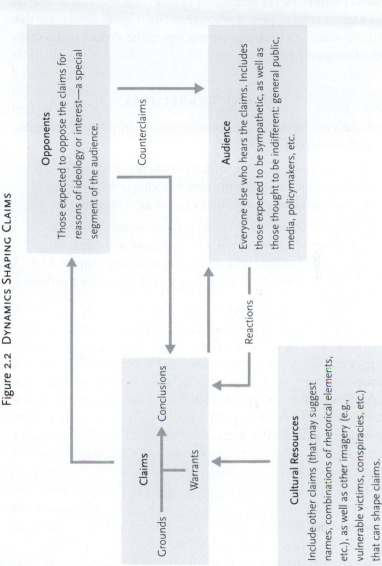

Opponents

Those expected to oppose the claims for reasons of ideology or interest—a special segment of the audience.

Counterclaims

Audience

Everyone else who hears the claims. Includes those expected to be sympathetic, as well as those thought to be indifferent: general public, media, policymakers, etc.

Reactions

Claims

Grounds

Conclusions

Warrants

Cultural Resources

Include other claims (that may suggest names, combinations of rhetorical elements, etc.), as well as other imagery (e.g., vulnerable victims, conspiracies, etc.) that can shape claims.

claims themselves, the remainder of this book will concentrate on the various sorts of people who create, distribute, alter, challenge, or otherwise react to claims—the actors in the various stages of the social problems process.

MAKING CONNECTIONS

- *Claims are rhetorical arguments structured by grounds, warrants, and conclusions.*

- *The concepts of claims and claimsmakers introduced in this chapter set the stage for the next two chapters' discussion of activists as claimsmakers and experts as claimsmakers.*

- *In Chapter 5 you will learn how claimsmakers use the media to present their claims. You will also learn how the media alter the claims they present. As you read that chapter, keep in mind what you have learned in this chapter about cultural resources.*

CASE STUDY
Battles over Bathrooms

Restrooms, or public bathrooms, often become a focus for claims-making. They are viewed as sanctums, places where individuals should have privacy. After all, these are places where people's bodies—their "private parts"—may be exposed. While people enter bathrooms to eliminate waste, widely understood as both necessary and yet somehow an embarrassing reminder of our animal nature, the fact that these are places where clothing will be disarranged also seems to give restrooms sexual overtones. These are back regions, where people retreat from public life and then wash, primp, and otherwise prepare to return (Cahill et al., 1985). Restrooms evoke complicated feelings that lend themselves to being woven into social problems claimsmaking. Most obviously, Jim Crow segregation required that there be separate sanitary facilities for "whites" and "colored," but worries about the dangers of restrooms have long figured into claims that sexually transmitted diseases (including HIV/AIDS) might spread through contact with a restroom toilet seat, and during the 1970s, opponents of the Equal Rights Amendment rallied support by warning that the amendment would inevitably lead to "unisex" facilities.

Note a taken-for-granted assumption that underpins our thinking about restrooms: that there should be—it is only natural for there to be—designated, separate spaces for males and females. (Of course, there are lots of exceptions—facilities on airplanes, for example.) Some designers argue that a more efficient solution might be to have a single restroom that contains an open area with sinks and mirrors where everyone needing to use the restroom could mingle while washing up, surrounded by stalls with floor-to-ceiling walls and doors (often found in Europe) that ensure privacy during elimination (Sanders & Stryker, 2016). Other commentators notice that claimsmakers find it awkward to address topics related to elimination, human waste, and sewage disposal (George, 2009).

Recent claimsmaking about restrooms has focused on growing awareness that the seemingly fundamental, binary male/female distinction is overly simplistic. Transgender people, including but not limited to individuals who feel uncomfortable with the gender they were assigned at birth, individuals who choose medical therapies to change their gender, and people who make other nonbinary choices have attracted attention, thanks in part to celebrities who were open about their own choices regarding gender. While transgender is a multifaceted topic, restrooms have become the focus for resisting the legitimacy of transgender claims (A. L. Stone, 2019). Should an individual be allowed or expected or required to use the bathroom that matches their birth gender, or should they use the restroom that corresponds to their gender identity? In particular, which restroom should a transgender woman (that is, an individual considered male at birth who now identifies as female) enter?

Opponents of transgender rights use such cases as typifying examples, implying that some males might claim to be female solely to gain access to women's restrooms; that is, claiming to be transgender may be nothing more than a guise to enable such males to gain access to spaces that will allow them to violate women's privacy and perhaps to commit sexually predatory crimes. Proponents of transgender rights argue that this is a ridiculous scenario, that such sexual crimes have not been reported, and they further insist that forcing transgender women to use men's restrooms is not only psychologically harmful but places them at risk of violence at the hands of the men they might encounter in the restroom. (On the concerns of transgender men, see Stein, 2018.)

Public opinion is pretty evenly split on this issue. A May 2017 Gallup poll found that 48 percent of Americans felt individuals should use restrooms that correspond to their birth gender, while 45 percent favored their using restrooms that correspond to their gender identity (J. McCarthy, 2017). This split reflects political differences: 71 percent of Republicans and 69 percent of conservatives favored transgender people using the restroom for their birth gender, while 63 percent of Democrats and 72 percent of liberals supported their using the facilities for the gender with which they identify. There were also age differences: respondents 18–29 were much more likely than those in older age categories to accept people choosing restrooms based on gender identity. This, in turn, may explain why many colleges and universities have been quick to establish all-gender restrooms as a way of both signaling their responsiveness to transgender concerns and enhancing their prestige within higher education (A. K. Davis, 2018).

Notice how the restroom with its mix of connotations—bodies, gender, and privacy—once again serves as a cultural resource for claimsmakers. Transgender issues have a long history; surgical procedures for sexual reassignment date back at least one hundred years. However, such operations were relatively rare. In recent decades, there is vastly more information available for people who might feel uncomfortable with their birth gender, a broader array of choices of treatments, and growing social support for their right to choose to alter their gender. At the same time, these developments encounter resistance, and worries that these changes fly in the face of what is natural. Which returns us to that place where we are reminded of our natural selves—the restroom.

Claims supporting transgender rights borrow from all of the earlier campaigns arguing that some groups—such as racial minorities, women, or the disabled—have a right to equal protections under the law. While considering oneself transgender might seem to be an individual decision, individuals who don't conform to traditional gender expectations may find themselves targets of hostility, and policies emerged to provide some protections. For instance, in 2016, the U.S. Departments of Education and Justice warned that school districts should not discriminate against transgender students and stated that districts that required transgender students to use restrooms and other facilities designated for their birth gender would risk losing federal funding.

In response, some state legislatures and school districts sought to require transgender individuals to use facilities for their birth gender. Most famously, North Carolina passed a "bathroom bill" in 2016 that required using birth-gender restrooms. This law attracted a good deal of national attention, resulting in various groups threatening to boycott the state, and the legislature revised the law in 2017, removing the restrictions on students using restrooms. However, that same year the Trump administration rescinded the Obama administration's instructions to school districts.

While this issue continues to be actively debated, it is worth recalling those earlier claims calling for controlling who could use which restrooms, such as the separate facilities under segregation. At the time, defenders of these arrangements argued that they were natural, that it was unthinkable the restrooms could be integrated, and yet, more than fifty years after the Civil Rights Act of 1964 was passed, this issue seems moot.

QUESTIONS

1. Are there other places or situations that, like restrooms, have also inspired frequent claims and counterclaims?

2. In what ways does claimsmaking for and against transgender rights reveal similar cultural assumptions?

3. Is restroom access for transgender individuals likely to remain a contentious issue, or is it likely to fade—and why?

3

Activists as Claimsmakers

laims cannot exist by themselves; people—claimsmakers—must advance them. It's tempting to equate claimsmakers with activists—people like Martin Luther King Jr.—who become passionately involved with an issue, dedicate their lives to a cause, and march and demonstrate until their claims receive attention. Indeed, this is part—but only part—of the story.

When we think of activists, we envision people who stand outside the halls of power. Because they do not hold powerful political offices or have strong ties with those who do, it is fairly difficult for these **outsider claimsmakers** to get others—the media, the general public, and particularly the officials who can make policies that might actually do something about the troubling social condition—to pay attention to their claims (J. Best, 1990). This is why activists so often resort to attention-grabbing tactics: demonstrations, sit-ins, and so on. Activists hope that these activities will lead to media coverage and that attracting publicity for their cause will bring their claims to the attention of the public so that, in turn, both the media and the public will press policymakers to take action. That is, activists envision the claimsmaking process as shown in Figure 3.1a, where the thicker arrow between the claimsmakers

Figure 3.1   CLAIMSMAKING BY OUTSIDER AND
INSIDER CLAIMSMAKERS

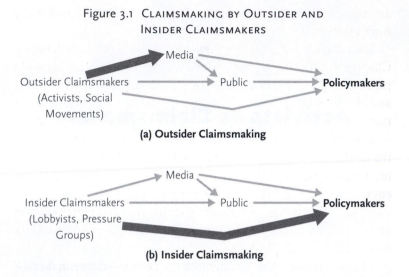

(a) **Outsider Claimsmaking**

(b) **Insider Claimsmaking**

and the media identifies the media as the most important audience for outsiders' claims.

However, there is an alternative, more direct route to successful claimsmaking. Some people already have contacts with policymakers. Such people include lobbyists, major political contributors, government officials, and well-established interest groups such as the National Rifle Association (NRA), which is concerned with protecting the rights of gun owners, or the National Association for the Advancement of Colored People (NAACP), which is concerned with advancing the rights of African Americans. Those who are already well connected to policymakers form what is sometimes called the **polity** (Useem & Zald, 1982); the polity consists of those groups whose interests are routinely taken into account by policymakers, so they are often able to influence policymaking. People with such connections can act as **insider claimsmakers**; often they pursue their claims outside the glare of the media spotlight, without arousing much public attention. The activities of insider claimsmakers are depicted in Figure 3.1b, where the thicker arrow runs directly from claimsmakers to policymakers.

The activities of insider claimsmakers will be considered in Chapter 4; this chapter will focus on outsider claimsmakers—in particular, activists such as Dr. King. Activists often belong to broad **social movements**, general causes such as the civil rights movement or environmentalism. Each social movement may contain several distinct **social movement organizations** (SMOs), such as the civil rights movement's SNCC (Student Nonviolent Coordinating Committee) and CORE (Congress of Racial Equality), or the environmentalist movement's Greenpeace and Sierra Club. As we shall see, although the larger society may view a movement's SMOs as allies that share a common cause, activists frequently think of other SMOs within the same social movement as rivals.

Social movements frequently face opposition. Movements seek to promote change, and the status quo inevitably has its defenders. The most vigorous defenses usually come from those who have vested interests in the status quo; these opponents benefit from existing social arrangements in ways that would be threatened if the changes promoted by the movement were to occur. For example, some white Southerners, who saw themselves as benefiting from legal segregation, opposed the civil rights movement. Moreover, it takes effort to change social arrangements, and even when people may not strongly oppose activists' claims, they may see no good reason to exert the effort that change requires; sociologists refer to such reluctance to alter existing social arrangements as **inertia** (Becker, 1995).

Chapter 2 described position issues—that is, topics that evoke controversy, inciting active disagreements about whether a particular condition should be considered troubling, or what that condition's causes might be, or what should be done to address the condition. In such position issues, claims inspire counterclaims, and **countermovements** may arise to promote these counterclaims.

Some sociologists associate the term *social movement* with liberal or progressive causes and prefer to restrict the term *countermovement* to more conservative causes. However, it makes better analytic sense to speak of social movements as calling for change, and of countermovements as resisting change. When abortion was generally illegal, there was a movement of abortion rights advocates, which was opposed by a countermovement that favored restricting abortion. Once abortion became widely legal, however, it became more reasonable to speak of a pro-life movement calling for change, and a pro-choice countermovement trying to defend the existing right to abortion. This example illustrates that countermovements are conservative in the sense that they seek to preserve the status quo; when political liberals support existing social arrangements (such as laws protecting the right to abortions), they may organize countermovements to oppose claimsmaking by political conservatives (such as the pro-life movement).

Because most social movements—and countermovements—promote claims about social problems, and because images of activists tend to come to mind when we think of claimsmakers, this chapter will focus on key aspects of social movements and the role of activists as claimsmakers. (Chapter 4 will consider other sorts of claimsmakers.) We will begin this chapter's discussion of activist claimsmakers by examining three recent approaches adopted by sociologists to study social movements: framing, resource mobilization, and opportunity structures.

FRAMING

Most social movements present claims; they identify a troubling condition and call for social changes to address the problem (Benford & Hunt, 2003). These claims can, of course, be studied in terms of their rhetoric—that is, by using the concepts developed in Chapter 2. Social movement scholars, however, often adopt a slightly different vocabulary: they speak of **framing** to describe how activists construct their claims.

Like the frame around a picture, activists' frames place a social movement within a larger context; frames locate the key issues and set them off so that they are easily understood. Like the wooden frame of a house, activists' frames also provide a structure, a framework around which elaborate claims can be assembled.

The same issue might be framed in many different ways. Some frames emphasize morality, appealing to people's sense of right and wrong. Some frames elicit outrage or other powerful emotions that lead people to join and stick with a cause (Gould, 2009; Whittier, 2009). Other frames evoke particular ideologies or political philosophies, such as Marxism or libertarianism. Still other frames emphasize political struggles between groups with competing interests. What may seem to be a single social movement—the civil rights movement, the environmental movement, and so on—can be composed of activists who frame the issue in very different ways (see Box 3.1).

Frames encourage viewing the world from a particular perspective; they give meaning to what might otherwise seem confusing, so that once someone adopts a given frame, everything seems to be clearer, to make sense. For example, the feminist movement calls attention to the various ways in which social arrangements disadvantage women; a feminist frame gives activists a particular vantage point from which they can view women's place in the world.

There are obvious parallels between constructionist scholars' examinations of claimsmaking rhetoric (as discussed in Chapter 2), and social movement analysts' discussions of frames. Frames have three components: **diagnostic frames** identify the nature of the problem (that is, *diagnostic frame* is another term for what constructionists call *grounds*); **motivational frames** explain why action needs to be taken (akin to the constructionists' *warrants*); and **prognostic frames** specify what needs to be done (similar to the constructionists' *conclusions*) (Snow & Benford, 1988). For our purposes, these are

Box 3.1 Diversity in Rationales for Opposing Vaccines

Social movements are usually alliances of people who may share a cause but not necessarily other views. Some parents refuse to have their children vaccinated, even though public health authorities strongly recommend following childhood vaccination schedules. What is striking is the different sorts of reasons parents articulate for not following these guidelines.

Every state exempts parents under some circumstances. All states allow exemptions for medical reasons (that is, the parents can provide documentation from a medical provider that vaccination would endanger the child's health), and most allow religious exemptions for those whose religious faiths prohibit vaccinations. In addition, many states allow parents to claim an exemption based on their personal philosophies or beliefs. Those who choose to be exempt for these reasons tend to be relatively advantaged—white, well-educated, with above-average incomes.

These parents adopt an ideology that they—not physicians or public health officials—are the experts on their own children. Some of them weigh the evidence available to them and decide to comply with some vaccines and refuse others. Some argue that vaccines are unnatural, that they interfere with the child developing natural immunities to disease. Others worry that vaccines introduce dangerous chemicals in the child's body—a viewpoint that often involves considerable suspicion about the motives of both vaccine manufacturers and the public health officials who oversee vaccination programs, sometimes including arguments that there has been a conspiracy to conceal the truth about vaccines' dangers. Still others choose to vaccinate their children—but on their own schedule, rather than at the ages recommended by medical authorities. In other words, the "anti-vaxxer" movement is actually a coalition of people with differing views about vaccines.

Source: Reich, 2016.

essentially similar classification schemes, one favored by those who think of themselves as sociologists of social problems, the other by scholars of social movements.

One reason that social movement analysts favor the language of framing is their interest in how social movements recruit new members. A key issue for most activists is enlisting supporters to their causes. Social movements need to attract new members, to convince people to share the activists' concerns and support the movement through donations and investments of time and energy. Because social movements typically promote unfamiliar ways of looking at society and its problems, they must frame issues in ways that will appeal to prospective members. In other words, activists need to align their frames with those of the people they hope to enlist in their movements (see Box 3.2).

Frame alignment refers to the ways in which social movements must address the existing frames or ways of looking at the world held by prospective members (Snow, Rochford, Worden, & Benford, 1986). Movement participants—activists—have a particular frame, with its diagnostic, motivational, and prognostic elements, but the people they might like to recruit to the movement already have their own ways of understanding the world. The goal is to bring these frames into alignment so that others will come to adopt the activists' frame (and presumably join the movement). For example, the feminist movement seeks to introduce people to a feminist frame so that they can recognize how sexism affects their lives, and so that they will support feminist efforts to challenge sexual discrimination. Frame alignment usually takes one of four forms:

1. *Bridging.* In **frame bridging**, activists seek support from people thought to hold frames similar to their own. For example, liberal activists interested in a new issue are likely to seek supporters among those already known to be sympathetic with other liberal causes, just as conservative activists generally try to bring their new concerns to the attention of known conservatives. That is, activists seek to enlist people

Box 3.2 The Name Mirrors the Frame

The term *homosexual* originated among nineteenth-century sexologists who sought to make sexual behavior a topic for scientific research; they also spoke of *sexual inversion*. Both terms seemed clinical to the people they described. Some early activists described theirs as a *homophile* movement, favoring that term because it emphasized love rather than sex.

However, a new set of activists emerged in the 1970s, and they favored *gay*. The gay liberation movement encompassed both males and females, but women complained that their concerns were treated as less important, and demanded equal billing, so it became common to speak of *gay and lesbian* issues. Over time, other sexual identities made analogous calls for mention so that the inclusion of bisexuals led to the abbreviation *GLB*, and adding references to transsexuals (later transgender) produced *LGBT*. Some expand this to *LGBTQ* to encompass either queer (suggesting a more radical, edgy orientation) or questioning (for those who are exploring their sexual identities). Others call for adding an *I* to acknowledge intersex (people with ambiguous reproductive or sexual anatomy).

We tend to take the categories and names that we use to classify people and problems for granted. But all of these terms have histories, sometimes contentious histories in which claimsmakers struggle to get a particular term accepted. In this example, individuals with a variety of identities campaigned to gain recognition as part of a larger gender-nonconforming social movement.

Source: Wilcox, 2014.

who have already supported other, similar causes because it should be easy to build a bridge between fundamentally similar frames.

2. *Amplification.* In **frame amplification**, activists call on values or beliefs that they presume many people hold in order to rally others to their cause. Although the prospective supporters may not have been active in other movements, they are presumed to hold basic

assumptions that should make them sympathetic to the activists' cause. For instance, recent campaigns to register sex offenders and then restrict their rights have drawn on popular stereotypes about the predatory nature of sex offenses and people's sense that society ought to be protected from such predators. Frame amplification often seeks to arouse emotional reactions, such as compassion or outrage, so that people feel compelled to join the movement.

3. *Extension.* In **frame extension**, activists enlarge their frame to encompass concerns that prospective supporters are thought to have. In this case, the activists' core values or beliefs may not overlap those of their prospective supporters until they extend their frame. To return to an example raised in Chapter 2, vegetarian activists tend to be concerned with primarily ethical issues: they believe that it is morally wrong to eat meat (Maurer, 2002). However, relatively few Americans share that concern, and vegetarians have had more success gaining support by extending their frame to emphasize the health and ecological benefits of vegetarian eating—appeals that can attract supporters who worry about health or environmental issues more than the morality of eating meat.

4. *Transformation.* In **frame transformation**, activists call on prospective supporters to reject the familiar worldview that they take for granted and adopt a new and different frame. This transformation may be limited to how one thinks about a specific troubling condition (for example, the campaign to redefine drunk driving sought to persuade people to stop thinking of it as a somewhat amusing, minor offense, and start viewing it as a serious crime that all too often leads to terrible consequences). In other cases, activists may try to convert supporters to a completely different view of the world (think of efforts to recruit adherents to unfamiliar religions).

These four forms of frame alignment pose increasingly difficult challenges to activists. Frame bridging is the most straightforward task: claims are made to prospective recruits who are thought to be ideologically predisposed to being sympathetic to the claims. Frame amplification depends on emphasizing values and beliefs that the activists already share with the audience for their claims, in order to mobilize them to action; and frame extension requires activists to modify their own frame to make it more attractive to potential recruits. Frame transformation presents the greatest challenge: recruits are asked to abandon their familiar view of the world in favor of the activists' frame.

Different SMOs within the same social movement may have distinct frames that appeal to different prospective members. Often, for instance, a movement may contain both moderate and radical SMOs, the former advocating limited reforms to the existing social system, while the latter call for more significant changes. Activists from a movement's moderate and radical wings usually frame the troubling condition and its solution differently, and they may clash in **frame disputes**, disagreements over how to think about the problem (Benford, 1993). In many cases, activists from different camps within the same social movement present their frames to different audiences: as a general rule, moderates seek to appeal to older people in the middle class (who have relatively secure places within the existing social system, and who therefore are likely to resist radical calls for dramatic social change); and radicals are more likely to seek supporters among those who are younger or poorer (who have far less invested in maintaining the status quo, and who therefore should be more open to pursuing fundamental changes).

Successful framing draws on cultural resources; it incorporates familiar values, beliefs, imagery, and other cultural elements that prospective members find persuasive and convincing. Feminists, for instance, invoke familiar notions of fairness and equality, and argue that women have a right to equal treatment. But framing cannot be a one-way process. When activists interact with prospective members, they usually discover that some appeals are more persuasive than others in convincing people to join the movement. After all, prospective social movement members have many messages competing for their attention—television shows, news reports, advertisements, and on and on. Activists cannot simply present a frame and wait for the world to take notice; that would leave too much to chance because it would be too easy for the activists' frame to be overlooked. Rather, activists must seek out potential supporters, try to frame their message in ways that others will find interesting and convincing, and then pay close attention to what does and doesn't work. If activists find that their claims have generated counterclaims, they may need to reframe the issue to take this opposition into account. Similarly, when one version of a frame fails to elicit much response, it will need to be modified until it begins to be effective (see Box 3.3).

This need to devise frames that will attract supporters, counter opposition, and eventually influence social policy can raise issues of integrity for activists (Benford, 1993). Activists at the core of an SMO often have more ideologically coherent frames than many other movement supporters have, and they may view frame extension—altering their frame in order to make it more appealing—as a violation of their principles, as "selling out." Frame disputes within a movement often revolve around questions of compromise: should activists present what they believe to be a more correct, more principled view of the issue even if it risks rejection by many prospective supporters who will find it too difficult to understand, or even unpalatable; or should they frame the issue in weaker but more appealing terms so that prospective members will find it easier to digest? Frames inevitably reflect a combination of how activists view the world, and what they believe will be an effective message.

RESOURCE MOBILIZATION

Adopting a frame that justifies belief in a cause is not enough to make a claim successful; activists cannot trade on outrage alone. Social movements also need to deal with a variety of mundane problems. Organizing a successful demonstration means picking

Box 3.3 Learning to Frame One's Own Story

While some activists make claims about troubling conditions that do not affect them directly, many are drawn to movements that address issues in their own lives. In a sense, they embody their social problem, and are in a position to testify how they have been affected by it.

Take the Dreamers—undocumented young people who accompanied their parents when their families illegally entered the United States. In some cases, they might have been infants or very young children when they crossed the border; they may have grown up in the United States without ever understanding their true immigration status. The DREAM Act was intended to give them a path toward becoming U.S. citizens.

Those who joined the movement encouraged one another to tell their personal stories in ways that would make people sympathize with their plight and support their cause. Prospective activists received coaching on ways to make their claims more compelling, with males and females receiving somewhat different guidelines.

Male Dreamers were encouraged to present themselves through "masculine" performances that emphasized their strength and competence; when they talked about the injustice of their circumstances, they were to highlight their outrage at its unfairness, without seeming to solicit pity from their audience. In contrast, females were urged to display more emotion, to emphasize their love for their families and their desire to help their communities; ideally, they would convey inner strength while still embodying "feminine" virtues. Obviously, the somewhat different scripts for males and females drew upon and reaffirmed the larger culture's ideas about gender so that their performances would support their claims.

Source: Cabaniss, 2018.

a good time and place to maximize participation. People who might be willing to participate must be contacted and encouraged to come (demonstrations designed to attract a big crowd might require Internet postings, posters, telephone calling systems, and other ways of getting the word out); it might even be necessary to make arrangements to transport people to the event. Large demonstrations also require a lot of planning: tasks might include training people in dos and don'ts, scheduling speakers and other events, assigning monitors to supervise demonstrators, preparing first-aid stations, and possibly even arranging to post bail for people who get arrested. In addition, press releases need to be issued to inform the media that the demonstration will be taking place, and it may be a good idea to designate spokespeople to explain the demonstrators' purpose to the reporters covering the event.

In other words, one way to think about activists is in terms of the resources required by a social movement's activities. Movements need money, members, skills, and so on. These may seem like mundane considerations, especially if we think of social movements in romantic terms, consisting of plucky little guys struggling against powerful interests. But without sufficient resources, movements will have difficulty getting started, let alone enduring. Successful movements must assemble the resources they need. Sociologists refer to this gathering of resources as **resource mobilization** (J. D. McCarthy & Zald, 1977).

The resources that activists need are almost always scarce: it is hard to raise enough money, because the people who give money have lots of other ways to spend it; it is hard to get people to devote time to the movement, because there are other things they could do; and so on. The struggle to assemble resources means that SMOs—even SMOs that are theoretically allies in the same social movement—find themselves in competition with one another for the same scarce resources. They compete for members, for donations, for media coverage, and so on. If one SMO is especially effective in mobilizing resources, rival organizations are likely to find resources harder to come by (see Box 3.4).

For example, the civil rights movement—now recalled as a grand, unified movement to end segregation—was characterized by internal competition and disagreements (Haines, 1984). Different civil rights organizations had different frames that led them to favor different strategies. For many years the NAACP had pursued a legal

Box 3.4 A Tale of Two SMOs

Consider two SMOs that began in 2011 in reaction to the global economic crisis. US Uncut organized protests against major banks and corporations to draw attention to the ways they avoided paying taxes; Occupy criticized the large share of wealth going to the corporate class. In other words, they promoted similar causes at roughly the same time. However, Uncut received relatively little press coverage, while Occupy gained massive coverage. Why?

To begin, Uncut launched its campaign in February, when there were other, competing social movement stories: the Arab Spring was attracting global attention, and protests by state workers in Wisconsin and Ohio were also receiving coverage. In contrast, Occupy's campaign began in September, when other social movement news was receiving less attention. Public opinion polling data also suggests that people became more frustrated with the economy as the year went on, so they may have been more receptive to movement messages.

Occupy had other advantages. It was more media savvy and used social media to spread its message. Whereas Uncut organized relatively small, simultaneous demonstrations in cities across the country, Occupy managed to attract a good-sized crowd (something over 1,000 protesters) to Wall Street (itself a location near the headquarters of important media organizations), which meant that reporters could easily cover the events it staged. Occupy's protests were more dramatic and resulted in a number of arrests, which made the events seem newsworthy. In short, the relative visibility of the two protests reflected differences in the sorts of resources they mobilized to draw attention to their causes.

Source: Shih, 2019.

strategy, mounting court challenges to the constitutionality of segregationist practices. Dr. King's SCLC (Southern Christian Leadership Conference) favored high-visibility protests in communities such as Birmingham and Selma, Alabama. More radical organizations, such as CORE and SNCC, adopted riskier, more confrontational tactics such as sit-ins and freedom rides. Because potential donors could choose which organizations they wanted to support, the various SMOs were rivals for those donors' dollars. The NAACP, for instance, believed that it made sense to invest in a long-term legal campaign, and it opposed spending donors' money to bail out SNCC's demonstrators who engaged in protests that were certain to lead to their arrests. SNCC, on the other hand, argued that the NAACP's approach was too slow, and tried to rally support for its riskier activities. Establishing and maintaining alliances with other SMOs takes work.

In contemporary America, much social movement activity revolves not around convincing individuals to dedicate their lives to activism, or even around organizing thousands of people to march in the streets, but around fundraising. Although activists do sometimes organize large demonstrations, much of their activity focuses on seeking media coverage for their cause, lobbying policymakers, and so on. These activities cost money, and activists spend considerable time soliciting contributions from people who support the movement's cause (but may not feel they have the time or energy to work directly on movement activities). Note that we can distinguish between **beneficiaries** (who stand to benefit directly if a movement is successful) and **constituents** (who support the movement) (J. D. McCarthy & Zald, 1977). Some people belong to both categories, but many movement supporters are **conscience constituents**—that is, people who contribute money or even join demonstrations because they believe in the cause, although they do not expect to be direct beneficiaries (think of Northern whites who donated to civil rights SMOs).

The growing importance of contributions led to the emergence of sophisticated fundraising efforts using, for instance, direct-mail techniques. Mailing lists of people known to have contributed to previous fundraising campaigns were used to raise additional funds. Fundraising efforts become more sophisticated as new technologies become available; in recent years, SMOs have begun raising funds via the Internet, using social media, websites, and e-mail to solicit donations. Of course, this emphasis on bringing in money means that SMOs become dependent on the support of constituents with whom the activists have no direct contact; most of an SMO's members act only as contributors, who may never actually encounter other members face to face. This poses a challenge: how to keep people emotionally committed to both the SMO and the larger cause and willing to continue their support when they have few direct connections to the movement. In response, SMOs maintain websites, send members frequent e-mail messages, and seek to convey a sense that their members constitute an electronic community (Eaton, 2010). Sending messages to current and prospective members turns into yet another occasion when troubling conditions must be reconstructed with compelling rhetoric—in this case, arguments that funds are needed urgently to respond to an important opportunity or, more often, to a looming threat. Both pro-life and pro-choice activists, for instance, raise money by warning that, unless supporters rally to their cause (by donating money to support their SMO's activities), their opponents are likely to win. Alternatively, SMOs may seek funding from other sources, such as foundations, but this support may come at a cost.

Increasingly, then, successful activism requires sophisticated skills—organizing, fundraising, media relations, lobbying, and the like. These skills tend to be portable: individuals who learn skills in one SMO can move on and apply what they've learned at another SMO, or even in another movement. Just as some veterans of the civil rights movement took what they had learned in that campaign and used their new skills to help organize antiwar protests, the women's liberation movement, and the gay liberation movement, people today pursue careers as activists, sometimes working for different causes over the course of their careers. Typically, these individuals do have ideological commitments, so they tend to move among social movements with which they are sympathetic: one individual may work for several liberal SMOs, while another becomes active in various conservative causes.

Resource mobilization is important because it reflects an SMO's ability to promote its claims. Organizations with more members and a bigger budget are better able to afford the services of skilled activists (who may in turn be attracted to working in campaigns that have plentiful resources and better chances of success). SMOs with money can afford further fundraising efforts, so they have better prospects for garnering future resources. Moreover, SMOs with greater resources find it easier to draw attention to their message: they are better able to gain coverage in the media; and, other things being equal, they are more likely to influence policymakers. Mobilizing resources is not glamorous, but it provides an essential base for would-be activist claimsmakers (see Box 3.5).

OPPORTUNITY STRUCTURES

Activists must worry about more than devising a persuasive frame and mobilizing necessary resources. Timing also matters. All too often, social movements face great obstacles. After all, movements seek to change existing social arrangements, and those arrangements work to the benefit of powerful people who can be expected to use their considerable resources to resist changes that might be to their disadvantage. On occasion, however, these obstacles to change are reduced, and activists must be alert for and ready to take advantage of such opportune moments. Various cultural and political circumstances can create opportunities to promote activists' claims.

Cultural Opportunities

Cultural opportunities arise when people become more willing to listen to the movement's claims (McAdam, 1994). Perhaps the most obvious cultural opportunity is the occurrence of a newsworthy event that focuses attention on a troubling condition. The September 11,

Box 3.5 Challenges for Young Activists

Teen activists face challenges in getting their claims covered by the media. Two movements that seek to mobilize young members are the virginity pledge movement (which asks youth to promise to postpone sexual intercourse until marriage) and gay–straight alliances (groups that promote discussions among gay and straight students within particular high schools). Both movements depend on mobilizing active participation from teens.

The media tend to treat teen activists with care. On the one hand, it recounts their stories as first-person typifying examples (why this person wants to postpone sex, how that one has experienced prejudice against gays and lesbians at school). However, media coverage is less likely to provide a forum for young people to speak *as activists*; statements about the movement's purpose usually come from adult leaders. Indeed, as a movement becomes more familiar, critical coverage becomes more common, and critical media reports and counterclaimsmakers are more likely to suggest that a movement's teen members are being manipulated by the adults behind the movements. That is, there is speculation that the virginity pledge movement is a tool of religious authority, or that gay–straight alliances serve to promote adults' gay agenda. The inference is that the young activists who join these movements do not really understand what they are doing, so they are portrayed as being less than full member-activists within the movement. Activists' credibility as claimsmakers depends not just on the content of their claims, but how their identities—their ethnicity, gender, and age—make what they have to say seem more or less credible.

Source: Kettrey, 2018.

2001, terrorist attacks, for instance, suddenly moved terrorism from a peripheral concern to the central focus of national attention. Other, less dramatic events—a natural disaster, a brutal crime, and such—can have similar effects. They lead to a widespread sense that a particular troubling condition, previously neglected, must now be addressed. Activists who have been struggling to have their claims heard may suddenly find themselves in demand—reporters seek them out for interviews, legislators invite them to testify at hearings, and so on—because they are the ones who understand and have ideas for what to do about the troubling condition that is now the focus of concern.

Another sort of cultural opportunity emerges when a **master frame** becomes familiar (Snow & Benford, 1992). A master frame articulates a broad orientation that can be easily adapted for application to many issues. For instance, after the civil rights movement first drew national attention to blacks' struggle for equal rights and then succeeded in dismantling the system of institutionalized segregation in the South, the idea that demanding equal rights might be an effective way of framing social issues spread to other social movements. Within about ten years, activists were campaigning for women's rights, gay rights, children's rights, and the rights of the disabled, prisoners, and the elderly. This master frame remains influential: the abortion issue has been framed in terms of fetuses' *right to life* and women's *right to choose*; divorced men campaign for *fathers' rights*; an active *animal rights* movement has emerged; and so on. Like dramatic events, the availability of master frames creates cultural opportunities that can make it easier for activists to promote their claims.

Political Opportunities

Political opportunities to promote activists' claims arise when the distribution of power among different groups shifts so that changes that previously would have been successfully resisted can now be implemented. Political opportunities may derive from shifting priorities, when formerly irrelevant concerns are redefined as relevant. One reason the civil rights movement gained momentum in the early 1960s was that former colonies—particularly the African colonies of Britain and France—were gaining independence. The Cold War was at its height, and the United States wanted to minimize the Soviet Union's influence in these newly independent nations. The concern that African nations might be repelled by the treatment of African Americans in the United States created a new pressure to do something about the system of segregation found in the Southern states. In this case, shifting foreign policy concerns created new opportunities for civil rights activists trying to change domestic policies (Bloom, 2015).

Another form of political opportunity emerges when, for some reason, opposition to a movement becomes weaker. Those who might be expected to resist the activists' claims may be losing influence, or they may be distracted by other concerns. Perhaps more important for the social problems process is the fact that support for claimsmakers may become stronger. Successful claims lead to sympathetic media coverage, public opinion polls that reveal growing support, and political leaders' joining the cause. Support for "an idea whose time has come" can grow to the point that opponents may decide to drop their opposition. For instance, the basic principles of equal rights for African Americans and for both men and women advocated by the civil rights and the feminist movements, respectively—principles once considered quite controversial—have achieved broad acceptance.

Activists need to assess political opportunities and devise appropriate tactics for exploiting them. A tactic that is effective at one moment may be less effective at another. For instance, McAdam (1983) traces the history of tactical choices in the civil rights movement. The movement's activists devised a variety of protest tactics—sit-ins, large-scale demonstrations, and so on. Some of these tactics proved ineffective: they failed to attract media attention or to weaken the system of segregation. But others worked better, and news of these successes spread, leading activists in other communities to copy the effective tactics. Still, these successes were temporary; a tactic remained effective only for a time. News of the new tactic also inspired opposition; the movement's segregationist opponents searched for tactics of their own—responses that could minimize the movement's impact—and news of these successful opposition tactics also spread. In addition, each time civil rights activists used a particular tactic, it became more familiar and less newsworthy, so the media coverage dwindled. These processes created a cycle of tactical innovation in which a novel tactic would emerge, work for a while, then grow less effective, causing the activists to invent a new form of protest to keep the movement advancing. Similarly, activists discover that their choice of targets matters: claims that don't attract much attention when directed at an unfamiliar target may become newsworthy when aimed at a prominent target (see Box 3.6).

Just as some circumstances can improve political opportunities, others create obstacles, occasions when claimsmaking probably can't succeed. Public attention is finite; if the media are devoting their attention to other newsworthy events, they aren't likely to cover a particular social movement's claims (see Chapter 5 for a more thorough discussion of how the media choose what they will cover). In the weeks immediately following September 11, 2001, media attention concentrated on terrorism, so there was almost no chance that claims about other issues could receive much attention. Similarly, when rival claimsmakers—activists for another social movement, or even for another SMO within the same movement—are occupying center stage and hogging the limelight, opportunities for promoting one's own claims are reduced. Rather than struggling to be heard under such adverse circumstances, it may be wiser to conserve resources and wait for a more promising opportunity.

Similarly, opportunities are unfavorable when opposition to a cause seems to be growing stronger, or when support for that cause seems to be growing weaker. Under such circumstances, activists need to consider what's wrong and make the necessary changes. Perhaps the existing frame is losing its appeal; perhaps more resources need to be assembled. At these times it is better to back off and wait for a better opportunity, rather than forcing the issue and facing certain defeat.

For example, Taylor (1989) traces the history of the National Women's Party (NWP), which long promoted an Equal Rights Amendment (ERA) to the Constitution that would guarantee women

Box 3.6 When Do Counterdemonstrations Occur?

Claims may inspire counterclaims, and social movements may lead to countermovements. In some cases, countermovements actually seek to confront members of social movements so that a movement demonstration may attract a counterdemonstration. Protesters then find themselves facing people demonstrating in opposition to their cause. What are the conditions that make counterdemonstrations more likely?

In general, counterdemonstrations occur when a movement seems to threaten the status quo. A weak social movement that seems ineffective is unlikely to attract counterdemonstrators, probably because those opposed to the movement's cause view it as unlikely to be effective, so there is little need to register their opposition. In contrast, a movement that seems to have some momentum—one that is attracting new members, garnering more media coverage, gaining more support, and planning large demonstrations—is much more likely to inspire counterdemonstrators to come out and protest. In other words, the closer a movement seems to be to having success in influencing the public, the press, and policymakers, the more likely those opposed to the movement's goals will recognize the importance of demonstrating that not everyone endorses the movement's claims. In a curious way then, the presence of counterdemonstrators can be a sign that a social movement's opponents view it as a threat, as worthy of being treated seriously. This helps explain why social movements' (and countermovements') rhetoric often emphasizes their opponents' strength, and the urgent need for people to stand up and support their cause.

Source: Reynolds-Stenson & Earl, 2018.

full equality under the law. During much of its history, and particularly during the years following World War II, the NWP confronted poor political opportunities for success. This was a period of **abeyance**; that is, the NWP maintained a modest organizational structure, continued monitoring political developments, and waited for brighter opportunities. A good opportunity arose in the late 1960s, after the civil rights movement had captured Americans' attention, making the equal rights master frame more familiar and more acceptable. In particular, new calls for women's liberation began to gain notice, and as a new wave of feminist activism began to emerge, the NWP joined the new feminists (such as the newly formed National Organization for Women, or NOW) and encouraged them to campaign for the ERA (although that particular campaign was again narrowly defeated). By tending the feminist flame during the decades of abeyance, the NWP had conserved its resources until more promising opportunities developed to use them.

Summary

Social movements can experience decades of frustration, periods when activists cannot seem to interest anyone in their cause— when they face indifference, ridicule, even repression. It helps to be patient, to wait until cultural and political opportunities develop that offer more favorable conditions for claimsmaking. For instance, the civil rights movement and the feminist movement have had long histories featuring both periods of frustration and periods of progress. These familiar examples teach other activists the importance of continuing the struggle, of hanging on until opportune moments arise.

THE ADVANTAGES OF OWNERSHIP

Activists whose efforts are particularly successful can gain **ownership** of a social problem (Gusfield, 1981). Ownership is established when particular claims or frames become generally recognized and acknowledged as the best way to understand a particular issue. It is an ambiguous status; no one receives an official certificate of ownership, but some claimsmakers become the recognized, go-to authorities on a troubling condition. If a dramatic event brings that problem back into the news, it is the owners who are asked by reporters to provide commentary and who are consulted by policymakers.

Ownership relates to framing, resource mobilization, and political opportunities. The owners' frames become influential in shaping how others approach the problem and its solution; the owners' perspective may not be the only possible way of thinking about the troubling condition, but it becomes familiar, almost taken for granted by the press, the public, and policymakers. Precisely because they are well known, owners find it much easier to mobilize resources. People who want to contribute or otherwise become involved in a cause tend to know about and turn to a problem's owners, just as reporters looking for sources to comment on an issue are likely to think first of approaching the owners. And, of course, precisely because owners find it easier to garner resources, they have an easier time maintaining their ownership in the face of competing activists. As a result, owners are well placed to take advantage of opportunity structures. When, for instance, current events draw attention to a troubling condition, owners tend to be far better prepared to exploit whatever opportunities develop: they have contacts with the media and with policymakers; they are probably better placed to assess political opportunities; and they may even be integrated into the social problems process well enough to act as insider claimsmakers (see Box 3.7).

A social problem can have multiple owners. Position issues marked by intractable disagreements often feature SMOs that own the opposing sides in the debate. For example, the NRA long ago established itself as the leading SMO speaking on behalf of the rights of gun owners and in opposition to gun control. For a long time, proponents of gun control lacked a comparably influential SMO; in recent years, however, the Brady Center to Prevent Gun Violence and the Violence Policy Center have emerged as the most visible antigun SMOs—the owners of gun control advocacy. And, as noted earlier, social movements often encompass a range of frames, from more moderate groups advocating modest reforms, to more

Box 3.7 Owning Child Sexual Exploitation in Canada

The Canadian Centre for Child Protection (C3P) is a charitable organization with a subsidiary tip line, Cybertip.ca, for Canadians who want to report child sexual exploitation or child pornography. Although it is a private entity, not a government agency, C3P has effectively gained ownership of these problems in Canada.

Canada's media turn to C3P for information about these threats to children, and C3P's spokespeople draw upon their own analyses of the tips they receive to construct the problem in alarming ways. They emphasize that it is a big problem, probably undercounted by official statistics. And they characterize the problem in terms of technology: dangers lurk on the Internet, but parents are less technologically sophisticated than their children, and teenagers in particular cannot appreciate the dangerous possibilities of sexting. This makes C3P's investigators essential, not just in recommending guidelines for needed laws and official enforcement, but as partners in investigations. They have campaigned to give these investigators— who are, remember, private citizens—forms of official police powers, and as might be imagined, they dismiss counterclaims that question this official standing.

This is an example of claimsmakers depicting a troubling condition about which most people will agree they know little. By being the most active figures making claims, and having the ability to depict the problem in ways that make themselves seem indispensable, C3P solidified their ownership of the child sexual exploitation issue in Canada.

Source: Kohm, 2020.

radical SMOs pushing for more significant changes. Owners may emerge at different points along this spectrum. Within the 1960s civil rights movement, for example, the well-established NAACP favored deliberate pressure to gain favorable court decisions, while more radical SMOs, such as SNCC and CORE, became well known for organizing more confrontational activities, such as sit-ins and freedom rides. A few highly visible SMOs shared ownership of the large, broad-based civil rights movement.

Some SMOs own particular issues for extended periods. The NRA has led the fight against gun control for decades, and the NAACP has been a leading voice in the movement for African Americans' civil rights since its founding in 1909. Such owners must constantly strive to keep their issue—and their ownership—visible to the press, the public, and policymakers. Maintaining such a presence serves two purposes. First, of course, it keeps the owners' particular claims—their frame—for interpreting the issue visible and familiar so that others find it easy to continue to think about the topic in the owners' terms. Second, it helps preserve the owners' status *as owners*. Attention—and contributions—tend to go to the most familiar advocates. Although ownership is harder to achieve in the first place than it is to maintain after being gained, it must always be nurtured.

Long-term ownership requires flexibility. Narrowly focused, single-issue movements are at a long-term disadvantage; it is too easy for public attention to drift away from an issue, and once that happens, supporters, media coverage, and access to policymakers may also dwindle. It helps to develop a broader set of interrelated concerns. The NAACP, for instance, has addressed a wide array of issues related to racial discrimination during its long history. In its early years, for example, the NAACP devoted considerable attention to its campaign against lynching. But as lynching declined and then disappeared, the NAACP turned to constructing other race relations issues, such as campaigns against discrimination in education and employment, opposition to hate crimes, and so on. As political opportunities shift, it can become easier or harder to promote particular claims, but to the degree that the NAACP maintains ownership over the full spectrum of issues related to African Americans, it can remain actively involved in the social problems process.

In contrast, narrowly focused SMOs run the risk of succeeding— and thereby losing their reason for existing. Consider the March of Dimes, a charitable organization originally launched to fight the problem of polio, a disease that left children severely disabled. Once polio vaccines were developed, the threat of polio virtually disappeared, and the organization faced a crisis. It could, of course, declare victory and disband. But why dismantle a successful fundraising apparatus? Instead, the March of Dimes redefined its purpose, declaring that it would continue to operate but would now dedicate its efforts to fighting birth defects. This was not just a new but also a broader definition of the SMO's purpose: there are many different birth defects, so although further successes might result in eliminating some of these problems, the organization would continue to be needed to address the problems that remained.

When claimsmakers begin drawing attention to a troubling, previously neglected condition, there are three ways ownership of the issue might evolve:

1. *No one assumes ownership.* This situation is most likely when a newsworthy event, such as a dramatic crime, catapults an issue into the public eye. A variety of commentators may offer their takes on this troubling condition, perhaps suggesting different ways of thinking about the issue. However, it may be that none of these claimsmakers will assume ownership of the topic, work to keep the issue visible, manage a prolonged campaign to change public policy, and so on. Under these circumstances, even topics that receive a burst of intense publicity can shift away from public attention, forgotten as soon as the next dramatic event commands notice. Without owners to remind people of a problem's importance, issues can fade (this possibility is discussed further in Chapter 5).

2. *Activists establish a new SMO that can assume ownership.* A familiar example is the emergence of Mothers Against Drunk Driving (MADD). Although drunk driving had a long history, MADD gave the issue not

just new visibility, but a new frame as a threat to children menaced by drunk drivers. MADD lobbied legislators, observed courtroom proceedings, established local chapters around the country, and generally took control over what had been an ownerless issue.

3. *An existing SMO assumes ownership of the new issue.* This can work well for the SMO, which can otherwise become a familiar part of the landscape and run the risk of being taken for granted. Assuming ownership of another issue, so long as it is at least tangentially related to the SMO's original program, is a way of making its claims seem fresh. At the same time, having an experienced SMO—which has already found ways to mobilize resources—assume ownership improves the prospects for keeping the issue in the public eye.

Ownership, then, affects the prospects of both an issue and the activists who promote it. Unless someone assumes ownership, it is hard for the social problems process to proceed; it is too easy for public attention to shift away as soon as the next new issue arrives on the scene. Owners are needed to tend the topic, to remind people of its importance, and to revise their claims so that the topic remains fresh and interesting. But ownership also benefits the owners: their claims seem better established; their authority seems more legitimate; and as they become familiar figures with a larger network of social contacts, they can begin to transform themselves from outsider to insider claimsmakers.

ACTIVISTS: PRINCIPLES AND PRACTICALITIES

Discussions of social movements often emphasize their principled character. That is, they depict activists as individuals committed to a particular cause, seeking to promote a higher good. But sincerity is not enough. As claimsmakers who seek to influence the social problems process, activists need to convey their message to, and influence the behavior of, the media, the public, and policymakers. That is, they need to confront the practical problems posed by social movements.

This chapter has explored four such problems (see Figure 3.2). First, activists must develop effective frames; that is, they must construct their claims so that others will find them convincing, so that people will support the activists' SMOs. Principled statements that cannot persuade others threaten to stall the social problems process before it has really begun.

Second, activists must mobilize sufficient resources to promote their movement's goals. Activists who prove unable to attract and manage members, money, and other necessary resources probably will not be able to keep their SMOs functioning long enough for their cause to succeed.

Third, activists need to be able to recognize and figure out ways to take advantage of opportunities. Current events and the shifting

Figure 3.2 ACTIVISTS' CONCERNS IN MAKING EFFECTIVE CLAIMS

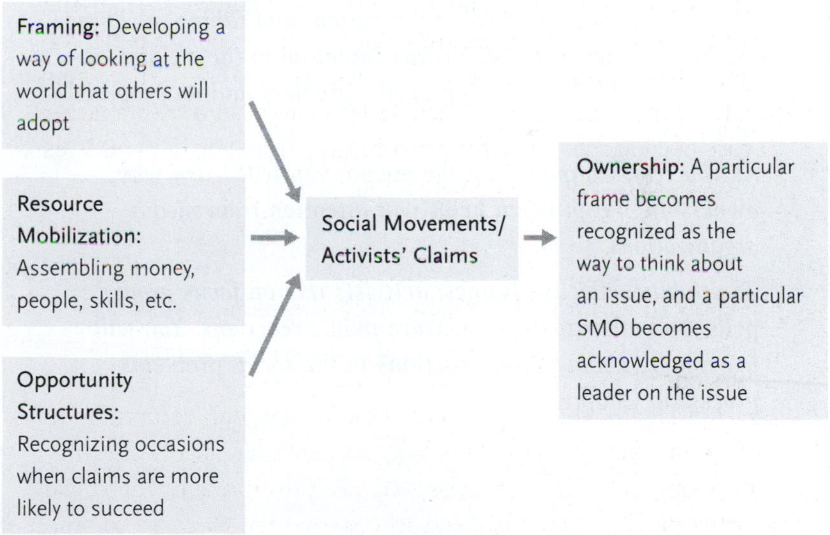

Framing: Developing a way of looking at the world that others will adopt

Resource Mobilization: Assembling money, people, skills, etc.

Opportunity Structures: Recognizing occasions when claims are more likely to succeed

Social Movements/ Activists' Claims

Ownership: A particular frame becomes recognized as the way to think about an issue, and a particular SMO becomes acknowledged as a leader on the issue political landscape can aid—or hinder—social movements. Activists need to be careful not to miss promising opportunities, just as they should avoid expending their resources when they have no chance to advance their cause.

Finally, activists can acquire and maintain ownership over an issue. Owning a social problem allows enduring influence, a means of keeping an issue—and the activists' leadership—visible so that the activists' frames remain familiar and widely accepted, resources are easier to mobilize, and the activists stay in position to take advantage of whatever opportunities develop.

Although they are the most obvious examples of claimsmakers, activists are not the only people who promote social problems claims. They often acquire allies—claimsmakers who, in addition to their commitment to principles, bring special knowledge or expertise to the social problems process. These expert claimsmakers are discussed in Chapter 4.

MAKING CONNECTIONS

- *Through framing, resource mobilization, and taking advantage of opportunities, activists attract attention to their claims in order to establish ownership over a problem and its proposed solutions.*

- *As you read Chapter 5 on the media, you will learn why ownership of a problem helps win attention from media organizations.*

- *To establish effective frames, activists rely on focus groups, polls, and other tools to measure public reactions. You will learn more about public reactions in the social problems process in Chapter 6.*

CASE STUDY
FRACKING AND SOCIAL MOVEMENTS

Fracking—a term for hydraulic fracturing—is the process of drilling into the earth and then directing a high-pressure mixture of water, sand, and chemicals into the rock, causing it to release the natural gas it contains. First used in the 1960s, the technique was refined and became widespread after 1998; it now accounts for a substantial majority of the natural gas production in the United States. Its adoption has caused the price of natural gas to fall, leading to less dependence on coal (a dirtier—more polluting—source of energy); it is generally understood to have aided energy policy. The energy industry strongly supports fracking.

At the same time, fracking has attracted considerable criticism, particularly from environmentalists. At a local level, the process can lead to both surface and groundwater pollution (often typified by videos of people living near fracking sites being able to ignite the water coming out of their kitchen taps), significant air pollution, and even earthquakes. More broadly, while natural gas may be cleaner than coal, burning it contributes to global warming.

Extraction industries, such as drilling for oil, mining coal, or fracking, tend to be geographically concentrated where geologists have located deposits of exploitable resources. This means that there are locales and states where drilling and mining are economically important; for example, coal in West Virginia and Pennsylvania, and oil in Texas and Oklahoma. While everyone consumes energy, relatively few people live in the immediate areas where extraction occurs. Many people benefit from the lower costs of energy resulting from fracking, while only a very few wind up with flammable tap water. Although many activists opposed to fracking are concerned about its effects on climate change, they tend to concentrate on local campaigns aimed at arousing concern among those most likely to directly experience fracking's troubling effects. Here, they rely on the ideas of the broader environmental justice movement, which argues that poor and ethnic minorities tend to experience disproportionate burdens from living close to polluting industries and therefore should be interested in joining social movements opposing those industries.

Indeed, most fracking sites are in rural, often economically challenged regions, where landowners may be pleased by offers to lease
their mineral rights for substantial sums and can hope to receive
royalties if the wells on their property prove productive. In contrast,
urban residents are more likely to object to fracking within their cities. It is therefore no accident that the antifracking campaign that
has attracted the most attention from sociologists was a 2014 referendum in Denton, Texas (a small city of about 130,000 residents,
including about 30,000 students at the University of North Texas
and Texas Woman's University) (Auyero, Hernandez, & Stitt, 2019;
Soyer & Ziyanak, 2018). Local activists started the Frack Free Denton
campaign to get voters to support the referendum by using a wide
range of tactics, including door-to-door canvassing; postings on
websites, blogs, and social media; and even a flash mob of college
students performing an antifracking dance. These activists' rhetoric
depicted fracking as widespread and too close (there were already
281 wells within the city limits) and as hazardous and disruptive
(due to noise and truck traffic), while bringing little benefit to the
city. In response to this grassroots effort, the fracking industry created a countermovement (Denton Taxpayers for a Strong Economy)
and hired a public relations firm to manage their campaign, which
included ads on television, on billboards, and online. The vote wound
up favoring the fracking ban, but the industry immediately challenged Denton's right to halt fracking in court, and the Texas legislature passed a bill restricting localities' right to ban fracking without
prior state approval, which the governor signed into law in 2015.

Efforts to get states to ban fracking have been somewhat more
successful: Vermont passed a ban in 2012, New York's governor
banned the practice in 2014, and Maryland banned it in 2017 (Mazur,
2018). While it is possible that other states will follow, media coverage of the issues has declined. Part of the challenge facing antifracking activists is that the immediate negative consequences of
fracking—such as undrinkable, occasionally even flammable tap
water or disturbances caused by heavy truck traffic—are largely felt
by those in the locales where drilling is occurring. But it has proven
difficult to mobilize support, even in those places. Jerolmack and

Walker (2018) found considerable support for fracking in the Pennsylvania community they studied. Residents were quite aware of the potential problems associated with fracking, and they mobilized—to encourage the industry to expand there and to bargain collectively for the most favorable leasing rates. The local culture celebrated individualism, self-reliance, and private property rights. The residents were suspicious of outsiders (including some celebrities) who staged antifracking events in their area. Even people who wound up seriously harmed by the effects of fracking, such as those losing a suit for damages after their drinking water became contaminated, remained committed to the idea that fracking had benefited their community. This example suggests that although sociologists adopting an environmental justice frame consider people affected by fracking to be victims who ought to be mobilized by enviromental justice campaigns, many of those people reject that frame's critique of fracking.

Critics of fracking argue that it may cause much broader harm, that the chemicals released into the air and water may constitute an ecological and public health catastrophe (Wylie, 2018), but they have had difficulty mobilizing a broad-based antifracking movement. The environmental justice movement encompasses lots of causes, many of them rooted in local opposition to fracking or other related industrial developments, such as proposed oil pipelines (Bakardjieva, Felt, & Teruelle, 2018). But these campaigns face both local resistance (at least in rural settings, public opinion tends to strongly favor exploiting local resources because it stands to benefit the local economy) and indifference beyond the confines of the locality because the general public is likely to view a local campaign as a local issue. Framing the question in local terms—should our city, county, or state ban fracking—is unlikely to attract much concern from the general public, which is more likely to focus—when it *does* focus on environmental issues—on broader topics, such as climate change. After all, environmental justice is just one strand in the larger environmental movement, which tends to promote global—not local—concerns by warning that the fate of the planet is at stake. Fracking may contribute to global warming, but so do lots of other aspects of social life. Ordinary citizens are unable to weigh the relative costs and benefits of fracking to produce natural gas versus burning coal as the means to power electrical generation plants. Banning fracking will not in itself have much effect on global temperatures. Also, the antifracking movement's most startling typifying example—igniting water from those kitchen faucets—has become old news, and it has found it difficult to attract new attention to what has become a familiar issue.

There is a tendency to study successful social movements that result in real change (even if advocates continue to argue that further changes are needed). Thus, the civil rights movement, the women's movement, and the LGBTQ movement can all point to victories, even as they call for further progress. But we need to appreciate that those movements had long histories, and that for much of those histories, change came slowly. It is impossible to predict the future of the antifracking cause, but there is no reason to be confident that it will succeed in the immediate future.

QUESTIONS

1. How do the challenges facing activists trying to make claims about local, national, and global issues differ?

2. Under what circumstances will individuals find claims based on economic interests versus other concerns compelling?

3. How important do you consider fracking as an issue, and how can you explain your views?

4

Experts as Claimsmakers

Colonial Massachusetts was established by Puritans, and ministers were key figures in that society. They saw evidence of God's hand everywhere in the world, and their sermons sometimes commented on current events, interpreting them in religious terms. A bad harvest might be evidence of God's wrath, and problems among people were caused by sin, by individuals breaking God's commandments. Virtually any event could be interpreted within this religious framework. Ministers, then, were colonial New England's principal experts; their theological training qualified them to explain and evaluate most aspects of life. Their religious frame was seen as authoritative because it was promoted by professionals representing the society's leading institution.

The ministers' religious perspective seems less authoritative today. In at least public discussions of social problems, modern Americans rarely speak of *sin* (and when politicians or even religious leaders do invoke such language, they often come under criticism). Rather, contemporary Americans are more comfortable with a kind of medical vocabulary; when talking about social problems, we are more likely to speak of *diseases, syndromes, disorders,* or *addictions*—words that seem grounded in medical, scientific classifications. Consider how contemporary discussions of Aquinas's classical list of the seven deadly sins often redefine these behaviors as medical problems; for example, lust might be characterized as *sex addiction*, gluttony as *food addiction* or *compulsive eating*, anger as an *anger management* problem, and sloth as *chronic fatigue syndrome*. (At the same time, modern medicine sometimes seems to promote those same deadly sins by treating their absence as medical problems that also may require treatment; consider drugs to enhance sexual performance [lust], cosmetic surgery [pride, envy], liposuction [gluttony], or concerns about workaholism and type A personalities [sloth] or low self-esteem [pride].) At least when they talk about social issues, contemporary Americans are less likely to accept the judgments of religious leaders, and more likely to defer to doctors.

The declining influence of ministers and growing clout of doctors illustrate how constructions of social problems reflect shifting patterns of institutional influence. In societies where religious authorities hold sway, social problems often are discussed in religious language; where medical authorities are more influential, social problems tend to be understood in medical terms. At different times and in different places, ideas about which people with which sorts of knowledge ought to be considered experts vary. *Experts* are presumed to possess especially authoritative knowledge, and other people—including activists, the media, and policymakers—may defer to this expertise.

In short, experts rank among the most influential claimsmakers because they are thought to have special knowledge that qualifies them to interpret social problems. Some experts are what Chapter 3 referred to as *insider claimsmakers*; their status as experts can give them easier access to policymakers so that they are part of the polity. This chapter examines the role of experts as claimsmakers in the contemporary social problems process. It begins by exploring the central place of medical authorities in constructing social problems, then turns to other sorts of experts.

MEDICALIZATION

Sociologists who have noted the increased use of medical language to characterize social problems speak of **medicalization** (Conrad, 2007), the process of defining troubling conditions as medical problems. A century ago, it was generally recognized that some people drank too much; that is, their drinking was blamed for causing problems at work and in their homes. The common label for these people was *drunkards* (Gusfield, 1967). Being a drunkard was seen as, if not a sin, at least a moral failing; drunkards were doing something they shouldn't do, and they needed to reform (the solution to being a drunkard often involved making a pledge to practice temperance; that is, the drunkard would promise to stop drinking).

Today, the term *drunkard* has virtually disappeared from our vocabulary. Of course, there are still people who drink too much, and whose drinking is thought to cause job problems and family problems. But we call these people *alcoholics*, and we speak of the *disease* of *alcoholism*. Alcoholics may receive *treatment*, often at *clinics*, where some of the costs are reimbursed by *health insurance*. In short, alcoholism has been medicalized, in that we now view it as a medical problem that should be addressed through medical solutions.

Consider another example: some students do not do well in school. Traditionally, those students were blamed for their poor performance: perhaps they were of lower intelligence, or perhaps they weren't trying hard enough. Today, claims suggest that poor performance at school may be caused by medicalized conditions, that these students have *learning disabilities* or *attention deficit hyperactivity disorder* (ADHD) (Conrad, 2007). Medical language—words such as *diagnosis, symptom*, or *therapy*—increasingly frames discussions of students' difficulties, and doctors now prescribe drugs to large numbers of children to help them become more attentive.

Why is medicalization important? There are two obvious ways it makes a difference. The first is that medicalization seems to shift responsibility away from the individual. In our culture, we routinely hold individuals responsible for what we view as deliberate behavior—acts that people choose to perform. Drunkards were once seen as weak because they gave in to drink, and poor students used to be viewed as lazy; in both cases, the individuals were held responsible for their own problems. In contrast, we generally do not hold people responsible for their illnesses; we don't blame them for becoming sick. Therefore, saying that people have the disease of alcoholism or a learning disability means that they shouldn't be blamed for their problems, that they merit sympathy and support, rather than criticism.

A second consequence of medicalizing a problem is that it provides a familiar frame—sometimes called the **medical model**—for thinking about the issue. Medical problems are described as diseases, disorders, syndromes, or disabilities. The people with these problems are ill; they display symptoms. They need to become patients, who can receive treatment from medical personnel—doctors, nurses, therapists—who often work in hospitals or clinics, and who can be reimbursed through the patient's health insurance. In other words, medicalization is a claim arguing that some problem should be owned and controlled by medical experts and organizations.

Medicalization, then, frames troubling conditions in particular ways (see Box 4.1). At first glance, our culture seems to construct sins or crimes differently from illness: sinners and criminals are held responsible, blamed for their actions, and punished; people who are ill are not blamed and receive treatment instead. However, the medical model also focuses on the individual rather than the larger society. In a medicalized view, people have diseases or syndromes that lead them to drink too much, to eat too much, and so on; and they must confront and overcome these problems through healthy behavior. By focusing on individuals' choices, medicalization shifts attention away from the ways in which larger social arrangements, such as poverty, shape these troubling conditions.

Medicalization grew markedly during the twentieth century. In part, this shift reflected dramatic changes in the practice of medicine:

Box 4.1 Criminalizing Disease

Medicalizing—defining troubling conditions as medical problems—is so common that we might be tempted to assume that medical definitions trump all others. However, a moment's thought reveals that even phenomena that are acknowledged to be illnesses can be defined in nonmedical terms.

HIV is unquestionably a disease, yet it has often been criminalized—that is, defined as a criminal problem. When the first AIDS cases were reported in 1981, the disease was viewed as very frightening because it seemed to be spreading rapidly and killed most infected individuals within eighteen months. Although most medical authorities argued that the new disease ought to be addressed using standard public health measures intended to reduce transmission, infected people were not just stigmatized but were blamed for having become infected, and there were calls to criminalize transmitting the disease (by making it a crime for, say, people who knew they were HIV-positive to fail to warn prospective partners). More recently, the advent of pre-exposure prophylaxis (PrEP)—in which an HIV-negative individual can take medication to protect against infection—has led to debates about whether PrEP will encourage people to behave "irresponsibly." Such concerns move beyond issues of health and medicine and frame questions in terms of morality.

Is HIV a medical problem? Or should it also be understood as a crime problem or a moral problem, or perhaps a religious problem? Although the medical frame has considerable social authority, it can be challenged by other definitional frameworks. Such judgments are inevitable, although we may not notice them when there is considerable consensus; they only become apparent when debating constructions call them into question.

Source: Hoppe, 2018.

doctors and hospitals became subject to tighter professional standards, so the quality of care rose; at the same time, advances in medical science led to new medications and treatments. All this meant that the chances of medical care actually helping patients rose sharply; people began to expect more of medical authorities, and the prestige and authority of physicians rose.

The rising stature of medicine encouraged the expansion of medical authority into a broader domain of social problems. In particular, psychiatrists (who are trained as physicians) began to claim that many troubling behaviors—including juvenile delinquency, unconventional sexual activity, drug addiction, and crime—should be recognized as symptoms of psychiatric problems. After World War II, the American Psychiatric Association began developing its *Diagnostic and Statistical Manual of Mental Disorders* (the so-called *DSM*), a huge catalog of all recognized mental disorders, which has continued to expand with each new edition (Kirk & Kutchins, 1992). The growing number of available diagnoses means that more and more behaviors can be understood in medical terms.

In addition to psychiatrists, whose medical training clearly placed them within medicine, practitioners in a variety of other quasi-medical professions adopted the language of *disease*, *symptom*, and *treatment*. Among these were clinical psychologists, licensed clinical social workers, and many others, including some with little or no professional training. Drug treatment, for instance, increasingly was provided by "professional ex-s [sic]"—recovered drug users who did not necessarily have professional credentials, but who were employed by drug treatment centers to lead therapeutic groups and who used medical language to describe what they did (J. D. Brown, 1991).

Often medicalization consists of little more than adopting a medical vocabulary. Take what is called the disease of *alcoholism*: its symptoms include drinking and getting into trouble at work and at home; there are no clear biological symptoms that distinguish alcoholics from nonalcoholic drinkers (Appleton, 1995). Similarly, treatment for alcoholism is to get people with drinking problems to choose to drink less (most often, total abstinence is recommended). The leading program for dealing with alcoholism, Alcoholics Anonymous (AA), is a resolutely amateur operation. There are no professionals; all of AA's members are people who identify themselves as recovering alcoholics. Individuals attend meetings with fellow alcoholics and discuss AA's twelve-step program for achieving sobriety.

AA insists that alcoholism is a disease, but that the cure is to stop drinking, continue attending AA meetings, and follow the Twelve Steps. Note that AA's solution for alcoholism—that is, helping the individual with a drinking problem to make a commitment to stop drinking—is not all that different from the way drunkards were expected to reform by taking a pledge of sobriety, although the language of medicine seems to impart special authority to treatment as a solution. The twelve-step model has been adapted to help people deal with a variety of troubling behaviors—including drug abuse, overeating, and gambling—that have also been characterized as addictions or diseases.

In short, various medical authorities, with very different sorts of credentials, claim ownership of many contemporary social problems. As noted in Chapter 3, ownership can bring important benefits. Experts who gain ownership of a social problem usually gain a good deal: their social visibility and prestige rise, they become more powerful, and typically they stand to benefit financially from the increased business that people afflicted with the problem bring to them. This means that experts often have a vested interest in promoting claims that depict social problems from their perspective (see Box 4.2).

In a classic constructionist case study, for example, Stephen Pfohl (1977) argued that pediatric radiologists played a leading role in bringing attention to battered child syndrome—what would later be called *child abuse*. Initially this problem was typified in terms of physical injuries to children too young to explain how they had been hurt. Pediatric radiologists—specialists in interpreting children's X-rays—argued that they could distinguish fractures caused by accidents from those caused by abuse. These claims not only promised to improve the protection of vulnerable children, but

Box 4.2 It Isn't Just Medicalization

Medicalization is just one example of a particular professional frame that can shape how social problems are constructed. We can see analogous processes with other professions. Consider *economicization*—the adoption of an economic model for thinking about social problems.

The basic assumptions of economics are familiar: we live in a world of finite goods, and most people seek to maximize their satisfaction by making choices that lead to an optimal outcome. Obviously, we are used to economists explaining what we think of as the economy—money, finance, and so on. However, there is evidence that advocates increasingly incorporate the basic economic model in their claimsmaking rhetoric. One simple way to do this is to argue that it would be more cost-effective to adopt some approach in addressing some troubling condition. For example, claimsmakers may argue that, say, establishing and funding preschool programs, while expensive in the short run, will more than pay for itself in the long run because children with improved early education are more likely to succeed as students, remain in school, and perhaps avoid other pitfalls such as delinquency, drug use, or poverty. Whereas earlier claims might have argued in terms of the morality of helping the disadvantaged, economicized claims frame the issue in terms of costs and benefits, insisting that the economically rational choice is to pay for preschools.

Just as a growing number of troubling conditions are being defined as medical problems, so, too, are there more claims being framed in economic language. Note, too, that as medicine and economics have become more influential in discussions of social problems, other professions—such as the ministry—seem to be losing much of their former influence.

Source: Best, 2018.

also gave pediatric radiologists—who represented a small, relatively low-prestige medical specialty—ownership of a life-threatening disease, so the specialty's status rose. Expert claimsmakers often experience such gains, and thus wind up doing well by doing good.

Experts often seek to defend their professional turf and even expand their domain of ownership. The process may be gradual. Consider the changing scope of pediatrics (Pawluch, 1996). When this medical specialty emerged in the early twentieth century, pediatricians focused their efforts on problems associated with infant feeding; the milk supply was often tainted, causing many infants to become seriously ill. However, improved techniques for managing the purity of the milk supply soon made infant feeding much safer, so the major service that pediatricians had been providing was becoming less needed. In response, pediatricians began to expand their domain to emphasize the treatment of, first, other childhood diseases, and then normal, healthy childhood development. As birth rates fell, of course, there were fewer children for pediatricians to treat, but the specialists began to extend their services to treating patients in adolescence and even early adulthood.

These efforts need not be seen as cynical and self-serving. Experts generally believe that they have valuable knowledge and offer useful services, and they are continually looking for new opportunities to apply their expertise. In periods when their services are already in high demand, they have less time to extend their domain, but when business is slack, the prospect of attacking new problems becomes much more attractive. In this way, professional domains expand and the professionals' interests are advanced.

Ideally, experts' gains can be consolidated into institutionalized ownership. For instance, rising health care costs increasingly require patients to have medical insurance. But what sorts of treatments should health insurance cover? Professionals who provide different treatments want medical insurance to cover their services so that more patients will seek those services. Thus, the federal government's decision to define alcohol and drug problems as medical problems, and to require health insurance programs to cover some of the costs of their treatment, institutionalized these experts as owners of the alcohol problem (Weisner & Room, 1984). As Chapter 3 noted, owners have advantages in promoting their constructions of social problems; when ownership is coupled with such experts' institutionalized arrangements, experts' authority becomes entrenched.

In recent years, medicalization has taken new directions, with troubling conditions becoming subjects of **biomedicalization** (Clarke, Shim, Mamo, Fosket, & Fishman, 2003). Experts argue that biological processes are the root cause of many troubling conditions, which means that effective solutions must then address biology. For instance, the scientific revolution in genetics has led to claims that it will soon be possible to identify particular genes that cause various troubling conditions. Clearly, genetic anomalies cause some medical disorders, such as Down syndrome. But biomedical proponents argue that it will soon be possible to identify the genetic roots of all manner of behaviors, such as homosexuality or alcoholism, and research funding increasingly supports biomedical studies. This assumption that biology is at the root of many troubling conditions also fosters **pharmaceuticalization**, the process of defining prescription drugs as the solution (Abraham, 2010). Some of these claims may be borne out; others may prove false. At least for the foreseeable future, however, medicalization is likely to remain our society's leading form of expert claimsmaking.

THE ROLE OF SCIENCE

Medical authority may be seen as a subcategory of a broader form of expertise: science. As with medicine, the advances made possible by the expansion of science, particularly during the past two centuries, have given scientists considerable authority in our culture. Society has been transformed by the growth in scientific knowledge; think of the Industrial Revolution, the exploitation of new forms of energy (steam, electricity, petroleum), faster transportation, speedier communication, and so on. Increased scientific knowledge made these changes possible.

Science depends on an appreciation of evidence. A scientific theory must generate falsifiable predictions; that is, those predictions must be able to be tested, and if they are proved wrong, the theory is rejected. Scientists do research to produce evidence that can support or challenge their theories' predictions; the more supportive evidence they find, the more confidence scientists have in their theories. This system of reasoning has proved very powerful and has provided the foundation for all sorts of technological and medical advances, and in our society scientists are considered to have considerable authority when speaking about matters for which they have gathered evidence.

This is not to say that scientific evidence is infallible. Science is socially constructed; it is one of the ways people make sense of the world. To be sure, we have considerable confidence in well-established scientific findings, but it takes time for findings to become well established. Research can be flawed, and evidence can be incomplete or incorrectly interpreted. Scientists may debate issues among themselves, questioning one another's reasoning and evidence. Scientific progress can be a slow process; such debates can continue for years, even decades, until the evidence compiled becomes sufficiently compelling for a consensus to emerge among scientists (see Box 4.3).

Unfortunately, the deliberate pace of science is not well suited to news media eager to report on dramatic scientific breakthroughs. For instance, the media may publicize reports of the initial study on a particular topic, even though that research may eventually prove to have been flawed. A dramatic example was the media's reaction to a 1989 report by two researchers who said that they had observed a cold-fusion reaction in their laboratory. The implications were staggering—harnessing cold fusion would provide limitless, inexpensive energy—and the media began to speculate about the social changes this discovery would bring. Alas, other scientists soon concluded that the researchers had misinterpreted their results—that they had not found a way to produce cold fusion—and the media quickly dropped the topic.

Scientific experts' claims derive much of their rhetorical power from the understanding that scientists have special knowledge and access to particularly strong evidence, so their views deserve respect.

Box 4.3 Identifying Sonic Attacks

Beginning in November 2016, about two dozen members of the diplomatic staff at the U.S. embassy in Havana reported hearing high-pitched sounds and then experiencing a variety of physical symptoms, including headaches, vertigo, and confusion. This cluster of ailments led to the government blaming "acoustical attacks" by someone presumably cooperating with the Cuban government, and some medical researchers claimed to have found evidence of changes in the brains of those affected. These claims attracted considerable media coverage. At the same time, scientists independent of the government argued that the medical findings were weak and ambiguous, and that there was no known means of directing ultrasonic beams to target individuals; some suggested that the sounds reported by the embassy workers actually were made by insects.

The sociological literature contains many reports of sudden onsets of various symptoms; these tend to be explained as instances of collective delusion, mass hysteria, or other similar labels. The basic pattern is that the affected group is experiencing some sort of stress and hearing about another individual's symptoms often leads to others reporting similar issues.

It is worth noting that the first symptoms were reported shortly after Donald Trump's election. The Obama administration had made the controversial decision to reopen an embassy in Cuba, and it was expected that the Trump administration might adopt a harder line, which must have created some stress among the embassy staff. While the Trump administration did not close the embassy, it adopted a number of measures that discouraged normalizing relations between the two countries, and the argument that Cuba was involved in an attack on the embassy could help justify these policies.

Source: Bartholomew & Pérez, 2018.

The media's tendency to treat the results of a single piece of research as definitive leads to confusion in the case of ongoing scientific debates. Until sufficient evidence becomes available, scientists—

like other experts—do not necessarily agree. Their evidence and interpretations may differ, even conflict. The press, the general public, and policymakers often find such disagreements frustrating, because they tend to look to scientists for not just authoritative, but correct, information. Apparent contradictions call scientists' authority into question.

For example, one week the media might report that a medical journal has published a research report concluding that drinking alcohol increases the risk of contracting a particular disease. The following week the media might announce that another group of researchers has concluded that moderate drinking improves one's health. What should people think? It is possible that both reports are correct—that is, that drinking raises the risk of contracting a particular disease but generally improves health. Or perhaps one of the studies is flawed (or even both are flawed). Over time, additional research is likely to lead to an eventual scientific consensus, but it is important to recognize that disagreements are normal within science and many other expert communities. Experts may disagree about which are the important questions to ask, about the best way to arrive at answers to those questions, about how to interpret the available evidence, and so on.

In general, research questions and answers are most clear-cut in the physical sciences (such as physics and chemistry), less so in the biological sciences (such as medicine), and the least so in the social sciences. The physical sciences have fewer disagreements about what constitutes compelling evidence, and debates among physical scientists often can be settled decisively; in contrast, social scientists often cannot agree about what constitutes convincing evidence. In addition, it is important to appreciate that disagreements among scientists can center on very different sorts of questions, and that the authority of science depends on the sort of question being asked (see Box 4.4).

Consider, for instance, the debate over climate change. At the most basic level is the question of whether the planet's temperature is indeed rising. Scientists have devised various ways of measuring temperatures going back through time. Although there may be some disputes about the accuracy of particular measurements, or about which methods of measuring temperature changes are most accurate, these are relatively technical matters, and there is considerable scientific consensus that cycles of global warming and global cooling have occurred in the past and that temperatures have risen about 0.74°C over the past one hundred years or so. Accurately measuring changes in temperature presents a relatively clear-cut research challenge—the sort of question that scientists are clearly qualified to answer. It is, of course, more difficult to predict what will happen in the future, although again there is fairly widespread consensus that temperatures are likely to continue to rise over the next century (but considerable disagreement about how much they are likely to rise, with estimates ranging from 1.8°C to 4.0°C).

A second issue—over which there is more debate—concerns the causes of climate change. Although some argue that the current global warming may be a natural process—just part of the long-term cycle of planetary heating and cooling—most scientists agree that at least some of the warming is due to humans' impact on the planet. Most commonly these claims focus on the role of greenhouse gases (for instance, emissions of carbon dioxide from vehicles and smokestacks) in retaining heat in the atmosphere. Note that these explanations are not mutually exclusive; perhaps the planet would be warming naturally in any case, but human activities are exacerbating the trend. At this level, the scientific issues are not as straightforward, and even experts who agree that global warming is occurring may disagree over the extent to which people's activities contribute to this process.

The debate's third level is far more contentious. Even if we assume for the moment that everyone agrees that human activity plays a substantial role in causing climate change, what should be done? Here, debates can address many different issues, including what the consequences of global warming might be, what sorts of policies

Box 4.4 The Limits of Scientific Authority

Although we pay a good deal of lip service to the authority of scientists, this may exaggerate their influence. Consider climate change. Presumably this is a heavily publicized issue in which people might imagine that scientific expertise would be relevant, and yet public opinion shows considerable confusion and disagreement. Claimsmakers insist that there is general scientific consensus that climate change is a significant problem, so why aren't scientists' views decisive?

Carmichael & Brulle (2017) examined a large set of public opinion polls on climate change and sought to explain shifts in attitudes. They discovered that scientific information had a minimal effect. In one sense, this is not surprising: the public doesn't follow the scientific literature; what people know about science—much as what they know about claimsmaking—is mediated by media coverage. And media coverage was influenced not by scientific developments but by various sorts of claimsmaking advocates, including environmental social movements (that generally supported claims about climate change), and environmental countermovements (that sought to challenge climate change claims). Coverage was also influenced by the amount of attention Congress was giving to the issue (which, of course, also included both voices warning about climate change and those dismissing climate change warnings). In other words, what shapes the public's confusion is that the media (which love to report on dramatic controversies) tend to convey the sense that climate change is an issue that is being hotly debated, even if there may be relatively little disagreement among scientists about the overall evidence regarding climate change.

might reduce climate change, what the costs of those policies might be, whether the prospective benefits justify those costs, who should bear the costs, and so on. At this stage, purely scientific issues are less central; science may offer fairly compelling evidence about the extent and causes of climate change, but scientific knowledge cannot specify the correct course of policy. Consider nuclear weapons, for example: scientists were able to design and build nuclear weapons, but the decisions to use—or not use—those weapons were made by political leaders, not scientists. Scientific knowledge ordinarily is not sufficient to set social policy.

In short, we need to understand that when scientists participate in debates over social issues, the relevance of their expertise varies, depending on the particular questions being considered. While people—including some scientists—may like to imagine that scientific findings are sufficient to guide policy, in practice policymaking is shaped by other considerations, especially values (Pielke, 2007). In addressing a question such as how much the planet's temperature has increased during the past century, scientific expertise is likely to play the central role. However, many commentators would argue that science cannot provide authoritative answers to questions such as whether the prospective benefits of implementing a particular policy to reduce greenhouse gases will justify the policy's costs, or how the costs of controlling emissions should be distributed among richer and poorer countries. The willingness of audiences to grant authority to scientists is likely to depend on how relevant they believe the experts' knowledge to be (see Box 4.5).

Contemporary debates over scientific authority often focus on constructions of risk. The modern fascination with risk can be dated to the 1960s, when the surgeon general announced that smoking was hazardous to health, activist Ralph Nader drew attention to unsafe automobiles, and author Rachel Carson warned that pesticides were causing significant environmental damage (Meyer & Rohlinger, 2012). These highly visible claims led to concerns about other risks, which in turn produced all manner of warnings—about the dangers of cholesterol, secondhand smoke, toxic waste, and so on. Such claims often couple scientific evidence (suggesting, for example, that a particular chemical may be carcinogenic) with warnings that the danger is widespread and the issue urgent. Increasingly, the media cover scientists' warnings that this or that condition poses risks to individuals' health, to environmental safety, and so on. Although the

Box 4.5 Conservatives Losing Confidence in Science

Expertise confers social status, for it is not enough that experts claim to have special knowledge; it is also necessary that other people ratify that expertise and defer to the experts' judgments. For decades, surveys have asked the public to rate the amount of confidence ("a great deal," "only some," and so on) they have in various institutions. These data make it possible to track changes in the level of confidence of both the public overall and in various subgroups of the population, such as people who describe their political orientation as conservative, moderate, or liberal.

In 1974, there were only modest differences in how people with different political orientations rated their confidence in science; if anything, conservatives expressed slightly more confidence in science than the other two groups. However, in the intervening years, the levels of confidence expressed by liberals and moderates remained essentially stable, while conservatives' confidence in science fell until they were the group least likely to say they had a great deal of confidence in science.

Such shifts have consequences for the social problems process. To the degree that there is general agreement about the authority of some type of expert, claims from such experts need not be divisive. However, if views of experts become politicized—as when conservatives have less confidence in scientific authority—then experts' claims have less power. In particular, conservatives' skepticism about the scientific findings regarding climate change have made policy debates much more contentious.

Sources: Gauchat, 2012; McCright & Dunlap, 2011.

evidence regarding some risks—such as the link between smoking and lung cancer—is overwhelming, scientists disagree about the extent and significance of other risks.

It can take time for scientists to agree on assessments of risk. The most compelling scientific evidence comes from experiments, but it is usually impossible to design experiments to study risk. We cannot take identical groups of infants and make sure that they have identical experiences going through life—except that we can expose the experimental group to a particular risk and keep the control group from being exposed to that risk. Such a study might produce very strong evidence, but it would be time-consuming, expensive, and unethical. In practice, researchers must settle for much weaker evidence; they might, for example, identify people exposed to a particular risk, try to match them with similar folks who have not been exposed to that risk, and then study whether the two groups have different rates of particular diseases. It is always possible to challenge the results of such studies—for instance, were the two groups matched on every relevant variable?—and it takes a great deal of evidence (such as the countless studies on smokers' health) to make a convincing case.

It is difficult for nonscientists—a category that includes most activists, members of the media, the general public, and policymakers—to assess claims about risk that refer to scientific evidence. Debates over social problems often ignore such issues as comparative risks (for instance, the number of people at risk, the number of people likely to be harmed, and so on). All kinds of activities (for example, driving to work) carry risks. Often we take these risks for granted and ignore them, even though they may be far greater than are the heavily publicized dangers of, say, exposure to secondhand smoke. Scientific evidence—particularly calculations of risk—is not well understood, and such issues often lead to confusion in the face of what is thought to be expert claimsmaking.

EVIDENCE, INTERESTS, AND ADVOCACY

A major reason why people defer to experts is their presumption that experts command knowledge that other people don't have. Although all knowledge is socially constructed, we consider experts' knowledge to be more likely to be accurate than gossip, rumor, or other less authoritative sorts of knowledge that, we know from experience, often prove to be wrong. Thus, we tend to consider expert knowledge to be relatively correct. We defer to medical authorities because we assume that they know how to diagnose diseases, are able to understand the causes and workings of those diseases, and can recommend the best possible treatments. Similarly, we presume that scientists have done careful research and compiled evidence that offers the best available information about how the world works.

In other words, we turn to experts for sound information based on high-quality evidence, and experts' status as relatively authoritative claimsmakers depends on such understanding. Experts are commonly assumed to be impartial judges—their medical diagnoses or scientific findings grounded in facts rather than opinions. Yet experts often have an interest in promoting claims, and when they become advocates for particular positions or policies, they are not necessarily guided solely by their expert knowledge.

We have already noted that experts stand to benefit from the ownership of social problems; recall how the status of pediatric radiologists rose after they drew attention to battered child syndrome. Experts also may have social ties to parties with interests in social issues. Scientific research can be extremely expensive, and many scientists derive funding from corporations, government agencies, and so on. These funders may have an interest in the researchers' findings. For example, both medical researchers and their pharmaceutical company sponsors may have financial stakes in a new drug, and they may hope that the drug proves safe and effective, just as scientists employed by a corporation may be under pressure to affirm that the firm's waste disposal practices are safe. Other scientists may be closely associated with particular social movements, such as environmentalism.

Even though we tend to idealize scientists as objective, impartial observers, they may have allegiances that help shape their conclusions. Some legal trials feature psychiatrists hired as expert witnesses by the prosecution and the defense, who testify, respectively, that the defendant's mental state was such that the trials should or should not proceed. The point is not that experts' social ties make science illegitimate—a very large share of scientists have such commitments—but that scientific knowledge is not produced or disseminated in a social vacuum.

In some cases, scientists' allegiances may be to the particular perspectives or approaches that characterize their disciplines. For instance, sociologists and other social scientists also act as expert claimsmakers. Just as medical authorities bring their professional training to bear when they medicalize troubling conditions by characterizing them using the language of diseases, symptoms, and other medical concepts, social scientists have their own orientations and conceptual tools. Economists, for example, argue that people can be understood as rational actors who make choices to maximize their own satisfaction. This proves to be a powerful underlying assumption, in that it can be extended to analyze all manner of choices. Thus, economists tend to see social problems as the products of people's choices, and to promote policies that will encourage people to make particular choices. For example, one way to discourage smoking is to raise tobacco taxes; if tobacco is more expensive, at least some people may choose to stop smoking.

Sociologists, too, apply their discipline's perspective to the analysis of social problems in their works (including this book). Sociologists argue that people shape one another's actions, and that social problems are products of particular social arrangements. Thus, where a psychiatrist may approach a social problem in terms of individuals whose thinking is disordered because they suffer from a syndrome of some sort, or an economist may see it in terms of arrangements that reward some choices more than others, sociologists are more likely to point to the way culture and social structure constrain and shape people's activities. C. Wright Mills (1959) called this mode of thinking the *sociological imagination* (discussed further in Chapter 5). This book, for instance, emphasizes understanding the social problems process through which actors socially construct social problems.

In other cases, experts may have allegiances to particular ideological positions. Liberal and conservative experts can approach social problems in very different ways: they focus on different causes, and they recommend different solutions. So-called think tanks—private nonprofit organizations dedicated to policy analysis and advocacy—often have an ideology that shapes their experts' recommendations (see Box 4.6). These experts maintain connections with media outlets and politicians who share their ideological orientations, so advocates from different positions have access to expert knowledge that can be used to buttress their claims.

Although we might like to imagine that experts are completely independent, impartial authorities, without interests or ideological commitments, this perfect objectivity is, in practice, impossible to achieve. Experts are part of the larger social order. At a minimum, they believe in the value of their professions: psychiatrists consider psychiatry a valuable perspective, just as sociologists promote the value of the sociological imagination. Experts can further be expected to believe that the problems they have chosen to study are important and worthy of their attention and that the solutions they have been working on are promising. They may also have more obvious interests (such as a financial stake in the outcome of their research) or ideological preferences. Such social connections do not necessarily mean that the experts are wrong, but they do suggest that experts may be less than perfectly objective, and may think less critically when they confront ideas that fit their prejudices, so their claims should not be automatically accepted.

Expert knowledge is imperfect because it is produced by scientists, physicians, and other experts who are themselves actors in the larger society. It should be no surprise that experts' ideas evolve as

Box 4.6 A Think Tank Decries Sink Estates

Think tanks are now found in many countries. In the United Kingdom, the Policy Exchange was established in 2002 by three members of Parliament from the Conservative Party as a think tank that
would serve as a resource for that party, by producing policy papers
on a variety of issues.

Slater (2018) describes the Policy Exchange's role in shaping
housing policy in Britain, where public housing projects are termed
estates. Journalists had coined the term *sink estates* as a label for
estates that were plagued by poverty, crime, and other troubling
conditions, and the term had been in fairly common use in the press
since the late 1990s to describe particularly troubled estates. Policy
Exchange revived the term, expanded its meaning to suggest that
public housing generally was troubled, and then argued that policymakers should strive to move away from public housing and allow
the market to regulate housing.

Slater argues that this construction ignored evidence that people turned to public housing precisely because the market did not
offer affordable choices. There are hundreds of thousands of empty
homes in the United Kingdom, but the costs of buying or renting
would be beyond the budgets of people who go to public housing.
In his view, people apply for public housing because they are too
poor to afford to pay for housing in the market. Policy Exchange,
however, argues that public housing—those sink estates—makes its
residents poor, and that the solution lies in eventually ending public
housing. Just as in the United States, think tanks in other countries
offer arguments and explanations about the causes of and solutions
to troubling conditions.

new information becomes available. But it takes time for novel ideas
to emerge and gain acceptance. As evidence accumulates, consensus is likely to develop, but this process cannot occur overnight.
This is why expert knowledge is best understood as a special type
of claim, part of the larger social problems process.

OFFICIALS AS EXPERT CLAIMSMAKERS

Another important category of expert claimsmakers consists of officials, particularly those employed by government agencies, such as the Centers for Disease Control and Prevention (CDC) or the Environmental Protection Agency (EPA). Such agencies have various responsibilities: they may compile information (collecting data to measure the crime rate, the unemployment rate, and so on); they may administer regulations (regarding workplace safety, pollution, or other issues); they may fund research through grants to experts outside the government; they may disseminate information to the citizenry; and so on. The work of many agencies bears on one or more social problems. Because the federal government spends billions on the budgets of its various agencies, these officials can draw on substantial resources. Usually they are able to compile more and better information about troubling conditions than unofficial claimsmakers can, giving officials' claims special authority in many social problems debates. Official agencies often achieve a level of ownership for social problems.

Agencies compete with one another for budget allocations and other scarce resources. Often multiple agencies have an interest in the same social problem. For instance, alcohol issues are the concern of several federal agencies: the Bureau of Alcohol, Tobacco, Firearms and Explosives (ATF); the National Institute on Alcohol Abuse and Alcoholism (NIAAA); the National Highway Traffic Safety Administration (NHTSA), which is concerned with alcohol-related traffic fatalities; and on and on. Imagine how many federal agencies must be concerned with a particular aspect of racial inequality. Just as social movement organizations find themselves competing with one another, officials—at least some of the time—view other agencies as competitors, both for resources and for ownership of particular social issues.

Protecting and, if possible, expanding an agency's turf becomes a central concern for officials, and claimsmaking provides one weapon for bureaucratic infighting. That is, drawing attention to a particular troubling condition, devising a program to deal with the problem, and then administering that program can serve two ends. On the one hand, it is easy to imagine that most officials are sincere, that they have joined an agency because they believe that it does important, valuable work. Like other claimsmakers, officials probably believe their own rhetoric and adopt the frames they promote. At the same time, officials have instrumental reasons to promote claims: successful claimsmaking is likely to serve the agency's interests, to increase its power, influence, and budget (see Box 4.7). Whatever their convictions, officials often have an interest in the claims they promote. For example, officials of the U.S. Bureau of Narcotics undoubtedly saw marijuana as a dangerous drug when they first called for a federal law against it in the 1930s, but that law also helped protect the bureau from further budget cuts (Dickson, 1968).

Officials may recognize that their agencies could address certain additional troubling conditions if they could help launch the social problems process. Indeed, agencies often control significant, flexible resources that can be used to jump-start the claimsmaking process. In the 1960s, for instance, the U.S. Children's Bureau (CB) was under fire from critics and losing control of some programs that were being shifted to other agencies (Nelson, 1984). At the same time, CB officials had long been in contact with the American Humane Association, an organization that had historically been concerned with the physical abuse of children. The CB began funding the research that drew national attention to what was initially called *battered child syndrome*, soon to be renamed *child abuse* (Pfohl, 1977). Child abuse became a visible, dramatic subject of considerable public concern, and in the process helped restore the CB as an important agency of the federal government. As an owner of the child abuse problem, the CB could extend its programs—funding further research, helping develop legislation requiring doctors and other professionals to report child abuse, and so on.

Box 4.7 Medical Language as Official Denial

In 2013, detainees at Guantánamo Bay protested their indefinite detention by refusing food. In response, the military running the camp forcibly fed the hunger strikers. Critics of the detention policy charged that this force-feeding constituted torture. In response, the military denied that it had committed torture by medicalizing the procedure.

When addressing the issue, military spokespeople avoided the term *force-feeding*, instead speaking of *enteral feeding*, language that presented the practice as a medical procedure. They also emphasized that detainees were given choices—they could eat a regular meal or a nutritional supplement—and that some hunger strikers underwent the procedure "calmly." In their accounts, enteral feeding was described as uncomfortable but not painful, and the military argued that it followed essentially the same procedures used in hospitals and nursing homes when patients refused food. The point was to keep the detainees alive; the feeding was not intended to punish the detainees or force them to break their hunger strikes. In other words, military spokespeople denied that this was a form of torture.

In contrast, critics argued that detainees reported that the procedure was both frightening and painful, and that it involved an abusive invasion of the body and thereby constituted a violation of medical ethics. Such debates reveal how claims and denials about the meanings of events are constructed using carefully chosen arguments. In this case, the military attempted to medicalize its practices by adopting a medical vocabulary and drawing parallels with similar practices in familiar medical settings to insist that this was lifesaving, not abusive.

Source: Del Rosso, 2018.

Although the expert claimsmakers in these examples were federal officials, analogous processes can occur in state or local governments, wherever officials become involved in drawing attention to troubling conditions. In some cases, national attention on a problem may lead local officials to call for action in their communities; in other locales, officials may be slower to acknowledge that the problem exists in—and requires action in—their jurisdictions. The policies of different cities toward homelessness, for instance, depend on how local officials respond to the issue (Bogard, 2003). In other cases, claimsmaking by officials may focus on purely local issues—such as whether an old building should be demolished to permit new development or be preserved as part of the community's historical heritage (Lofland, 2003).

Officials working in government agencies usually have special knowledge or expertise that justifies their participation in claimsmaking. They are insiders, and their activities often occur behind the scenes, out of the public view. In sharp contrast are the claimsmaking activities of elected officials—presidents, senators, and the like—who may seize on an issue and become active claimsmakers. These officials may lack special expertise, but their visible positions make it much easier for them to attract media attention and help publicize a cause.

EXPERT CLAIMSMAKERS IN THE SOCIAL PROBLEMS PROCESS

Chapter 3 explored the role of activists and social movements in claimsmaking; this chapter has concentrated on the claimsmaking of experts—particularly medical authorities, scientists, and public officials. In many cases, claimsmaking campaigns feature alliances between activists and experts. Activists often contribute enthusiasm, passion, and whatever organizational resources their movements may control, whereas experts provide authoritative knowledge. (This is obviously an oversimplification: many activists become quite knowledgeable, and experts can become highly dedicated to claimsmaking campaigns.)

Knowledge is an important commodity in claimsmaking. Remember that social problems claims begin with grounds statements—that is, statements about the facts concerning the troubling condition. When claimsmakers are trying to draw attention to a neglected condition—one that hasn't attracted much attention—often they discover that little information is available and no experts are studying the problem yet. One solution is for activists to begin to collect their own information. For instance, it was only after gay and lesbian activists in some cities tried to gather reports of homosexuals who had been assaulted that official efforts to collect hate crime statistics started (Jenness & Grattet, 2001). Similarly, residents living near toxic waste sites may begin to collect their own evidence of health problems as a way of arousing concern about the risks they face (P. Brown, 1992). In such cases, amateurs try to generate the sort of knowledge that experts have failed to collect, in order to fill what would otherwise be a gap in their claims. Figure 4.1 illustrates how both trained professionals and those without formal training as experts can make use of professional knowledge when making claims.

Just as activist claimsmakers must be alert to the responses of others—particularly the media, the public, and policymakers—so, too, must experts be concerned with feedback from other actors in the social problems process. Because experts are likely to consider the knowledge that they contribute to the social problems process especially valuable, they may be disappointed that their statements are not more influential. Audiences may have trouble interpreting what experts have to say, particularly when the experts present their findings using a professional, technical vocabulary. To bridge the gap, experts may discover that they need to popularize their work, to translate their findings into lay language.

Another problem is that audiences may have impossibly high expectations for experts' contributions; as we have suggested, experts may add to our understanding of a troubling social condition, but their knowledge usually is not sufficient to identify policies that can

Figure 4.1 EXPERTS' ROLE IN THE SOCIAL PROBLEMS PROCESS

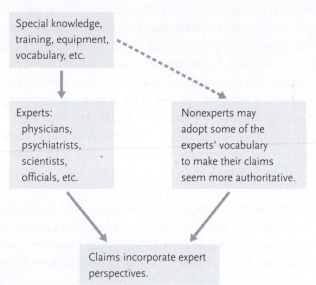

make the problem disappear. Ultimately, whether experts' claims—or, for that matter, the claims of activists—are widely understood depends on the treatment they receive in the media.

MAKING CONNECTIONS

- *The role of experts in the policymaking process is discussed further in Chapter 7.*

- *The media rely on experts to make claims about social problems. In the next chapter you will learn how experts and the media collaborate in the social problems process.*

- *In Chapter 9, the role of experts in evaluating the outcomes of social problems and making new claims about problems will be discussed.*

CASE STUDY
EXPERTISE AND OPIOIDS

What sort of problem is drug addiction? Is it a crime problem, a medical problem, or something else?

To begin, drug addiction may affect different sorts of people. At the end of the nineteenth century, drug addiction affected diverse populations: there were thousands of Civil War veterans who had suffered painful wounds and had been receiving maintenance doses of morphine for decades; their addiction was seen as a medical matter. In addition, many thousands of ordinary women habitually treated pain using various patent medicines that contained some type of opium derivative; and there was a much smaller population (often associated with the underworld as thieves, prostitutes, and the like) who smoked opium or dosed themselves with morphine or laudanum (Courtwright, 1982). In those days, people who argued that addiction was a social problem were usually thinking of opium dens, not veterans or housewives.

The Harrison Narcotics Act of 1914 began federal efforts to redefine addiction as a criminal problem by trying to restrict access to opiates and cocaine. Early court decisions ruled that physicians could not prescribe opiates to maintain a patient's habit, so doctors' medical judgments became irrelevant. The federal government then embarked on a long history of campaigns and "wars" intended to halt the use of various drugs, even—during the Prohibition era (1920–33)—alcohol. Law enforcement officials became the principal experts who shaped understandings of drug problems, although physicians generally retained control over drugs being prescribed for legitimate medical treatments. Thus, in recent decades, the concerns about crack (in the late twentieth century) and meth (at the beginning of the twenty-first century) were largely viewed as crime or law enforcement problems. While some medical experts continued to insist that addiction should be understood and addressed as a medical problem, their views had relatively little influence in the United States compared to other countries that relied more heavily on medical expertise (MacCoun & Reuter, 2001).

However, the next major drug problem—opioid addiction—broke this pattern, and people began to turn to medical authorities for expertise. There were several reasons for this that reflected the way medicine had contributed to the problem. First, in the 1990s, the American Pain Society promoted the idea that pain was a fifth vital sign (along with body temperature, pulse, blood pressure, and respiratory rate) and argued that managing pain should be a central goal in medical care. More physicians began prescribing enough pain medication to help patients manage their pain for weeks as they recovered from injuries and medical procedures. Second, an idea began circulating that addiction was an extremely uncommon outcome when nonaddicted patients were prescribed narcotics. Since narcotics were effective in controlling pain (which was increasingly considered important), and there was thought to be minimal danger of addiction from prescribed narcotics, doctors were encouraged to issue more prescriptions. Third, pharmaceutical manufacturers with new opioid products organized extensive campaigns aimed at encouraging physicians to prescribe their drugs to manage the pain problem (McGreal, 2018).

At the same time, there were warnings—largely ignored at first—that growing numbers of patients were becoming addicted to their opioid prescriptions. A patient whose own physician might have refused to write prescriptions for further refills because he or she was concerned about the patient's dependency on opioids could shop around to find another willing doctor, and this was not difficult to do. Unscrupulous doctors discovered they could make big money simply by writing lots of these prescriptions. Drug manufacturers, which were selling dramatically more opioids than ever before, turned a blind eye to what was happening. And those who were able to get opioid prescriptions filled discovered that they could make money reselling their pills.

In other words, the massive increase in the availability of opioids produced for theoretically legitimate medical purposes caused a significant rise in the number of addicts, including large numbers of people who were introduced to the drugs as patients. While most patients with opioid prescriptions were leery of becoming dependent on the drugs and sought to stop using them as soon as possible, some—particularly those whose lives were stressed in other ways— were less careful. Addiction began to spread, particularly in rural Rust Belt areas where economies were offering fewer opportunities, and authorities noted that deaths from overdoses were increasingly concentrated in settings like West Virginia. The impact was significant: in 2017, there were nearly twice as many deaths from drug overdoses as from motor vehicle accidents; Americans' overall life expectancy actually declined slightly. The greatest increases in overdose deaths were among those ages 25–54, with those involving synthetic opioids other than methadone showing a dramatic rise (Hedegaard, Miniño, & Warner, 2018).

Of course, most drug addiction problems can be described in terms of overdose deaths. But, unlike earlier concerns about heroin, crack, or meth, which tended to be described as crime problems, the opioid problem—with its spectacularly higher death toll—was thoroughly medicalized. The authorities referred to the opioid *epidemic*, and even law enforcement authorities began warning that "we can't arrest our way out of this problem." Press coverage tended to depict opioid addicts as white, middle-aged members of the working and lower-middle classes, in contrast to portrayals of addicts as younger, lower-class members of ethnic minorities in earlier drug problems. These opioid addicts became sympathetic figures, people who had fallen on hard times, even as media focused blame on the troubled medical system that had produced the epidemic. Instead of recommending arrest and imprisonment, the emphasis was on treating addiction as a public health crisis and trying to save those who had overdosed by using products such as naloxone nasal sprays (approved for use by nonmedical personnel to reverse the effects of an overdose). There were calls to promote drug prevention and drug rehabilitation, for example, by increasing the number of beds in residential rehab programs so that addicts who decided that they wanted to enter a program could do so without waiting. And there were calls for the development of safe-injection sites (clean places where addicts could use drugs under medical supervision).

To be sure, the medicalized construction of the opioid problem coexisted with more traditional attitudes that held that addicts were responsible for their own bad choices, and that others were more deserving of sympathy and support (Russell, Spence, & Thames, 2019). And it was certainly the case that neither law enforcement nor medical policies offered quick, easy solutions to drug problems. But after a long series of campaigns that defined various drugs as crime problems and drug users as criminals, opioids were being treated as first and foremost a medical problem, and there was widespread agreement that social policies to address this problem ought to be guided by medical—rather than law enforcement—expertise.

QUESTIONS

1. Why does expertise tend to transfer from one social problem to the next similar problem (for instance, from familiar drug problems to a new one)?

2. Under what circumstances can experts lose ownership of a social problem?

3. There have always been calls to medicalize drug problems, but in the past they had little effect. Why weren't they more successful?

5

The Media and Claims

Analyses of the mass media's role in the social problems process often focus on the issue of **bias**. Conservative critics charge that the media systematically present a liberal point of view:

> The argument over whether the national press is dominated by liberals is over. Since 1962, there have been 11 surveys of the media that sought the political views of hundreds of journalists. . . . And the proportion of liberals to conservatives in the press, either 3-to-1 or 4-to-1, has stayed the same. That liberals are dominant is now beyond dispute. (Barnes, 2004)

Meanwhile, liberals counter that the media have a conservative bias:

> Even the genuine liberal media . . . [are] no match—either in size, ferocity, or commitment—for the massive conservative media structure that, more than ever, determines the shape and scope of our political agenda. (Alterman, 2003, p. 11)

These critiques address the news media that report information (such as newspapers, newsmagazines, and radio and television news broadcasts), but also the entertainment media (such as television dramas, novels, or movies) and so-called infotainment that uses entertaining formats to discuss social issues (such as television talk shows, or "reality" shows that depict police at work).

All forms of **media coverage** tend to alter how social problems are constructed, although not necessarily in the ways that critics of media bias imagine. The social problems process typically begins with claimsmaking that precedes the media's involvement; usually activists or experts present the initial, or **primary, claims** (J. Best, 1990). Unless these claimsmakers are insiders who have ready access to policymakers (see Chapters 3 and 4), they probably hope that the media will cover their claims, thereby bringing those claims before a larger audience than the claimsmakers could hope to reach on their own. Newspaper stories, talk show episodes, or movies with plots involving troubling conditions can bring claims to the attention of millions of people in the general public, as well as policymakers. However, media coverage almost inevitably alters the claims that it presents.

Media workers face their own constraints: they work under deadlines, so they rarely have time to become thoroughly familiar with the claims they cover; their presentations are usually constricted (for example, newspapers can print only so many inches of news per day [journalists call this the *newshole*], and television news programs have only so many broadcast minutes available); and they need to make their coverage interesting enough that the audience won't stop reading or watching. The media, then, translate and transform claimsmakers' messages into what we will call **secondary claims**, typically by making them shorter, more dramatic, and less ideological than the original primary claims.

Because there are many claimsmakers and the media can cover only a limited number of stories, claimsmakers find themselves competing for media attention. Savvy claimsmakers realize that they need to package their claims so as to interest the media in covering them. The media prefer to cover new, seemingly fresh material, so it is important to present claims in novel ways (the first sit-in or peace march may get a lot of coverage, but each additional sit-in or march is likely to get less, unless it offers an interesting new angle). The media like to be able to plan their coverage in advance, so it helps to issue press releases and schedule press conferences so that reporters know when and where they can find someone willing to talk with them. The media favor claims presented by interesting people, so claimsmakers need to find spokespersons who seem engaging (note how often claimsmaking campaigns use either celebrities—interesting in their own right—or highly dramatic figures, such as parents who have suffered the loss of a child, to present their claims). Television seeks visually interesting material that can accompany a story, so claimsmakers favor marches, demonstrations, and other easy-to-film ways of presenting their claims. In the competition for media attention, claimsmakers who take the media's needs into account have an advantage (Sobieraj, 2011).

Hilgartner and Bosk (1988) suggest that the marketplace for social problems can be understood as composed of multiple **arenas**. Each arena is a venue where social problems claims can be presented; the pages of a newsmagazine, a TV talk show, or the hearings of a congressional subcommittee are all arenas. Each arena has a limited **carrying capacity** for presenting claims: magazines have only so many pages per issue, talk shows schedule a set number of episodes per season, subcommittees hold only a limited number of hearings, and so on. In Chapters 3 and 4, we considered the perspective of claimsmakers, who understand that they are competing for attention in various arenas. In this chapter we will adopt the perspective of those who work in the media. We can think of them as managing different arenas and having the job of sorting through all the competing claims and choosing which ones will receive attention in their arena.

In general, sociologists who have observed how news reporters and editors decide which stories to cover and how to cover them conclude that bias—in the sense of an underlying political ideology—is less important in shaping how the news is covered than the nature of the work that reporters and editors do. This chapter begins by considering the nature of those jobs—and the parallel considerations that shape how social problems are treated in entertainment and social media—before examining the forms that secondary claims tend to take. The chapter ends with a caution against exaggerating the media's influence.

WHAT'S THE NEWS?

The term **news work** draws our attention to the fact that reporters and editors have the job of locating and presenting news to the larger public. Like all other occupations, news work has constraints (Schudson, 2011; Tuchman, 1978). Some constraints are economic: it costs money to collect and produce news, and news workers operate within budgets, so newspapers and television news operations can afford only so many employees; the newshole (that is, the number of available column inches or broadcast minutes) can contain only so many stories; and so on. Other constraints are cultural. News workers have their own understanding of what they should do; that is, their sense of professionalism also shapes their coverage.

News workers operate under pressure. They have schedules and deadlines; newspapers and magazines need to reach the printer on schedule, just as radio and television programs need to be ready in time for their broadcasts. News workers cannot simply sit back and wait for news to happen and come to their attention; rather, they must try to plan ahead, to anticipate what might be and ought to be covered. Many news organizations assign reporters to beats—types of news that are expected to generate suitable stories; for example, a reporter on the police beat covers stories about crimes. News workers also are drawn to predictable events; a scheduled demonstration or even a press conference can be attractive precisely because reporters and editors have some sense in advance of what sorts of stories those events might generate.

News workers also judge some stories as being more deserving of coverage than others. Most obviously, they consider some stories to be more important, or, as they say, more newsworthy. Important stories involve consequential events, things about which people need to know. But importance depends on the news workers' audience. Imagine a passenger jet crashing and killing, say, 150 people. How much attention should a newspaper give that story? If the crash occurred in the city where the newspaper is published, we can imagine this dramatic local story consuming most of the front page. If it occurred, say, in a city a thousand miles away, and if there were other compelling stories competing for the paper's attention, the crash story might well be pushed off the front page. If the crash occurred in a foreign country (and especially if no Americans were killed), it is likely to receive no more than a paragraph or two, somewhere well inside the paper. In other words, it is not just the death toll that makes a story seem important, but also the story's perceived relevance to the paper's readers.

In addition to being of varying importance, stories strike news workers as being more or less interesting to their audience. Television news, for example, favors stories that can be accompanied by videotaped footage showing something happening. The earliest television news broadcasts featured newscasters facing the camera and reading stories to the audience. Television workers soon realized, however, that theirs was a visual medium, and that audiences found these "talking heads" boring. There is, then, a strong preference for having some sort of videotaped action to illustrate the story, even if the activity shown is mundane; this explains why stories about ongoing trials—where cameras are often forbidden in the courtroom—routinely feature footage of trial participants walking into the courthouse to accompany the sound of a reporter describing what happened in court that day.

There are, of course, other ways of making stories interesting. Like claims generally, news stories often begin with typifying examples. For example, a story on homelessness might begin by describing the experiences of one or two particular homeless individuals; such an introduction puts a human face on the story and gives the problem "human interest" (see Box 5.1). Stories that seem less interesting can easily lose out in the competition for media attention; news workers will favor covering stories that can be presented in an interesting manner.

Another quality of an attractive story is novelty. Notice the very word *news*—that is, "what's new." In general, news workers prefer stories that are current (especially "breaking news") and that seem different. "Fresh" news is preferred to stories that seem too familiar, that have grown "stale." After all, if there isn't something new to report, why should news workers expect the audience to pay any attention? This means that familiar, troubling conditions that affect many people—such as world hunger—may not attract nearly as much media attention as the latest sex scandal or lurid murder.

In assembling the stories they report, news workers apply other professional standards as well. For example, when the story's subject is clearly an issue about which people disagree, many news workers consider themselves obliged to *balance* their coverage by reporting the views of "both sides." This expression reveals an assumption that most issues have only two sides—pro and con, liberal and conservative, or whatever. The news media often resist reporting complex stories in which there are more than two competing positions; they prefer to construct the issue as a straightforward, two-party disagreement. Note, too, that news workers do not feel the need to balance coverage when they perceive a general unanimity of opinion (concerning what Chapter 2 called *valence issues*). If there is general, widespread agreement that, say, child pornography is bad, then reporters will not consider themselves obliged to balance their coverage by reporting the views of child pornographers.

Because most news workers keep track of coverage by rival news organizations, they often feel they ought to *follow one another's lead.* The very fact that another newspaper or newscast is covering a

Box 5.1 Being News

The concept of news work draws our attention to how the reporters and editors who create news coverage experience this process. But what about the individuals who find themselves being covered as the *subjects* of news stories? Many are political leaders, celebrities, even activists who have sought the news media's attention, who hope to see themselves covered. But what about ordinary people who have some newsworthy experience that suddenly catapults them into the media spotlight?

Palmer (2018) interviewed people who unexpectedly found themselves subjects of news coverage. Their experience has two parts. First, they find control of their own stories gradually shifting to the journalists, who have identified a story that can be told that may interest their audience. A reporter's sense of what makes a "good story" may be very different from how individuals define the contours of their own lives, but the former carries more weight because it is the reporter who decides which elements are needed to make a compelling story. The subjects of the story usually find themselves cooperating with the reporter's construction project to turn their lives into something newsworthy.

The second part of the experience is that, having allowed the press to present their stories to the public, the subjects of news coverage find that the people around them hold them accountable for that coverage. They may feel that there are errors in the resulting story yet have little ability to set the record straight, especially since the news media's attention may have already shifted to the next topic. The individuals who had their "fifteen minutes of fame" may find themselves living with a status or stigma that they never sought.

story suggests that that story must be newsworthy. When several news organizations rush to follow the same lead, the result can be a wave of news coverage. This often happens with social problems coverage, which is why criminologists have long understood that crime waves are not so much waves in criminal activity as waves in news coverage (Vasterman, 2018).

Considerations such as importance, interest, novelty, balance, and what other news organizations are covering shape how news workers construct the news. These are inevitably matters of judgment, with editors making choices—deciding which stories deserve more attention, which deserve less, and which can be ignored (see Box 5.2). In some cases, news workers may act as primary claimsmakers; that is, they might originate the claimsmaking through their coverage.

For social problems claimsmakers, the challenge is to construct claims that will strike news workers as sufficiently important and interesting to merit news coverage. Sophisticated claimsmakers learn to take the news workers' concerns into account: they make it easy to cover their claims by, for example, staging demonstrations and other events that will seem interesting and therefore newsworthy; they schedule these events and press conferences in advance so that news workers will know when and where to go to get their stories; they designate articulate spokespersons who can present the claims, answer reporters' questions, and help them identify suitable typifying examples; and they devise novel, visually interesting ways of presenting their claims—new forms of demonstrations, new evidence, and such—so that their message seems fresh and the story well suited for television. For instance, a small San Francisco prostitutes' rights movement managed to attract a great deal of media attention by organizing the "First Annual Hookers' Ball" (Jenness, 1993). Understanding the news media's concerns allows claimsmakers to package their claims in ways that will appeal to news workers, and thereby makes it more likely that those claims will, in fact, become the subjects of news coverage.

News workers are not naive; they understand that experienced claimsmakers tailor their campaigns to attract news coverage. On the one hand, news workers may be wary of being manipulated; they particularly want to avoid wasting time covering a story that will strike them and their audiences as familiar and boring. They want to be convinced that the information they're being given is

Box 5.2 Photojournalism and the Dead

Although it is common to hear complaints declaring that news photographs and video footage are too grim and grisly, images showing dead bodies are actually quite rare. Instead, the news media favor using images of crumpled buildings, mangled automobiles, or other evidence of violent events to accompany reports (in the text of a newspaper story or the words of a reporter narrating video) that describe the deaths. Journalists, their editors, and media critics debate what constitutes appropriate visual evidence and how to construct factual reports about deaths in ways that are responsible, respectful, and not offensive.

In general, U.S. news coverage avoids showing postmortem images of dead Americans; it is more likely to show people of other nationalities who have died. News reports of American deaths may be accompanied by photos of individuals who were wounded, of survivors being rescued, or of the emotional reactions of the living who are grieving or otherwise confronting deaths, or the stories may feature images taken when the now-dead individuals were alive. There are a variety of conventions used by journalists to simultaneously evoke the fact the someone has died while avoiding actually displaying images of dead bodies.

There are exceptions. In 2015, a photo of a drowned three-year-old Syrian boy—a refugee whose body had washed up on a Turkish beach—was widely disseminated and became emblematic of a terrible humanitarian crisis. But some news sources, including the *New York Times*, decided not to run the photo, and others used enlarged pixels to obscure the details of the body. Even widely circulated images are altered so as to report death in an appropriate manner.

Source: Fishman, 2017.

fresh, accurate, and interesting; they have no interest in attending yet another press conference where the same speakers make the same old claims. Still, depending on what rival stories are under consideration, it may be easier to cover a well-packaged story. There are, after all, "slow news days" when there seems to be a shortage of newsworthy stories, just as summer has long been known among journalists as the "dog days" or the "silly season"—months when the federal government and other news-generating institutions are less active, so competition for coverage is less intense and it is easier for offbeat stories to attract news coverage. A well-assembled claim can become very attractive to news workers if there aren't strong alternative stories competing for attention.

Geography also plays a role in this process. News workers are not evenly distributed across the country; rather, they are concentrated in larger cities (J. Best, 1999). In particular, three cities have exceptionally large concentrations of news workers: New York is the nation's largest city, and it remains the traditional base for such important news media as the *New York Times*, the *Wall Street Journal*, and the three major television network news broadcasts; Los Angeles is the second-largest city, and as the center of the entertainment industry, it has its own concentration of news media; and Washington, D.C., is, of course, the center of the federal government and attracts a vast army of news workers devoted to covering the government's actions. Events that occur near such concentrations of news workers are more likely to attract coverage.

Such geographic concentrations of news workers are important because where there are more reporters, there are more opportunities for claimsmakers to get their claims covered. There is nothing to keep people from making claims in a small town in a remote rural location, but it is more difficult to get news workers to travel there to cover the story. It is far easier for a claim to gain widespread attention if the claimsmakers bring their case to a major media center, to a location where many news workers will have convenient access to the story. Thus, even claimsmakers who begin in distant places tend to migrate to larger media centers.

All of this is to say that the news is a social construction, produced by news workers operating under various constraints that force them to make choices—to prefer stories that can be covered in ways that fit their sense of what good news ought to be. Claims-makers who ignore these considerations do so at their own peril.

CHANGING NEWS MEDIA

Note that the news media's forms shift over time. During television's first thirty years, the great majority of Americans relied on broadcast signals; even those living in fairly large urban centers might receive signals from only half a dozen stations. The three major networks (ABC, CBS, and NBC) originally ran fifteen-minute news broadcasts on weekdays, which were expanded to thirty minutes in the early 1960s, then later to six days per week; in addition, local stations offered their own news broadcasts a couple times a day.

Today, most households receive either cable or satellite television signals or other online services offering access to dozens, if not hundreds, of channels. Several channels offer round-the-clock news coverage. This shift has had all manner of consequences: the audience for the networks' evening news broadcasts has grown smaller as viewers turn to all-news channels at more convenient times; the audience for print journalism—both newspapers and weekly newsmagazines—has also declined as more people rely on electronic media for their news; and some cable networks have begun to adopt overt editorial stances (as the emergence of Fox News as an unabashedly conservative network illustrates) (Letukas, 2014).

For claimsmakers, one important consequence of these changes in the media is that competing twenty-four-hour news channels have a colossal appetite for fresh stories (see Box 5.3). In television's early years, when the networks broadcast five fifteen-minute news shows per week, it was far tougher to get an issue covered on national television than it is today. Television's carrying capacity for news has increased vastly. (On the other hand, as their advertising

Box 5.3 The Knockout Game Becomes News

The knockout game gained brief national media attention in late 2013. Crime waves are best understood as increases not in crime, but in media coverage. The knockout game involved youths striking a random, unsuspecting passerby with the goal of knocking him or her out with a single punch.

The knockout game story was not new; incidents of this sort had been reported for at least twenty years, and local media occasionally made much of reports about similar activities, sometimes resulting in fatalities, giving them various names such as knockout, happy slapping, polar bear hunting, and flash mobs. There is, of course, a long history of news coverage of unruly young people threatening the social order, most of which attracts only modest attention.

Late 2013's relatively intense coverage of the knockout game seems to have been the result of several factors. First, this version of the story combined key elements: it depicted the game as played by black youth against largely white victims, and it suggested that video records of the attacks were posted online. In addition, some attacks occurred in New York (a major media market) and involved Jewish victims, thus turning the story into one about anti-Semitism, something that major media tend to treat seriously, even if they might otherwise have been reluctant to emphasize knockout's racial element. And, finally, the story began receiving considerable attention on Fox News, which presented it as evidence of that cable network's willingness to cover stories other, "mainstream" media might ignore. The wave of knockout game coverage lasted a few weeks before the story dropped from view. There never were many reports, and the lack of further developments soon made the story seem less compelling.

Source: J. Best, 2019.

has declined, newspapers and newsmagazines have been shrinking in size, so their carrying capacity has grown smaller.)

As television channels have increased in number, they have increasingly aimed at targeted audiences. Theorists once worried about the "mass media" that would turn society into an undifferentiated mass receiving the same media messages (Turow, 1997). In practice, the media find it more profitable to practice **audience segmentation**, to aim at particular demographic groups; because people fitting a particular demographic profile (defined by age, sex, income, and so on) are more likely to watch programs aimed directly at their interests, the audience for those programs will be relatively homogeneous, and advertisers who believe that their customers will be concentrated in that segment of the larger audience will prefer—and even pay a premium—to place their ads on those programs. Thus, there are cable channels aimed at women, Spanish speakers, people in particular age groups, and so on, just as websites are aimed at people with distinctive interests or concerns. (A similar process changed magazine publishing: general-interest magazines such as *Life* that once sought to appeal to huge mass audiences folded long ago; the titles that remain aim at people with particular interests.)

Audience segmentation affects the media's role in the social problems process. Because different television channels or magazines seek to appeal to demographically distinct audiences, their coverage of claimsmaking will reflect their sense of which issues will strike their viewers or readers as interesting and relevant. Because advertisers often favor more affluent customers who can afford their products, the news media are less likely to target poorer audiences, which means that social problems coverage tends to downplay claims of greater concern to the poor and the powerless. Newspapers' economic reporting, for instance, tends to devote far more attention to the concerns of corporations than to those of workers or the unemployed (Kollmeyer, 2004). The consequence of audience segmentation for social problems claimsmaking is that, although it is becoming easier to gain media coverage for claims, that coverage often is tailored for the particular audience that follows the television programs or magazines that choose to cover the claims (see Box 5.4).

The obvious example of changing media is the emergence of the Internet (Maratea, 2014). The Internet is a boon to claimsmakers in that websites, discussion groups, and blogs can be established quite easily, and at minimal cost. Claims of all sorts can be posted and made accessible to anyone who knows how to use a search engine; in effect, the Internet has an unlimited carrying capacity. Because there is little in the way of filtering, the Internet offers a forum for even the most controversial claims, and sites can be *cloaked* so as to conceal the posters' identity (Daniels, 2009). However, it becomes difficult for news workers to evaluate the various claims that wind up posted in cyberspace. (In contrast, those working in print and broadcast journalism routinely sort through prospective stories and have standards for rejecting some claims.) Moreover, posting a claim does not guarantee that it will gain a large audience; bloggers have learned to encourage traffic to their sites by providing mutual links to other sites. Still, it seems likely that the Internet will have a long-term effect on claimsmaking. In some instances already, websites or bloggers have forced more established news media to cover particular issues by breaking stories about those issues.

Thus, the news media's structure is changing: Some media, such as newspapers and magazines, are losing part of their audience, shrinking their coverage, and becoming less influential. Others, such as television news, are expanding their coverage and shifting forms (by, for example, becoming more openly ideological). At the same time, new Internet-based forms such as blogs, websites, and electronic discussion groups are emerging. Thus far, these changes seem to make it easier to gain some sort of media coverage of claims, although, because the target audiences for different media tend to be smaller and more homogeneous, it is not necessarily easier to bring claims to the attention of a broad, general audience.

Box 5.4 What the News Means When It Mentions Gender Neutrality

News coverage often refers to social problems, but different reports may use the same term to mean very different things. Take "gender neutrality"—what does this term mean? It some cases, it may involve *degendering*, so that gender-neutral writing should avoid gender-specific terms (e.g., a term such as *fireman* assumes that this is a job done by males, and alternatives such as *firefighter* are preferred).

Alternatively, gender neutrality may be used to describe *androgynous* ideas that support the freedom to choose qualities associated with both masculinity and femininity (e.g., a child should be able to choose to play with boys' toys or girls' toys). A third way of thinking about gender neutrality is *gender inclusivity*, which invites a wider array of options.

Newspaper stories usually speak of gender neutrality in terms of equality between men and women, although the proportion of stories that also use the term to address claims from gay males, lesbians, or bisexuals has increased over time, and there have recently been news reports that use the term when referring to transgender people. While the vast majority of coverage uses the term to speak of degendering, a growing minority of stories use gender neutrality to address androgyny or gender inclusivity.

This example shows that the language used to describe social problems is constantly changing. We are used to the vocabulary of social problems changing, so that news media in different eras have favored the labels *colored*, *Negro*, *black*, *African American*, and *person of color*. But even a single term—apparently unchanging—can turn out to have different meanings as a social problem is constructed and reconstructed.

Source: Saguy & Williams, 2019.

PACKAGING SOCIAL PROBLEMS
IN THE NEWS

In short, the nature of news work and the structure of the news industry shape which stories are covered and the form that coverage takes. In particular, news about claimsmaking tends to display some fairly clear patterns.

The Advantages of Issue Ownership

First, remember that particular claimsmakers sometimes assume ownership of their social problems. That is, they become widely recognized as *the* authorities on the problem, as especially knowledgeable. One of the principal benefits of such ownership is that, when news workers find themselves covering a story related to a certain social problem, they routinely turn to the problem's owners for comments. This status is self-reinforcing; once the media have used particular activists or experts as sources for one story, they are more likely to seek out the same sources for future, related stories.

Of course, achieving ownership is easier for some people than for others. The news media frequently turn to government officials as sources for their stories, and other experts have credentials that make their comments seem particularly authoritative. The news media also favor covering people who are already well known; thus, when movie stars or other celebrities enlist in claimsmaking campaigns, they often draw press attention. (Another way to claim ownership and control the media message is for corporations or other interest groups to run advertising that presents their claims [Silver & Boyle, 2010].) In short, the news media prefer to collect their information from those who already have high status.

The flip side of ownership arises when the media define some claimsmakers as lacking the legitimacy to deserve coverage. We might call these *dispossessed* claimsmakers (that is, they are the opposite of owners). News workers may view people who are poorer—who lack power, wealth, or high status—as less newsworthy, and claimsmakers representing these people find it hard to get their claims covered. Similarly, those with views considered too far outside the mainstream—too unpopular or too radical—find it much harder to gain media coverage for their claims. Remember, the media often try to balance their coverage by presenting "both sides" of an issue—typically understood to mean liberals and conservatives, or Democrats and Republicans. Those who adopt other, very different positions—who are too radical or too reactionary, who hold unpopular beliefs or values—usually find it difficult to break into the news media that have the largest audiences. As a result, claimsmakers whose rhetoric strikes news workers as too far outside the mainstream—think of vegans, hate groups, or unfamiliar new religions—may find themselves ignored by the major media. Those newspapers, newsmagazines, and television networks with the largest audiences tend to concentrate their coverage on less controversial claims.

Dispossession also reflects the news media's efforts to appeal to their target audiences. Although we might imagine that newspapers or television news broadcasts want to gain the largest possible audience, audience segmentation leads them, in practice, to be more concerned with reaching some people than others (Hamilton, 2004). Advertisers are more likely to place their ads in media that reach particular types of consumers, and editors may favor stories that will appeal to their target audience. To the degree that social problems claims address troubling conditions thought to be of concern to that target audience, it is easier to get coverage; claims that may be of more concern to people outside the target audience have a tougher time getting covered. Again, advertisers—and therefore the news media—tend to be especially interested in reaching more affluent audience members and less interested in attracting poorer readers and viewers; therefore, claims about problems that face the poor may have a harder time gaining news coverage.

Not all social problems come to have owners, because claims-makers must themselves choose which issues are most important (J. Best, 1999). Consider the media coverage of school shootings that began in 1998; there were several heavily publicized incidents (most notably, of course, at Columbine High School in 1999). Various claimsmakers sought to explain these episodes, but the cacophony of explanations was remarkable. School shootings were blamed on insufficient gun control laws, violent video games, the Goth subculture, bullying, theaters admitting those under seventeen into R-rated movies, the gun culture, and so on.

This is a common pattern: reports of novel sorts of violent crime often lead to all kinds of commentators offering competing explanations and solutions. In the case of school shootings, none of these explanations emerged as dominant; that is, no single set of claimsmakers assumed ownership. Why not? Probably because school shootings were not central to the causes of any of the commentators who spoke out on the issue. Gun control activists, for example, saw school shootings as just one small part of the larger gun problem; they wanted to continue to draw attention to all of the aspects of that problem, rather than focus on school shootings. The emergence of ownership requires claimsmakers who are motivated to continue promoting an issue, as well as news workers who treat those claimsmakers as authoritative.

The Dominance of Landmark Narratives

Second, particular typifying examples—what are called **landmark narratives**—often come to dominate news coverage of a topic (Nichols, 1997). That is, a particular case may become the central focus of media coverage of a social problem—the subject of more newspaper and magazine articles than other, similar cases, or represented in more of the video clips that accompany numerous TV news stories on the topic. Just as the typifying examples chosen by claimsmakers are often quite atypical—more serious, dramatic, or troubling than most cases—so news workers choose landmark or iconic narratives not because they accurately reflect the larger problem, but because they are the stuff of compelling news. These cases serve as landmarks in two senses: they guide news workers' thinking about the nature of the problem and how it should be covered, and they shape the terms by which the news audience understands the problem.

Constructing Packages

Third, landmark cases often belong to larger constructions called **packages** (Beckett, 1996; Gamson, 1992; Gamson & Modigliani, 1989). A package is a familiar, more or less coherent view of a social issue, including its causes and what ought to be done about it. A package has a core idea, or frame; for example, arguments that climate change is substantially caused by humans' activities, that it poses a serious threat, and that steps need to be taken to minimize the problem are at the core of one familiar package. Similarly, arguments that climate change is not necessarily caused by humans' activities and may not constitute a serious threat are the frame for a rival package. Within a package, there is room for disagreement: people may accept the same basic frame yet disagree about specifics, such as the exact processes causing the problem or what needs to be done. Not everyone who shares the basic concern about climate change has to agree on every aspect of the package (see Box 5.5).

In addition, packages offer **condensing symbols**, shorthand elements—landmark narratives, typifying examples, slogans, visual images, and so on—that evoke the package. Editorial cartoons in newspapers depend on the fact that readers will understand such symbols; a figure in a Klansman's robe and hood denotes racism, a smokestack belching smoke symbolizes pollution, and so on. Similarly, a bumper sticker's slogan—"When Guns Are Outlawed, Only Outlaws Will Have Guns"—can encapsulate a larger package

Box 5.5 Ideology Affects Who Focuses on Which Focusing Events

Discussions of media coverage of social problems and social movements sometimes argue for the importance of *focusing events*. These are events that capture media and public attention, that cause people to focus; they often become typifying examples in claimsmakers' rhetoric.

When issues are contentious, that is, when people hold opposing views, it is often the case that there are media representing the respective ideologies of each perspective. Those media aim to reach audiences of people who share their ideologies, and often the media workers share similar views with their audiences.

In these situations, an event may strike those on one side of an issue as particularly revealing, as perfectly illustrating what they view as an important problem, and the media that serve the people who hold those views are likely to pay considerable attention to this incident, to treat it as a focusing event. Meanwhile, media representing the opposing position are likely to downplay—even ignore—the incident or, if they do cover it, to use a very different frame in interpreting it. To illustrate this process, Alimi and Maney (2018) draw upon focusing events in disputes between Israelis and Palestinians that received very different coverage in media directed toward each of the two groups. But it is possible to see similar patterns in politicized cable news coverage, where conservative Fox News and liberal MSNBC often focus coverage on particular events that seem to illustrate the larger ideological points that guide their coverage, so that an example that is receiving intense coverage on one network may be getting little or no attention on the other.

of ideas about guns and gun control. Condensing signals remind people of the larger package, which presents claims that define the nature of the problem, its causes, and a vision of what ought to be done about it.

Note that packages draw on the larger stock of cultural resources. Like primary claimsmakers designing their claims, news workers want to assemble coverage that seems sensible to them, and that also will seem sensible to their audiences. Their stories, then, incorporate the culture that they take for granted—values, symbols, worldviews, and so on. These underlying assumptions are invisible to those who share them, although they may seem quite glaring to others. Consider Americans' shock when they discovered that during the hostage crisis of 1979–80 (perhaps the first time serious tensions with the Muslim world became apparent), Iranian media had described the United States as the "Great Satan." In most cases, however, the way news coverage draws on cultural resources that are taken for granted goes unnoticed.

Media packages help organize people's thinking about social problems. News workers sort through many, if not all, of the available claims, select some as worthy of coverage, and give that coverage shape. The packages they choose may change over time. News workers' choices are influenced by the nature of the claims they encounter, but also by other considerations, including the need to produce news under the pressures of news work, the range of available stories competing for coverage, the desirability of tailoring coverage to the target audience, and so on. Social problems packages are one outcome of this process; they give the news media's secondary claims a sense of coherence: among all the things that might be said about race or crime or anything else, these become the most visible positions. It is relatively easy for the public to become familiar with the packages presented by the news media, and considerably harder for people to learn other ways to think about social problems.

Packages help make the media coverage of social problems seem more coherent; they turn a lot of information into a *story*—a word that is significant, because it reminds us that news is often presented as narratives (Nichols, Nolan, & Colyer, 2008). In the process, some elements are highlighted, while others are pushed to one side. This helps explain why analyses of media content regularly find that the depictions of people or events mirror popular images of problems, and are a less accurate reflection of official measures of a problem's dimensions. Our notions of who is likely to be victimized by a hate crime or what it is like to be poor not only derive from images presented in the media, but also shape the imagery the media choose to present.

It is possible to exaggerate the media's role in packaging social problems; they do not have a completely free hand. News workers have to derive and present packages that they believe will make sense to their audiences. American culture, for example, places great weight on the idea of individual responsibility; this idea runs through much commonsense thinking about life. We tend to hold individuals responsible for their circumstances; people who are poor, overweight, or addicted to drugs bear, most Americans agree, at least part of the blame for their troubles. It is, then, relatively easy to devise frames and packages in which individual responsibility plays a key role, but much harder, for instance, to present explanations that argue that individuals' actions are largely determined by social forces.

IS IT JUST ENTERTAINMENT?

We assume that the news media will cover social problems; after all, it is their job to report on serious matters. But social problems claims are also picked up by a wide range of entertainment media and are portrayed in what is called **popular culture**. Television talk shows, for instance, often present episodes focused on particular sorts of relationship problems, addictions, and the like. But even fictional genres, such as mystery novels, adopt topics from the news: when missing children became a national concern, fictional detective heroes tried to find missing kids; once stalking attracted notice, some of those same heroes confronted stalkers; and so on. And just as the demands of news work shape how the news media cover social problems, entertainment media are constrained by conventions that affect how they construct social problems (Maratea & Monahan, 2016).

Every pop culture genre has its own conventions and constraints—a formula that it follows. Television situation comedies need joke-filled scripts that will last about twenty-three minutes (thirty minutes less time for the commercials and the opening and closing credits), in romance novels the main characters fall in love, and comic book superheroes confront and defeat supervillains. The people who produce popular culture follow these formulas because they are known to work; that is, they appeal to each genre's respective audience. Romance authors, editors, and publishers, for instance, doubt that their readers want stories about people who can't find love.

These formulas shape how entertainment media deal with social problems claims. Although popular culture often reflects current social problems claims, with stories "ripped from the headlines," its depictions of those claims must conform to the different formulas' requirements (Gitlin, 1983). For example, to be dramatic, a confrontation requires an uncertain outcome; this means that the hero must face a villain who seems capable of winning. For instance, detective heroes—whether on television or in mystery novels—must be matched with powerful lawbreakers. As a result, fictional criminals tend to be far more powerful than their real-world counterparts: fictional child molesters belong to organized rings of wealthy abusers, drug dealers are millionaire industrialists, or gang leaders command hundreds of highly trained, well-armed followers. In comparison, real-life offenders, often people with very limited resources, offer poor material for entertaining plots (see Box 5.6).

Sociologists often complain that popular culture's conventions focus on individuals rather than on social forces. Novels, movies, and television series tend to match good people with heroic virtues against bad people with villainous vices, instead of exploring how social problems emerge from social arrangements. Thus, when racism appears in popular culture, it is often treated as a sort of personality defect: villains and other unsympathetic

Box 5.6 Ripping Popular Culture from the Headlines

Munchausen syndrome by proxy (MSBP) involves adults—usually mothers—who induce illness in children under their care. The term began to attract attention among psychiatrists during the 1980s and, after it figured into some high-profile court cases, began being featured in crime fiction plotlines in the 1990s.

MSBP is well-suited for crime stories, whose formulas often depend on surprising plot twists. The idea that a mother would deliberately hurt her child violates our cultural assumptions about the goodness of mothers. MSBP was featured in crime novels by bestselling authors and in highly rated television crime dramas (it was also a topic on major TV talk shows). These popular culture plotlines tended to involve children who died—a fairly standard bit of dramatic exaggeration, in that the vast majority of MSBP cases do not lead to death. Also, whereas there is a debate among experts about whether MSBP offenders are "bad" (that is, whether they are child abusers who should be subject to criminal penalties) or "mad" (that is, whether they are suffering from an unusual sort of mental illness and ought to be treated by psychiatrists), the crime fiction plots tended to adopt a criminal justice frame.

This illustrates the ways that entertainment media reconstruct social problems claims to fit their own needs. Crime fiction is a popular genre for books (bestseller lists often contain multiple crime-related titles), television (with its many detective and cop shows), and movies. There is a considerable appetite for fresh angles for these stories, and claims about a new or little-known kind of crime can often be worked into the genre's plots. This, in turn, helps make the claims—at least in the dramatic form into which they have been translated to meet formulaic demands—more familiar to the public.

Source: Bates, 2018.

characters express racist sentiments, thereby affirming their poor character. Where sociologists view racism as a widespread problem with roots in social arrangements and consequences for the larger society, popular culture often treats racism as a personal characteristic of flawed individuals, because the formula requires a hero triumphing over a particular villain. Similarly, talk shows and other genres that mix elements of news and entertainment feature the same emphasis on flawed individuals. They present problem gambling as a psychological compulsion that affects some individuals, rather than emphasizing how social institutions, such as government and the gaming industry, exacerbate the problem by promoting gambling.

In other words, the formulas used in entertainment media highlight stories about individuals (Berns, 2004). This individual focus is found in both fictional pop culture genres (such as mystery novels) and the quasi news of infotainment (such as talk shows). Entertainment media may address social problems claims, but regardless of whether primary claimsmakers view a problem as widespread and systemic (think of claims about racism, environmental degradation, or climate change), entertainment tends to translate those claims into stories about the struggles and successes of particular people. This focus on telling compelling stories about individuals is central to the formulas for many entertainment genres, and the people who work as creators and producers within the media understand the need to focus on typifying individuals.

This means that entertainment media have an especially difficult time adopting what C. Wright Mills (1959) called a **sociological imagination**—that is, viewing the world in terms of social arrangements and social forces. Mills noted that, in everyday life, people focus on their private troubles, such as not having a job. Adopting a sociological imagination requires seeing those private troubles in terms of larger public issues; for example, whereas an individual may have trouble finding a job, the larger society confronts the more general problem of unemployment. Sociologists, then, tend to downplay the experiences of individuals and focus on larger social patterns. (To use concepts from Chapters 3 and 4, the sociological imagination can be understood as the frame that sociologists as experts use to construct social problems.) No wonder sociologists—as well as many primary claimsmakers—often criticize the entertainment media's portrayal of social problems; by translating claims into dramatic tales about individual suffering and redemption, the media favor constructions that run counter to more sociological interpretations.

WHAT ABOUT SOCIAL MEDIA?

Do social media (think Facebook, Twitter, and the like) belong in a chapter on media coverage of claimsmaking? This chapter has been using the word *media* as shorthand to refer to what were traditionally called *mass media*, that is, methods of communicating messages to very large audiences, such as newspapers, television, film, and the like. So, the question becomes, are social media a form of mass media? Certainly lots of people participate in social media; Facebook reports having more than two billion active users, and there are individuals—mostly entertainers—with tens of millions of Twitter followers. So the total social media audience is huge. However, it is also diffuse. Facebook is individualized; each user maintains a set of friends. The median number of Facebook friends is 200, meaning that half of all users have fewer than that number; the average Twitter user has 700 followers. These are hardly mass audiences.

Social media are most likely to affect the social problems process as a means of drawing attention to claims. In addition to entertainers, those with vast numbers of Twitter followers include political leaders (who may use Twitter as a platform for making brief claims) and major news organizations (such as the *New York Times* and CNN Breaking News) that hope to redirect their Twitter followers to some of their coverage on their websites. We might think of these as institutional participants in social media. But of course, most communication via social media occurs between individuals, and they, too, can draw attention to claims. In a few spectacular cases (usually involving a good deal of deliberate marketing), a claim can "go viral" and reach millions of people (Madianou, 2013). In other cases, claimsmakers may try to package claims in ways that will maximize their chance of spreading widely.

Even if most people have only a few hundred people in their social media network, because each of those contacts has his or her own networks of friends or followers, there are possibilities for transmitting information quickly to large numbers of people through these connections. If you share or signal that you like something to those in your network, and if they choose to pass it along to their contacts, who in turn pass it along . . . it is possible for the information to reach truly large audiences.

The information that spreads in this manner is not necessarily accurate; in fact, there is some evidence that inaccurate information spreads farther and faster on social media than accurate information (see Box 5.7). People tend to have social media contacts who share many of their characteristics, not just age and social class but also opinions. In general, conservatives probably have lots of other conservatives among their contacts, just as liberals have more liberals. This means that information that spreads via social media networks tends to travel among those with similar views, who are more likely to pass it along and less likely to critically examine information they receive from one another. Critics warn that this creates "echo chambers" and "filter bubbles" in which individuals communicate largely with those who share their views. If mass media increasingly target segmented markets, social media replicate that segmentation.

Another aspect of social media is that it can serve as a forum for recruiting members to a cause. In recent years, social movements such as Occupy Wall Street, Black Lives Matter, Me Too (sexual harassment), and Never Again MSD (school shootings) have emerged with a strong social media presence, including popular hashtags on Twitter and Instagram. These campaigns have shown the ability to

Box 5.7 True, False, and Social Media

Many people now report that they use social media as news sources, counting on their contacts to pass along information that they will find relevant. Commentators warn that this is dangerous, that social media do a poor job of filtering out misinformation. Whereas news workers in traditional media (such as newspapers) had procedures that sought to ensure that their reporting was accurate, social media are not principally concerned with the accuracy of what is reported.

Vosoughi, Roy, and Aral (2018) examined more than 125,000 rumor cascades on Twitter. They use the term *rumor* to refer to the process by which a claim spreads (that is, when they call something a rumor, they are not implying that it is either true or false); a *rumor cascade* is an unbroken chain of retweets (if no one retweets something, the cascade has one link; if it is retweeted by one hundred people, it has one hundred links). They then classified rumors as true, false, or mixed (containing both true and false elements). Their findings were clear: true information was less likely to spread than false or mixed rumors. Social media actually treat bad information better.

Why does bad information fare better? Freed from the constraints of having to tell the truth, those spreading false information are able to craft more compelling accounts, making their messages more dramatic. These messages are therefore more likely to be remembered by those who hear them, who will then be more likely to pass these messages along. Messages coming from someone who shares our opinions and beliefs are likely to be something we want to hear, so critical thinking is at a premium on social media.

mobilize large numbers of followers fairly quickly through social media, and they have received considerable attention from traditional news media that tend to treat them in basically the same ways that they've always covered social movements. Although some sociologists suggest that these movements may be transforming activism (Milkman, 2017), others argue that the potential for social-media–driven campaigns may be limited. Traditional social movements often required commitments of time and energy from their members, whereas announcing that you share some sentiment with your contacts on social media demands little effort. Online declarations of support for social movements are sometimes dismissed as "slacktivism." The degree to which movements based on social media can endure is uncertain (Tufekci, 2017).

In other words, there is evidence that social media can become a factor in the social problems process, although social media are such a new phenomenon that relatively little research has been done on this topic. We will return to social media in Chapter 6, when we consider their uses in assessing public reactions to claimsmaking.

Critics worry that media constructions—whether in news or entertainment genres, or in social media—are important because they are influential. That is, it seems obvious that people who follow the news, consume entertainment, or surf the web must be affected by how these media portray social problems. But is this true?

THE MEDIA'S IMPACT

Commentators often assume that the media are extremely powerful and influential, that members of the audience are regularly affected by media messages. To be sure, most of us would deny that we, personally, are easily manipulated by the media. We are made of stronger stuff; we take an attitude of healthy skepticism toward the messages in news, entertainment, and especially advertising. But others, we worry, must be easily bamboozled by the media and may require protection.

The media's powerful influence may seem obvious, but it turns out to be fairly difficult to document. Consider claims that televised violence leads to violent behavior. Television is nearly universal in our society (which makes it difficult to construct experimental studies of its effects, since there is no natural control group lacking exposure to television), yet most people do not engage in violent acts. Similarly, most people who view commercials do not rush out to purchase the advertised products. Although claimsmakers often insist that media exposure has damaging effects, it is hard to observe and measure these consequences. Clearly, the media don't have the same effects on everyone.

If we are to understand the media's role in the social problems process, we need to specify what forms its influence might take. One thing we might mean is that the media can bring a social problem to public attention. As we have already noted, this is a central goal of many claimsmakers. When claimsmakers are calling attention to a new problem—that is, to a troubling condition that has been generally neglected or ignored, one that is unfamiliar to many people—getting media coverage can bring the topic out in the open. Media attention can make the public aware that the issue exists or encourage the public to think that something ought to be done to remedy the problem. This is sometimes called **agenda setting** (McCombs, 2004).

Just as a meeting may be guided by an agenda—a list of topics to be addressed, usually in order of importance—we can envision a society's members as needing to prioritize their concerns. All people have countless topics competing for their attention. Many of these concern the individuals' personal lives—routine errands, conversations with friends and relatives, and on and on. The media—particularly the news media—provide some sense of what's occurring in the larger world, suggesting what else deserves people's notice. Media coverage, then, can make people aware of a social problem—get it on society's agenda. Agenda setting can affect both public awareness (as will be discussed in Chapter 6) and policymakers' sense of what deserves their attention (a topic covered in Chapter 7).

Note that the media do not have a free hand in agenda setting. They are constrained. First, some events—say, a major disaster—may demand media coverage. Second, the media can be influenced to cover particular topics—by claimsmakers who convince the media that a problem deserves their attention, by officials who herald a particular new policy, even by other media outlets whose coverage suggests that a topic must be worthy of coverage. Third, as we have already noted, people working in the news and entertainment media are limited by the resources available to them, by their sense of the sort of coverage they ought to produce, and so on.

Nevertheless, in one sense the media make choices that are consequential. We have already noted that the media translate and transform social problems claims. In the case of contentious issues, topics (such as abortion) about which claimsmakers may advance contradictory claims, media coverage can structure the debate by assembling a small set of claimsmaking packages. Although the media cannot force people to adopt particular ideas, they make some constructions readily available, so it is easier to come to understand social problems in particular ways. In some cases, media coverage may give individuals a new perspective on their personal lives, to help them redefine their personal troubles as part of larger social problems.

The public and policymakers pay attention to what the media cover for a couple of reasons. First, they use the media as a source of information: media coverage may be how the public and policymakers first learn about particular social problems. Second, policymakers may begin to hear from members of the general public who, having learned about the problem via the media, may call for action. Although the media are by no means all-powerful, they do help shape the social problems process.

THE MEDIA IN THE SOCIAL PROBLEMS PROCESS

Part of the reason why commentators exaggerate the media's power is that the media play an especially visible role in the social problems process. Outsider claimsmakers view media coverage as almost essential for making the public and policymakers aware of their claims. More powerful people use press conferences and other public relations techniques to attract and shape coverage for their activities. Meanwhile, much lobbying and other insider claimsmaking is hidden from the public (unless an enterprising reporter draws attention to it). Media coverage remains the easiest way for most people to learn about social problems.

This chapter has argued that the media must also be understood in terms of their social arrangements. Figure 5.1 illustrates some of the key features of these arrangements. First, note the distinction between news and entertainment media; the figure portrays news coverage as occurring first and often shaping the entertainment media's coverage of social problems. Second, the figure draws attention to the role of cultural resources. News workers' sense of what is newsworthy, as well as how news stories should be assembled and reported, depends in part on their understanding of how the larger culture will make sense of claims; a parallel set of considerations will shape what will be considered entertaining. Finally, note that both news and entertainment media have their own organizational constraints—operating budgets, production schedules, established conventions and formulas, and so on—that also influence what the media produce.

In addition, the media constantly receive feedback. Most obviously they worry about the reactions of their audiences: Are people interested in the news or entertainment they produce? If not, the media are likely to modify what they're doing. The media may also hear from claimsmakers who offer congratulations or complaints about coverage, from segments of the general public who are not in their target audiences (and who often have their own criticisms), and from policymakers who may endorse or challenge what the media have done. The people who work in the media, then, should not be seen as all-powerful, as able to dictate what others think. Rather, they are connected to—and influenced by—the other actors in the social problems process. And just as the media transform

Figure 5.1 THE MEDIA'S ROLE IN THE SOCIAL PROBLEMS PROCESS

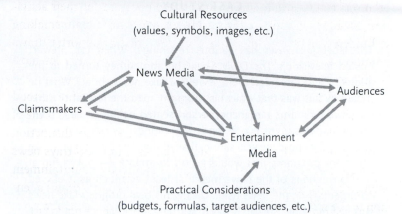

and translate primary claims into the secondary claims presented in news coverage or entertainment, the media's audience—the public—reworks those messages for its own purposes.

MAKING CONNECTIONS

- *The media are eager for new claims and fresh ways of framing problems. Chapters 3 and 4 explain how activists and experts frame their claims to attract the most media attention.*

- *Claimsmakers use the news media to encourage recognition of a problem. In Chapter 7 you will learn about the essential role that the media play in introducing a social problem into the policymaking process.*

- *In the next chapter you will learn how the public responds to media coverage of social problems.*

CASE STUDY
FAKE NEWS

The label *fake news* has various meanings. When Jon Stewart hosted television's *The Daily Show*, he sometimes turned to the audience and reminded them, "We're a fake news show." What he meant by this was that while his program aped the format of other TV news programs (an anchorperson seated behind a desk, often talking about current events and monitoring reports from roving reporters), its purpose was satiric. If anything, *The Daily Show*—like the many programs that would go on to imitate it—poked fun at the conventions of the news media at least as much as it offered commentary on the news itself. Calling his own program fake news was self-mocking, Stewart's way of warning the audience not to take the program's content too seriously.

The assumption that the news should present an objective view of what has been happening is a relatively recent development (Schudson, 1981). Early newspapers usually presented a slanted point of view, praising a particular political party and denouncing its opponents. It was only in the late nineteenth century that people began arguing that journalism should be professionalized, and that objectivity was a key value. This ethic spread to broadcasting; the original three major television networks were all constrained by the federal government's fairness doctrine, which required that coverage of the major parties should be evenhanded. However, the fairness doctrine was eliminated in 1987 and the media landscape changed with the emergence of cable news channels, the Internet, and later social media.

In the immediate aftermath of the 2016 election, there were reports of a new sort of fake news (Ball, 2017). A group of computer-savvy young men from an economically depressed village in Macedonia had been generating income by posting what purported to be news stories on social media (Silverman & Alexander, 2016). These stories were fictional (e.g., one reported that the Pope had endorsed Donald Trump's candidacy), and the press labeled them fake news. The reaction to this reporting was surprise that many people were now receiving their news, not from established journalistic sources such as newspapers or news broadcasts, but from what reached them via social media. (This reaction paralleled earlier shock that many young people reported using *The Daily Show* as a news source.)

By December 2016, the term *fake news* was being tossed around in political debates; one way to counter a report one disagreed with was to disparage it as fake news. Donald Trump used the term on several occasions before he was inaugurated, often to dismiss reports in the traditional media. However, when the new president declared that the crowd at his 2017 inauguration was the largest ever, critics compared photographs from the 2017 ceremony to those showing much larger crowds at other, recent inaugurations. The new press secretary explained that the president's claim was based on "alternative facts"—which critics argued was itself a form of fake news. How can we make sociological sense of the debate over fake news? Obviously, news—like all other knowledge—is socially constructed. But the term *social construction* does not mean false, bogus, dubious, fictional, or fake. Everything we know is a product of human efforts to understand the world—our knowledge comes from explorers, scientists, philosophers, journalists, and anyone else who adds to the stock of what humanity knows. Some of what they add comes to be considered true, other additions (think of works of fiction or lies) are known to be false by their creators. Some additions prove useful and become well accepted, while most fall out of favor and are largely forgotten. We encounter all kinds of social constructions every day of our lives, and we have to sort through them, assessing their truth and deciding what is useful and what is not.

People who produce knowledge also make decisions. Honest researchers must carefully gather their data to make sure that it is as accurate as possible; they must report their findings honestly; and they should clearly identify the limitations of their research. Obviously, reporting the news involves similar sorts of decisions. Reporters and editors must ask themselves which stories are the most newsworthy and what sorts of evidence are needed to document a report so that they are convinced it is accurate and so that their readers or viewers will also find it convincing.

In other words, it is necessary for those who work in the media *and* those who consume the media's messages to think critically about news (and all other media products, including entertainment). Thinking critically does not mean simply being negative. Declaring that a news report is "fake news" because one doesn't like what it says is not critical thinking. Rather, one needs to evaluate the report to assess its strengths and weaknesses. Do the sources seem appropriate—and was there an effort to identify and draw upon all relevant sources? Is the report consistent with other evidence? And so on.

Conspiratorial thinking has long been a theme in American culture (Walker, 2014). Our fiction is filled with tales of dark plots by villainous conspirators. But warnings of conspiracies often describe things that have happened or are happening in the real world. Rumors regularly tell of hidden schemes. And all manner of dramatic historical events—think the assassinations of Presidents Lincoln and Kennedy, or the Pearl Harbor and 9/11 attacks—have inspired small industries of conspiracy-mongering that can endure for many decades.

The proliferation of television channels and the rise of the Internet have altered how news is produced and consumed. Print journalism (newspapers and magazines) has lost readers, advertising revenue, and staff, and this makes it harder for journalists and editors to cover the news, which in turn costs them more readers. At the same time, it has become easy to make all sorts of information available via websites, blogs, and social media, and to target people who find particular messages appealing. People might once have found it difficult to locate others who shared unusual views (such as those who insist that the earth is flat or who favor fringe ideologies), but they now have little difficulty locating like-minded people and exchanging information with them. It is often unclear whether a report is the product of journalists attempting to uncover a story, check evidence, and then report what the evidence shows, or a claim that may be founded on little or no evidence.

All this means that it is easy both to produce inaccurate reports and to dismiss any report by labeling it fake news, even as there are also many sources that do fact-checking to evaluate claims. The twenty-first century is developing into an era where people who want to engage in critical thinking can locate the tools that will help them evaluate the news they encounter, but also one where those who can't be bothered to assess what they hear—or who deliberately seek out reports that will affirm their beliefs—also can find what they want. The result is a world where fringe beliefs can find plenty of social support, where it is ever harder to establish political consensus. In other words, fake news—in the form of rumor and conspiracy theories—has always been out there, but it is becoming ever more available. Individuals who wish to avoid fake news need to take responsibility for critically sifting through the many reports they will encounter in order to make sense of their world.

QUESTIONS

1. Find a recent instance where there is a disagreement among people who question the accuracy of each other's information. What are some ways to assess this disagreement?

2. How do fact-checking services such as Snopes.com or Politifact .com evaluate the accuracy of claims? What are the strengths and limitations of these services?

3. Are disputes over fake news likely to continue? Why or why not?

6

Public Reaction

Discussions of the social problems process usually assume that, at some point, claims reach and influence members of the general public. Sometimes there's a direct connection between the primary claimsmakers and the public, as when people hear a claimsmaker give a speech, or find themselves listening to a claim during a conversation. More often, of course, claims reach the public via the media; people encounter secondary claims while watching television, reading newspapers, magazines, or books, or searching the Internet. All this simply reflects the media's ability to reach very large audiences; claimsmakers who receive media coverage can be exposed to a far larger segment of the general public than they can hope to reach through face-to-face contacts.

As part of the audience for claims, members of the public are not completely passive; they can react in various ways. They may be energized and moved to action by some claims, deciding to contribute to a social movement organization, participate in a demonstration, write their legislators, or relay the claims to others they know. Some may treat a claim as interesting information—something to talk over with friends and acquaintances. Others may be indifferent, apathetic; they may find the claim boring and ignore it. Still others may react negatively, disagreeing with the claim and opposing its conclusions. Probably all claims elicit all of these possible reactions in different people.

Because the public is both large and diverse, because people can respond to claims in different ways, and because many of those responses are relatively private (in that people may keep their opinions to themselves or share them only with others they know well), interpreting the public's role in the social problems process poses special problems. Nonetheless, the other actors in the process want to understand the public's reactions. Claimsmakers use the feedback they receive from the public to modify their claims, in hopes of making them more persuasive; the media also attend to feedback from the public, in order to better devise news and entertainment that will capture the audience's attention; and policymakers may respond to public pressure to do something about a particular troubling condition. Thus, many people want to learn what the public is thinking, in spite of the difficulties in doing so.

This chapter will focus on the methods that claimsmakers, the media, and others involved in the social problems process—as well as sociologists—use to assess public reactions. It will consider several of these, beginning with the most familiar method—public opinion polls or surveys.

MEASURING PUBLIC OPINION

Public opinion polls have become a taken-for-granted part of our political landscape. We are used to hearing news reports that polls show one candidate favored to win the upcoming election, that the president's approval rating has risen higher or fallen lower, that the public is more or less concerned about particular issues, and so on. Before considering how public opinion figures into the social problems process, we need to consider how the very methods of polling can affect a survey's results.

The Impact of Polling Methods

Efforts to measure public opinion through polling came of age during the early twentieth century. Usually this research involves conducting a **sample survey**. Because it would be prohibitively expensive to contact, say, all voters or all citizens (what statisticians call the **population**), the poll approaches a **sample** of people within that population and asks them questions. The responses to the poll can be tallied to reveal, for instance, the proportion of sampled voters favoring Candidate A in an election; in turn, the sample's results provide a basis for generalizing about the population by projecting the likely outcome of the election.

Many people are suspicious of sample surveys because the samples seem too small to promise accurate results. National surveys often use samples of 500 to 1,500 respondents. How, critics ask, can such a small number of people accurately represent the huge U.S. population (over 300 million)? However reasonable this question might seem, it emphasizes the wrong issue. A relatively small sample—say, 1,000 people—can produce fairly accurate results, as long as it is a **representative sample**—that is, as long as the sample is not selected in ways that make it more likely that some sorts of people will be chosen than others. (Statisticians calculate that, for a population of 300 million, a poll with a representative sample of 1,000 will produce results accurate within about 3 percent, 95 percent of the time. Thus, if a survey shows that 54 percent of voters favor Candidate A, there is a 95 percent probability that between 51 and 57 percent of the population favors A's candidacy. Moreover, larger samples aren't that much more accurate: a 10,000-person sample—for which collecting the data would cost about ten times as much—will produce only slightly more accurate results: accuracy within 1 percent, 95 percent of the time [de Vaus, 1986].)

However, statistical theory's assumptions about representative samples often have to give way to the realities of survey research. It is both difficult and expensive to design perfectly representative samples, and unrepresentative samples can lead to inaccurate results. Consider some sampling problems that affect today's pollsters: an increasing number of households screen calls using answering machines or caller ID, and some of those people may choose not to answer the pollsters' calls; in addition, a growing proportion of the population has only cell phones (which the law requires must be hand dialed, making them more expensive to contact) (Link, Battaglia, Frankel, Osborn, & Mokdad, 2007). Can we assume that people who refuse to answer—or who can't be reached via landlines—have the same distribution of opinions as those who pick up the phone, or should we suspect that those who don't respond or can't be reached may have somewhat different opinions from those of the respondents? Refusal to take the pollsters' calls or having only a cell phone—like any other factor that may make the sample less representative—can damage the accuracy of a survey's results.

In addition, survey results are sensitive to many other influences. Pollsters know that the wording of a question can affect the results. Polling is expensive, and often the costs are covered by claimsmakers who hope to use the results to support their campaigns. As a result, many polls ask questions worded in ways that encourage people to produce the answers that the poll's sponsors favor. Of course, when the claimsmakers or sponsors release the poll results to the press, they tend to ignore the questions' wording, while emphasizing the favorable results.

Another important problem is that surveys usually try to distill people's thoughts about complex, multifaceted issues into one or two questions. The result is inevitably crude and oversimplified. For example, many discussions of abortion attitudes imply that people can be classified as either pro-life (opposed to abortion under any circumstances) or pro-choice (in favor of women having complete freedom to choose whether to have abortions) (J. Best, 2013). But the largest proportion of Americans' attitudes fall somewhere between those extremes: these people favor permitting abortion for "good" reasons (such as pregnancies resulting from rape or incest, or cases in which continuing the pregnancy might endanger the woman's life), but they have reservations about allowing abortions for less compelling reasons. A simple question asking whether the respondent favors or opposes abortion cannot hope to accurately measure these complicated attitudes (see Box 6.1).

We should also remember that answering a survey is a social situation. That is, respondents who are interacting with a pollster usually want to make a good impression, to be a good respondent. This means that some respondents may try to say whatever they believe the pollster might think they ought to say. For example, if a pollster asks whether X should be considered a serious problem, the very fact that the question is being asked suggests that at least some people consider X a problem, and some respondents may feel that they ought to agree that, yes, X should be considered a serious problem. But responding in that way to a question does not mean that the respondent actually spends much time thinking about—let alone worrying about—X.

In short, a variety of methodological issues—who is polled, how the questions are phrased, and so on—can affect the results of survey research. Every survey's results have been shaped by the choices that the people conducting the surveys have made, and those people may have designed their poll to produce particular results. This doesn't mean that all survey results are meaningless, but they need to be viewed with some caution. After all, media coverage of poll results is fairly common, and this measure of public opinion often becomes a factor in the social problems process.

Constructing the Meaning of Public Opinion

Typically, discussions of the role of public opinion in the social problems process have two distinct themes. First, analysts argue that public opinion is a product of claimsmaking and media coverage of social problems, that effective claims can make the public

Box 6.1 CHALLENGES CONFRONTING SURVEY RESEARCH

Public opinion surveys have always been viewed with suspicion by some people, and contemporary developments have created new challenges. Response rates—that is, the proportion of people who once contacted agree to complete a survey—have fallen. Billions of robocalls from telemarketers have led many people to block, or at least refuse to answer, calls from unknown numbers. Moreover, people who do begin to answer what purports to be a survey often discover that the "survey" actually is a guise for a sales pitch or a fundraising effort. It has become increasingly difficult to reach and ask questions to a representative sample of the population.

There is also considerable cynicism about the surveys themselves—concerns that the results cannot be trusted. Politicians routinely celebrate results that seem to support their positions, while dismissing numbers that seem less supportive. Even government survey statistics—which are collected by highly professional staffs using transparent methods (think of the census, or economic statistics regarding unemployment or the cost of living)—are suspected of being unreliable by substantial proportions of the population. Doubts about the motives and the methods of survey researchers become the subjects of contentious political debates (as in the case of the disputes over whether the 2020 census should ask respondents a question about their citizenship).

Survey researchers are aware that their work has always provoked skepticism, and they continually strive to devise new methods to deal with the growing challenges of getting accurate data from an increasingly unresponsive population. But doubts about their value surface whenever survey data are introduced into discussions about any social problem.

Source: T. P. Johnson, 2018.

aware of and concerned about some social problem. Second, policymakers are assumed to be responsive to public opinion; that is, it is assumed that high public concern about a social problem will in turn lead policymakers to try to do something about that problem.

Factors Affecting Public Opinion. Some evidence suggests that public opinion can be affected by media coverage. However, it is important not to exaggerate the media's influence; people are not passive recipients of media messages who automatically must accept whatever the media tells them. The media are probably more effective at agenda setting than at communicating particular messages. That is, they may be better able to influence what topics people are thinking about than what exactly people think about those topics.

For example, one study (Beckett, 1994) found that the proportion of people who expressed concern about crime in polls did not correlate well with official crime rates—concern for crime might rise even when the crime rate was falling; similarly, public concern about illegal drug use did not correlate closely with official measures of drug use. In other words, the shifts in public concern about crime and drug use revealed in surveys do not seem to have been responses to changes in the actual levels of those conditions. However, public opinion did correspond fairly closely with media coverage of crime and drug use, and particularly with officials' announcements about anticrime and antidrug policies (which were, of course, covered by the press). The media coverage tended to rise first, with public opinion following somewhat later; that is, opinions lagged behind media coverage. Thus, increased media coverage of crime and drug problems led to higher proportions of poll respondents expressing concerns about crime and drugs.

This example suggests that the public can be influenced to at least pay attention to heavily publicized social problems. And naturally the perception that this is true affects the behavior of claimsmakers, who work hard to promote their constructions of social problems by gaining media coverage, in hopes of arousing public concern. Of course, concern is not spread evenly throughout the population. On most issues, opinions vary with the respondents' characteristics: differences in race, social class (as measured by education or income), age, gender, and region often influence people's opinions. The media cannot affect everyone equally, but they can sometimes arouse fairly broad public concern about a particular troubling condition.

The Impact of Public Opinion. Survey results contribute to the social problems process in two major ways. First, polls offer feedback at earlier stages in the process. Claimsmakers use polls to determine whether their claims are effective or ineffective, hoping that their efforts—particularly if they have received a reasonable amount of media coverage—will cause public opinion to shift in the direction the claimsmakers favor. For instance, imagine that gun control advocates mount a campaign to promote a new law restricting guns. They may organize demonstrations, testify before legislators, appear on talk shows, and so on, in an effort to make the public aware of the issue. If polls taken following this effort suggest that a growing portion of the public is aware of and favors the proposed gun control law, the claimsmakers will view this result as evidence that their campaign has been effective. But, of course, if the poll results do not reveal a substantial shift in public opinion in support of their position, the advocates may look for ways to alter their claims, in hopes of making them more effective. Polls, then, provide feedback to claimsmakers.

The second major way polls affect the social problems process is that policymakers often follow poll results. In particular, elected officials may view evidence of widespread concern about a troubling condition as an indication that they need to take action, to develop a new policy to address the problem. This is not an automatic response. Poll results are one of the considerations that may influence officials, but they are by no means the only one. Still, it is possible to track poll results as "the voice of the people," and to justify policymaking as a response to what the public wants. Polls become one element in the construction of policymaking—a topic that will receive further attention in Chapter 7.

FOCUS GROUPS AND OTHER INTERVIEWS

Survey questionnaires are limited by the questions asked. Sampling does allow analysts to measure the relative distribution of opinions in large populations, but each respondent's views tend to be reduced to relatively simplistic responses to particular questions; moreover, as we have noted, those responses can be affected by precisely how the questions are worded, the order in which questions are asked, and so on.

Sometimes researchers try to circumvent these problems by organizing **focus groups**. Focus groups are sets of people to which a moderator poses questions that stimulate discussion on a particular topic. Group members may be chosen so that the group has a particular racial composition or level of education. Sometimes the members are acquaintances, who presumably will feel comfortable talking with one another about controversial social issues. Focus groups have several advantages over surveys. Individuals have more freedom to express their ideas about the topic, to qualify their remarks and explain what they really mean. In addition, the group is a social setting in which people can respond to one another's comments.

Focus groups often reveal that the public's views about social problems are more complex than the simple pro/con disagreements revealed by many surveys. Analysts tend to imagine that the public's views are internally consistent, and that they reflect the sorts of ideological consistency that claimsmakers often bring to the social problems process. Compared with these expectations, the views of members of the public often seem confused, ambivalent, or uncertain. These apparent inconsistencies can become evident in focus group discussions. Focus groups also allow individuals to express emotional reactions to issues (see Box 6.2).

Box 6.2 Focus Groups on PrEP as Problem or Solution

In 2012, the Food and Drug Administration approved Truvada, a drug that if taken daily can reduce the risk of HIV infection (a strategy called pre-exposure prophylaxis, or PrEP). Although many public health officials believed that it might help reduce the spread of HIV infections, the drug faced resistance within the gay community. Focus groups of gay and bisexual men revealed the broad range of attitudes toward PrEP.

On the one hand, many participants defined the drug as a social problem because they worried that it would encourage risky sex. That is, individuals taking Truvada might believe that the drug would protect them and thereby allow them to engage in riskier sexual behavior, such as not using condoms (long the centerpiece of safe-sex campaigns). These arguments parallel other concerns about medical developments that could reduce sexual dangers, such as birth control pills, HPV vaccines, and Plan B. In each case, critics opposed these medical developments because they might encourage sexual promiscuity and thereby threaten social morality. While focus group participants conceded that some users might have good reasons for using Truvada (such as an HIV-negative man with a long-term partner who was HIV-positive), they worried that many prospective users would be undeserving and irresponsible.

Other participants viewed PrEP as part of the solution to the HIV problem. They argued that the opposition to Truvada was morally judgmental and that such attitudes only got in the way of achieving the more important goal of eradicating HIV. In this view, risky sexual practices existed before PrEP and would continue to occur, regardless of whether the drug was available. Such focus groups allow people to disagree in respectful, constructive conversations and can help researchers understand the range of public reactions.

Source: Pawson & Grov, 2018.

Studies of focus groups reveal that individuals tend to draw on at least three sorts of information when discussing social problems (Gamson, 1992; Sasson, 1995b): First, they use popular wisdom—"commonsense" understandings about how the world works as expressed in aphorisms, stereotypes, and so on. Second, people refer to personal experiences—things that have happened to them or others they know. Third, they may adopt various information and ideas derived from media messages about the larger world, including not just news reports, but also the various forms of infotainment and popular culture that depict the workings of the world beyond our personal experience. Popular wisdom, personal experiences, and media discourse are resources that can be used to construct public definitions of social problems, and focus group conversations reveal how people weave these elements together. In general, groups that are able to integrate all three sorts of information—to combine their personal beliefs and experiences with information about the larger world—are more confident that their constructions are correct and more willing to defend their views.

Given the importance of experiential knowledge in focus groups, it should be no surprise that people with different backgrounds construct issues differently. Such background characteristics as race, social class, gender, age, and education affect how people think about social problems. For example, among groups given the task of discussing crime, references to racism in the criminal justice system were relatively common in all-black groups, but relatively rare in all-white groups (Sasson, 1995b). In some cases, African American group members presented conspiracy theories, arguing that powerful whites supplied guns and drugs to poor black neighborhoods as a means of keeping them disadvantaged (Sasson, 1995a). Such findings illustrate a strength of focus groups; survey researchers might not even think to ask questions that could reveal whether their respondents hold such views.

The results of focus groups can, in turn, influence claimsmakers. Like political consultants trying to understand voters' views during election campaigns and firms seeking to market their products to consumers, activists sometimes use focus groups to better understand what the public is thinking. Identification of the frames that emerge within focus groups can be used to revise claims so that they are tailored to influence the public more effectively. For example, when opponents of abortion successfully campaigned against public funding for abortions during the 1980s, abortion rights advocates organized focus groups that revealed that people who opposed such funding also objected to government intrusion in their lives (Saletan, 2003). Abortion rights advocates used this knowledge to craft a new argument—that the right to have an abortion was tied to a broader right to privacy; in this view, restrictions against abortion became another form of government interference in people's private lives. This new pro-choice campaign proved relatively effective.

As a source of information about public reactions, focus groups obviously have limitations. They are relatively costly in terms of time and money, and it is impossible to know how representative particular groups may be. Much depends on the moderator's skill in directing the conversation and making sure that the various participants have their say. Still, focus groups can be an important way of discovering what ordinary people think about social problems.

USING SOCIAL MEDIA AND ONLINE SEARCHES TO DETERMINE PUBLIC OPINION

Beyond surveys and focus groups, there are other ways to examine claims made by ordinary people about troubling conditions. These may involve access to some media platform intended to let members of the public express their views. The classic example—more common in the past than now—is writing a letter to the editor for publication in a newspaper (Doering, 2014). This is hardly a random sample: people who wrote these letters had to care enough about an issue to put pen to paper; and they had to be literate enough and have enough time and money to spend on the project. Only a tiny fraction of the population ever expressed themselves in this way. It also is important to appreciate that the newspaper editors must have been selective in choosing which letters to publish; they might have had all sorts of reasons—everything from objecting to a letter writer's views, to not having enough space to print a letter—for deciding not to publish all the letters they received. Still, such letters can tell us something about how members of the larger population thought about the issues of the day.

While people still write letters to the editor (probably most often via e-mail), the Internet now offers all sorts of new platforms that allow members of the public to express their views. Increasingly, physical newspapers are being replaced by news websites, and readers of a news story on a site may be invited to post their reactions. A story may elicit hundreds of these comments; it is not uncommon for the original story to fade into the background as people begin to add comments giving their reactions to some earlier comment. News organizations track these comments, and post lists of the stories eliciting the most reactions. Presumably this alerts readers to stories other people have found interesting, and also provides valuable feedback that the site can use to decide what to cover and how to cover it in the future. Similarly, websites keep track of how often particular items are forwarded as another way of identifying what the public finds interesting.

Such discussion threads appear across the Internet—appended to blog posts as well as news stories, and on various website forums organized to attract people who share some particular interest or point of view. Many of these sites focus on hobbies, celebrities, and other matters of only fleeting interest to hard-core enthusiasts, but others have been established to address social issues, often for people who subscribe to a particular ideology, and can be seen as part of the social problems process. Analysts are struggling to devise methods of assessing public reactions using these various electronic forums (see Box 6.3).

Box 6.3 Users Challenge Media Depictions of Bath Salts

"Bath salts" were a group of synthetic stimulants that briefly, prior to being defined as an illegal drug, were sold legally, mostly in convenience stores, under labels such as "plant food" or "bath salts." Although they were never an especially widely used recreational drug, they became the focus of sensational news media coverage that blamed them for terrible crimes and even insisted that bath salts users behaved like zombies.

The Internet offers websites where drug users can post accounts of their experiences, with an eye toward creating an online forum for helping people understand drug effects. The people who administer these sites review and edit submissions and decide which ones should be posted, so that these posts undergo an editorial process that parallels the sorts of decisions that shape news stories. The accounts that wind up being published tend to adopt a medical/public health frame that might give prospective drug users tips about what to expect and how to manage problems that might arise during drug use.

These websites offer another way of assessing how those directly involved in using drugs construct their experiences. As we might expect, bath salts users' accounts do not report zombification, and they often mock media exaggerations of the harmful effects of drugs. Such websites offer a perspective that is absent from sensational press coverage aimed at constructing drug use as an alarming social problem; instead, they provide yet another way of assessing the reactions of those with firsthand experience of what claimsmakers view as a troubling condition.

Source: Kavanaugh & Biggers, 2019.

Thus, the emergence of social media has led some commentators to try to discern public attitudes from tweets, Facebook posts, and the like. This turns out to pose difficult problems; it is hard to know how to measure social media content, or to know how accurate those measurements may be. The simplest method is to selectively quote individual comments to suggest a sense of the sort of things people are thinking, as when a television news program takes a moment to present comments from members of their audience. But it is impossible to know whether the few comments shown accurately reflect ideas in the larger public. A second method is to measure the frequency with which some term is used—whether it is "trending." But such counts may ignore a good deal of diversity among the various comments; the fact that a lot of people are using some word hardly tells us what they are thinking.

A more promising alternative is **semantic polling** (Anstead & O'Loughlin, 2015). This involves software that tries to interpret the meanings in large numbers of social media messages, to categorize them as reflecting particular sentiments. The difficulties here are obvious: the messages are being read and classified not by people but by computers that may have imperfect methods of interpreting what a particular set of words means. People promoting semantic polling argue that by having humans review a portion of the messages being classified and recoding those that the software seems to have misinterpreted, the computers can be taught to make more accurate assessments. And, even if they aren't completely accurate, semantic polls have the advantage of speed—results are available in close to real time.

Traditional survey researchers are skeptical of analyses of social media content. The people participating in these forums cannot be assumed to statistically reflect the general population, nor do we yet know very much about how well social media posts reflect—or affect—public attitudes. Like other methods used to understand public reactions, analyses of social media content produce imperfect results that need to be examined with considerable care.

In addition to the statements people post online for others to read, it is possible to track their other online activities. Individuals' searches for information reveal their concerns—what Mills in his discussion of the sociological imagination called private troubles.

A woman, for instance, may ask her search engine whether it is safe to drink wine while pregnant, or ask for signs that indicate her husband might be gay. But social scientists who collate the data may discover that lots of women are asking the same questions, and that there are patterns in these searches. For instance, women are more likely to wonder whether their husband is gay when they live in states where polls find that tolerance for same-sex marriage is lowest, a pattern that suggests that where intolerance is great, closeted gay males may choose to marry women (Stephens-Davidowitz, 2017). Similarly, people may perform a search using racial slurs, and areas where such searches are more common are less likely to, for example, vote for black candidates (see Box 6.4). While analyzing search terms is a relatively new technique, it may offer people in the social problems process, such as claimsmakers and policymakers, another way of assessing public reactions.

LEGENDS, JOKES, AND OTHER FOLKLORE

Public opinion polls, focus groups, and even social media posts involve somewhat artificial, formalized situations in which people know that their opinions are presented for analysis, and this knowledge may affect what the people who participate are willing to say. But talk about social problems also is the stuff of everyday conversations. It would be nice to know how members of the public construct social problems when they are not self-conscious about being observed. Studying folklore offers one way of examining such everyday constructions.

The term *folklore* refers to information that is disseminated informally, among the *folk*—that is, among ordinary people. Traditionally folklore was transmitted orally, rather than through writing: people told one another folktales, or taught each other folk songs, folk dancing, or folk crafts. You may have a mental image of a folklorist seeking out old folks living in remote corners of society, hoping

Box 6.4 Using Online Search Patterns to
Spot Hidden Attitudes

Using racial slurs is widely seen as inappropriate and unacceptable, so much so that even discussions of the topic use euphemisms such as "the N-word." However, just because people are reluctant to use some words in front of others doesn't mean that they won't enter them into a search engine.

Increasingly, it has become possible to track what people search for online. Researchers can identify patterns in these searches; for example, mapping the locations of the computers from which people entered search terms that included racist language reveals geographic patterns. Areas that had higher rates of racist-language searches showed lower rates of voter support for Barack Obama in the 2012 election, even after controlling for age, education levels, church attendance, or gun ownership (that is, the sorts of variables that social scientists assume might affect voting patterns). People's reluctance to voice racist sentiments in public need not restrain them in their private interactions with their search engine.

Similarly, it is possible to track search patterns minute-by-minute. In the aftermath of a 2015 domestic terrorism incident perpetrated by two Muslims, President Obama sought to reassure the nation with a prime-time address that most commentators praised. However, researchers found that anti-Muslim search terms (such as "kill Muslims") actually increased during and following the speech, suggesting that the president's claimsmaking rhetoric failed to persuade some listeners.

Social scientists are only beginning to explore the value of search terms as a way of understanding public reactions to social problems. Such research will undoubtedly increase in the future.

Source: Stephens-Davidowitz, 2017.

to capture traditional folk wisdom that is in danger of disappearing as the last generation to have this knowledge fades. This common image equates folklore with an elderly person perched in a rocking chair on a rickety, unpainted front porch, talking about the old days.

This is a mistaken image because it is far too narrow. *All* people have folklore—young people, people living in cities, everyone. Contemporary folklore spreads in new ways—in photocopied bits of humor posted in offices (Dundes & Pagter, 2000) or through faxes ("faxlore"), e-mail messages, and posts on social media—as well as by the traditional means of word of mouth. And some of the time, this folklore expresses ordinary people's reactions to social problems claims. Let's consider two common folklore genres: contemporary legends and joke cycles.

Contemporary Legends

Sometimes called *urban legends*, **contemporary legends** are stories that people tell one another (Ellis, 2001; Fine, 1992). In general, contemporary legends lack supernatural elements; they are far more likely to feature criminals than, say, ghosts. Typically the teller claims—and the listener believes—that the story is true, that the events in the story really happened. Often the teller offers evidence of the story's truth, such as identifying the place where it happened (perhaps a nearby shopping mall), or explaining the teller's connection to a person who witnessed or experienced the events: "This really happened to my roommate's cousin's neighbor." Folklorists refer to this sort of attribution as a *FOAF* (for Friend Of A Friend). Efforts to trace the story back to the FOAF inevitably fail; the roommate's cousin's neighbor may agree that the story is true but explain that "it actually happened to my mother-in-law's brother's friend."

As legends spread, the details tend to shift. A story about a horrible crime at a shopping mall may be revised so that it is relocated at the local mall; the shocking thing that someone said on a TV talk show may be said to have occurred on several different programs, and so on. Folklorists call the differing versions of the same tale **variants**. Variants often make the story more interesting to the audience; for example, the story is better if, instead of having happened at an unknown mall somewhere, the events are described as having actually occurred at a nearby mall.

Contemporary legends must be good stories—good enough for people to remember them and want to repeat them—in order to spread. Thus, effective legends tend to evoke strong emotional reactions, such as fear or disgust (Heath, Bell, & Sternberg, 2001). People are more likely to recall—and repeat—stories that pack a punch. Often legends warn that the world is far more dangerous than we might imagine: that gang members lurk beneath our parked cars or in our backseats, that terrible crimes occur in the mall where we shop, that having a drink with an attractive stranger may lead to having a kidney stolen, and so on (see Box 6.5).

What is the difference between a rumor and a legend? The distinction is somewhat blurry. Basically, *rumors* tend to be specific, confined to a particular time and place. They spread in conditions of uncertainty; they report "improvised news" when more authoritative information is not available, and they tend to be short-lived, one-of-a-kind stories (Fine, Campion-Vincent, & Heath, 2005; Shibutani, 1966). Rumors tend to have local relevance: they refer to a case of corruption by a local official, a local business in trouble, and so on.

In contrast, *legends* can survive over decades—they may lie dormant for a time, only to be revived. A story may pass through a city, disappear for years, but then reappear. Though a legend may include local references ("It happened at our mall"), the same story may be told as having occurred in many places. Legends often invoke familiar **motifs**; that is, the same elements recur in many legends. For example, many contemporary legends involve maniacs with sharp objects—the escaped killer with a hook replacing his missing hand, the man (disguised as an old lady) with a hatchet, Halloween apples laced with razor blades, and such—just as a surprising number of contemporary legends involve terrible crimes

Box 6.5 Creepy Clown Concern

In late August 2016, there were reports from Greenville, South Carolina, that clowns were trying to lure children into the woods. Soon there were clown sightings in other states. The press publicized some of these reports, and warnings also circulated on social media. No one actually identified an individual clown engaged in any troubling behavior, nor were there reports of anyone having been victimized, but concern mounted about what people began calling "creepy clowns." As Halloween approached, some schools announced that children would be forbidden from wearing clown costumes to their holiday festivities, and some major stores announced they would not be selling clown costumes. Concern about clowns vanished by November, probably because news of the presidential election monopolized much media coverage.

Strange as this concern might seem, it is not unique. People exhibit a range of reactions to clowns: some see them as figures of innocent fun; others find them disturbing. Evil clowns make frequent appearances in novels, films, and other forms of popular culture. Episodes in which people report sighting troubling clowns occur periodically in different locales, even in other countries (France experienced a clown panic in 2014).

These episodes are interesting, because they seem to fall outside the social problems process: There are no real claimsmakers nor any coherent claims, nor is there any evidence that the phenomena being reported even exist. Nor is it at all clear why attention is focusing on clowns, and yet some people get caught up in worrying about these topics. The fact that people become frightened is not proof that there is anything to fear.

Sources: Bartholomew, 2016; Radford, 2016.

at shopping malls. Legends can supply raw material for rumors; that is, familiar legendary elements, such as villainous conspiracies, can easily be reworked to become the stuff of a new rumor.

What do rumors and contemporary legends have to do with social problems? They often reflect contemporary claimsmaking: when the media report on the dangers of drugs, stories circulate about drug dealers giving small children LSD-laced lick-on tattoos; when gangs become a hot news story, tales of vicious gang initiation rites circulate; and so on. Many contemporary legends respond to current claims, but they also reconstruct those claims to fit the constraints of legend. Their need to be memorable means that legends tend to be melodramatic; these stories feature innocent, vulnerable victims preyed on by villains whose evil nature explains their crimes. Why would drug dealers distribute LSD to preschoolers? That's just the sort of bad thing those bad people do. Just as news and entertainment media reshape primary claims to fit the demands of their respective genres, legends rework the topics of the media's secondary claims to make them disturbing, dramatic, and memorable—the qualities of successful legends (see Box 6.6).

Rumors and legends often revolve around social conflicts. Many tales, for example, center around racial or ethnic conflict (Fine & Turner, 2001). Typically, these stories circulate within one ethnic group and describe the nefarious activities of people of another ethnicity. In the United States, for instance, there is a long history of both whites spreading tales about blacks, and blacks telling stories about whites. Sometimes these stories are mirror images of one another—the same story, only with the races reversed. A major race riot in Detroit in 1943 featuring open conflict between blacks and whites, for example, was inspired by rumors that a woman and her baby had been thrown off a local bridge (Langlois, 1983). But the story whites told one another featured a white woman and baby thrown off the bridge by blacks, while blacks shared a story of a black woman and baby thrown off the bridge by whites. In either case, the incident was apparently imaginary; there was no evidence that anyone had been thrown off a bridge.

Box 6.6 Old Tales in New Places

Contemporary legends tend to spread quickly and then disappear. Often they reappear some years later, sometimes after migrating to new settings. Thus, the tale folklorists call "Lights Out!" (warnings about gang members who drive around at night with their headlights off, wait for an approaching motorist to blink his or her lights in warning, and then follow and murder that motorist as part of a gang initiation rite) attracted considerable attention through faxes spread in the United States in 1993. In 2005, the same message, translated into Spanish, aroused alarm—even from top government officials—in Mexico. Even though there was some evidence that crime rates were actually falling, the Mexican media had been giving crime considerable attention, and the story tapped into those concerns.

Similarly, a story spread in Hong Kong in 2007 about two Hong Kong women going to a nail salon in Shenzhen (the Chinese city that borders Hong Kong); after DNA from their nail clippings had been sequenced, one of the women was kidnapped and her organs harvested. This is a variant of familiar organ-theft legends (such as a U.S. story about someone drinking with a stranger and later awakening in a bathtub filled with ice to discover that a kidney had been removed). The Chinese version featured a new element— victims being selected after their DNA had been examined—that reflected Shenzhen's heavily publicized emergence as a center for commercial DNA sequencing.

In both these cases, what had been a widespread, familiar legend in the United States found new life in another country where the tale's theme seemed consistent with local conditions—crime, an emerging industry—that had become a focus for social concern.

Sources: Soltero, 2016; Wong, 2017.

Stories based on ethnic tensions do not necessarily have such precise counterparts. Several stories circulating among African Americans, for instance, warn that particular companies have connections to racist groups (for example, that a fried chicken franchise is owned by the Ku Klux Klan); or report that a popular clothing designer appeared on a TV talk show and stated that he (or she—the story is told about different designers) did not want black people wearing the designer's clothes, so he (or she) deliberately designed clothing lines that would not fit blacks (Fine & Turner, 2001). Such stories share an underlying theme that African Americans have a subordinate place in a largely white-controlled economy. Not surprisingly, whites do not have many such tales about black-controlled firms (although they have circulated warnings that some businesses are controlled by other conspiratorial elements, such as satanists).

Other contemporary legends explore gender conflict. For example, women pass along warnings about methods that gang members, rapists, and other criminals use to prey on women, just as men share stories about seductive women who intend to harm males. Any social fault line—between ethnic groups, the sexes, bosses and employees, students and professors, and so on—can inspire rumors or legends.

Other social changes also inspire contemporary legends. For instance, numerous legends warn about the risks of AIDS, including the widespread story of a person who awakens after a sexual encounter to discover the message "Welcome to the World of AIDS" written on the bathroom mirror, and warnings that AIDS-infected IV-drug users leave used needles in the coin return slots of pay phones (Goldstein, 2004). Similarly, stories of organ thefts—that is, of stolen eyes, kidneys, and other human organs—have global popularity (Campion-Vincent, 2005). In less industrialized countries, these stories warn about westerners who only pretend to adopt children but actually harvest their organs to be used for transplants in the United States; Americans and Europeans tell one another about people awakening after sexual encounters only to discover that a kidney has been removed. The morals of these stories—warnings about imperialistic exploitation or the risks of casual sex—reflect issues that are themselves the subject of claimsmaking.

As these examples illustrate, the larger significance of rumors and contemporary legends is that they are, in a sense, ripped from the headlines. They translate topics of claimsmakers' concern— racial and ethnic tensions, the impact of immigration, the spread of AIDS, and so on—into melodramatic, disturbing stories, how-ever unlikely, that people tell one another, assuring their listeners that the tales are really true, that the events happened nearby, to someone who knows someone they know (see Box 6.7). To be sure, many of those who pass along these stories do not think of themselves as participating in the social problems process. Rather, they consider these merely memorable stories, troubling and worth repeating. They probably don't view themselves as claimsmakers, or these stories about social problems as claims.

Note, however, that many rumors and contemporary legends do share a worldview. They generally warn that the world is a danger-ous place, bedeviled by dangerous villains, and that one can't be too careful. Ordinary activities, such as driving in a car, visiting the shopping mall, and striking up a conversation with a stranger turn out to be portals into a world of violence and victimization. Thus, there is a sort of conservatism underlying most contemporary leg-ends, a worldview characterized by the suspicion that change is dangerous and needs to be approached with great caution.

Joke Cycles

A second form of contemporary folklore that builds on social prob-lems claimsmaking is the **joke cycle**. Joke cycles are sets of jokes that share a form ("knock knock" jokes) or a topic (jokes about blondes); a cycle often becomes quite popular for a time, before losing favor. Some folklorists seek to explain the emergence of particular joke cycles as reactions to awareness of social problems;

Box 6.7 The Menace of Momo

Folklorists originally understood contemporary legends as traveling by word of mouth, stories spreading in face-to-face conversations. But it quickly became obvious that these tales could travel in many ways, and social media have proven especially effective ways for them to spread. In particular, social media promote disturbing accounts of threats to children and young people. Often, these dangers are said to lurk on the same social media that spread the warnings.

For instance, warnings about Momo feature a disturbing face (originally a sculpture made for a Japanese gallery), along with a story that this face suddenly appears in social media content aimed at children (for instance, inserted into an animated cartoon available on YouTube). Supposedly, the face encourages children to perform a series of increasingly harmful acts, culminating in committing suicide.

Momo warnings have appeared in various countries. There was no evidence that children had actually been harmed, or even that the messages existed, but the story was disturbing enough to make it likely that those who encountered it would pass it along. Of course, as many critics pointed out, it was easy to interpret this legend's meanings. Parents are aware that their children spend a good amount of time online, and that they are often more familiar with technology and social media than adults. From the very beginning of the Internet, there have been warnings that child users might be victimized by cyberpredators and other menaces. The sense that children are vulnerable, and that parents may not know effective ways to protect them, provides conditions that make it easy for alarming legends to spread.

Sources: Herrman, 2019; Lorenz, 2019.

Dundes (1987) argued that the popularity of elephant jokes in the 1960s reflected public attitudes toward the civil rights movement, and the dead-baby joke cycle of the 1970s was a reaction to concern about abortion and contraception.

At first glance, these interpretations may seem peculiar, but Dundes noted that elephant jokes (for instance, "Why do elephants paint their toenails red? To hide in cherry trees") often ridicule the elephant's efforts to fit into a particular setting, and they often portray elephants as sexually dangerous. The timing of this joke cycle—it emerged in the 1960s, when the civil rights movement was at its height—suggests that this may have been an indirect means of expressing resistance to the cause of integration.

Similarly, the dead-baby joke cycle (for example, "What's red and sits in a corner? A baby chewing razor blades") presented various disturbing images and emerged during the early 1970s, shortly after the contraceptive pill became widespread and around the time that abortion was being legalized. It is not impossibly far-fetched to view joking about dead babies as linked to ambivalence about these changes. Although not everyone finds them convincing, such interpretations suggest that even the silliest-seeming joke cycles may be part of the social problems process.

Many joke cycles pose much less difficult interpretive problems. There is a long tradition of joke cycles that play on and reinforce racial, religious, or ethnic stereotypes (Dundes, 1987). Similarly, other joke cycles are grounded in stereotypes regarding gender or sexual orientation. Various joke cycles depict different target groups as being lazy, stupid, dirty, sexually promiscuous, or having other undesirable qualities. Repeating such jokes can be seen as a sort of claim about different sorts of people; of course, it is always possible for those telling the jokes to deny this, to insist that they're just joking.

The links between joking and claimsmaking are especially apparent with joke cycles inspired by dramatic current events— such as the explosion of the space shuttle *Challenger* in 1986; or the terrorist attacks on the World Trade Center on September 11, 2001 (Ellis, 2003; Oring, 1987). One important quality of such **topical joke cycles** is that we know the date they started spreading.

Obviously there were no *Challenger* jokes before January 28, 1986 (the day the explosion occurred).

Studies of topical joke cycles reveal that such jokes spread widely and very rapidly through informal channels. Media commentators, for instance, noted the existence of jokes about the *Challenger* within a few days following the catastrophe, although the jokes themselves were not circulated by the media (which viewed the jokes as in very bad taste and therefore unrepeatable). In such cases, both the number of jokes told and the number of people who report having heard them increased rapidly in the days and weeks following the event that inspired the jokes (Ellis, 1991). Of course, after a few weeks people stopped telling these jokes, presumably because those who might have enjoyed them had, by that time, already heard them, but also because the subject no longer seemed topical.

Topical jokes tend to spread where they have relevance. Local scandals may become the subject of local joke cycles, but they are unlikely to spread beyond that locality. For example, the on-camera suicide of Pennsylvania's state treasurer in 1987 inspired a joke cycle in that state, but those jokes did not spread widely beyond the area where he was a familiar figure (Bronner, 1988). In much the same way, the 1986 Chernobyl nuclear reactor disaster—which released radiation—did not become the subject of extensive joking in the United States (which seemed geographically far removed from the danger), but it did become the subject of a substantial joke cycle in Europe (where people worried about their exposure to radioactive contamination) (Kurti, 1988).

Why do people tell jokes about disasters? It is easy to argue that there is nothing funny about these events, and that such jokes are inappropriate. The most popular explanations are psychological—either that such jokes are symptoms of a "sick" society, or that telling jokes is cathartic and eases people's psychological strain. Sociologists might argue, however, that topical jokes, like contemporary legends that address subjects of current claimsmaking, offer an indirect way of expressing public attitudes toward troubling social conditions. Jokes often reveal skepticism of media constructions of events (Oring, 1987).

Here it is worth noting one other form of folk humor: the photocopies of jokes, cartoons, mock memos, and such that are posted in offices and other workplaces (Dundes & Pagter, 2000). This "office folklore" has become much easier to reproduce and disseminate, thanks to improved technologies, such as photocopiers, fax machines, e-mail, computer software, and smartphones, which allow people to create, modify, store, and transmit photos and other graphics very easily (Ellis, 2003). Often these bits of folklore suggest considerable skepticism about the workings of bureaucracies and the abilities of their leaders. Like legends and joke cycles, such office humor often addresses ethnicity, class, gender, and other familiar bases for social conflict. The fact that they are widespread suggests that their subversive reconstructions of different social problems are relatively popular, although—as is the case with all other types of folklore—it is always possible to shrug off objections by insisting that these postings aren't serious commentary, that they are just in fun. Still, such folklore remains one way in which ordinary people can express their thoughts and respond to more visible claimsmakers.

THE PUBLIC'S ROLE IN THE SOCIAL PROBLEMS PROCESS

Although opinion polls, focus groups, social media, and contemporary folklore all offer ways of understanding something about how the general public responds to constructions of social problems made by claimsmakers and the media, none of these methods can hope to tell the whole story. After all, the general public is very large and very diverse. It includes people who virtually ignore social problems claims, but also people who follow claimsmaking with enthusiasm. It includes people from a wide range of social groupings—different occupations, different ethnicities, different social classes, different genders and sexual orientations, different political ideologies, and on and on. These various groups have, if not different values, at least different interpretations of which values are most important and how they ought to be realized. There are, then, all sorts of differences that can affect how people in the general public will respond to particular social problems claims.

Moreover, even people who seem to respond in the same way—who, for example, give the same response to a survey question—may, in fact, be quite different. Some people may be energized by particular claims—they may become committed, inspired to join the cause, to devote their time, money, and energy to bringing about change. Others may become interested enough to follow the issue, read books or articles on the topic, watch TV coverage, and become well informed, although they may never actually enlist in the cause. Still others may be only dimly aware of the claims, knowing enough to tell a pollster that they think the problem is serious, but not moved to do anything more. In other words, what people mean when they respond to a survey question indicating their concern is not at all clear.

Similarly, people who hear and repeat contemporary legends or jokes may understand this folklore in very different ways. Some may indeed view themselves as participating in the social problems process, as expressing particular beliefs or attitudes; for example, probably many people who tell ethnic jokes understand that, in so doing, they are promoting particular stereotypes. But others may insist that this is just innocent fun, that it has no larger meaning.

Earlier chapters noted that claimsmakers often hope to affect public opinion, to make people aware of and concerned about a troubling condition, and that the media justify their own activities by referring to the importance of an informed public. Similarly, policymakers (discussed in Chapter 7) often argue that they are responsive to the "will of the people." Other actors in the social problems process, then, argue that public reactions play an important role. Claimsmakers, the media, and policymakers want to reach—and influence—the public, but those actors also pay attention to the public's reactions and try to adjust their own behavior in response (see Figure 6.1).

This book has emphasized the competitive nature of the social problems process: there are countless claims being promoted, and nearly as many media reports about troubling conditions. With all these bids for the public's attention, some claims inevitably must fail to attract the public's notice. This is why rhetoric—the way claims and media coverage are packaged—becomes important; the public is likely to ignore many claims and focus only on those that it finds particularly compelling.

This chapter has argued that all the ways in which social scientists measure public reactions, including public opinion surveys, focus groups, social media, and folklore, offer indirect, imprecise ways of interpreting what the public is thinking. We might wonder, then, whether we can hope to fully understand this stage in the social problems process.

Figure 6.1 THE PUBLIC'S ROLE IN THE SOCIAL PROBLEMS PROCESS

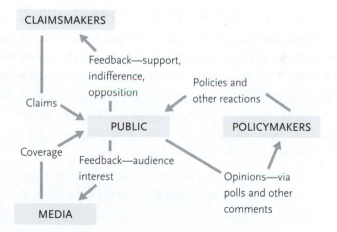

However, there is other evidence of public reactions. Over time, we can also witness changes in people's behavior that reveal responses to claimsmaking. For instance, motorists have become more likely to use seat belts; some of this change is doubtless due to laws that subject people who fail to buckle up to fines, but it is also true that a growing proportion of the population now buckles up automatically, as a matter of habit. Over time, the proportion of the adult population that smokes has fallen—again, partly because of higher taxes and restrictions on where smoking is permitted, but also partly because a growing proportion of people sees smoking as risky behavior. Although our ways of measuring these changes are imperfect, the incidence of child abuse and other family violence has probably fallen, people's willingness to express racist sentiments in surveys has dropped, and so on.

We can, in short, find evidence of actual changes in people's behavior that is motivated, at least in part, by the public's redefining what is wise, prudent, or appropriate. Although we cannot measure the public's reactions with precision, we can still recognize that the public is responsive to—and an active part of—the larger social problems process.

MAKING CONNECTIONS

- *Claimsmakers study public reactions and reframe their claims on the basis of the feedback they receive from the public. See Chapters 2, 3, and 4 for more about the claimsmaking process.*

- *Public opinion polls that measure the reaction to claims about a social problem also help determine which issues garner attention from policymakers. In the next chapter, you will learn more about the policymaking process.*

- *Public reactions to social problems change over time. Chapter 10 discusses how reactions to social problems have evolved throughout history.*

CASE STUDY
How Public Opinion Changes

How does public opinion change? The Gallup poll began asking Americans about their attitudes toward same-sex marriage in 1996. (From 1996 to 2005, the question was worded: "Do you think marriages between homosexuals should or should not be recognized by the law as valid, with the same rights as traditional marriages?"; beginning in 2006, the wording was changed slightly, so that the question began: "Do you think marriages between same-sex couples. . . .") In 1996, two-thirds of the population (68 percent) opposed making gay marriages legal. By 2018, those percentages had been reversed, with 67 percent now supporting same-sex marriages (J. McCarthy, 2018). This is a dramatic change.

Similarly, pollsters have been asking whether Americans favor legalizing marijuana since the 1960s. The proportion favoring legalization hovered around 25 percent through the end of the 1980s, when it began to climb, reaching about two-thirds of the population as 2020 approached (Felson, Adamczyk, & Thomas, 2019). Again, this is a large shift in public opinion. How can we understand these changes?

In both of these cases, age affects attitudes: A 2017 Pew Research Center survey on same-sex marriage showed that older generations were less supportive. To use common terms for generations, among Millennials (born 1981–97), 74 percent supported same-sex marriage, and that percentage fell with each older generation: Generation X (1965–80—58 percent); Baby Boomers (1946–64—51 percent); and Silent Generation (1928–45—45 percent) (Masci, Brown, & Kiley, 2019). Similarly, a 2018 Pew survey found generational differences in the percentage favoring legalizing marijuana: Millennials—76 percent; Generation X—65 percent; Baby Boomers—63 percent; and Silent Generation—35 percent (Daniller 2019). In other words, each generation was less supportive of change than the one that followed it.

One possible interpretation of this pattern is that young people are more tolerant than older people. Perhaps being young means that people aren't settled into stable adult lives, but that as people age—as they start their own families, move through their careers, and become more tied to their communities—they tend to become more conservative. These are called *age effects* because this explanation assumes that opinions change as people age. Such a pattern could explain why younger respondents are more open to the sort of change same-sex marriage and legal marijuana represent (Hart-Brinson, 2018).

Another explanation is that change is generational—that is, marijuana tends to be smoked by young people, and as those smokers age (and as older people who never tried the drug die), Americans' attitudes toward legalizing marijuana ought to grow increasingly favorable. This is called a *cohort effect.* Everyone belongs to an age cohort—people who were born around the same time (sometimes people talk about a cohort as those born in the same calendar year, or sometimes they speak of those born during a stretch of years, such as Millennials). If you think about it, you realize that our society tends to treat age cohorts as important: Most of us started first grade at about the same year as others in our cohort, and we went through adolescence more or less simultaneously, and so on. This means that dramatic historical events such as a war, an economic crisis, or some other memorable event are experienced when people in our cohort are at a particular age. For instance, the cohorts that lived through the Great Depression as children—who probably watched the adults in their family struggle during hard times—carried that formative experience throughout their lives (Elder, 1974). While homosexuality's and marijuana's histories have not during recent decades been marked by events of that magnitude, we can appreciate that there has been public drama around gay rights, including the rise of the gay liberation movement in the early 1970s, the HIV/AIDS epidemic that began in the 1980s, and the growing acceptance of gays and lesbians over half a century, just as marijuana has been a visible part of popular culture and the subject of various campaigns to legalize first medical and then recreational marijuana.

Focusing on cohort effects might lead us to assume that individuals who have firsthand experience with marijuana when they are young would retain their attitudes as they age. We can track this by comparing survey results from different years. However, the data actually suggest that we need a third explanation—what we can call *period effects*, which involve events having an impact on different cohorts. Imagine 25 percent of thirty-year-olds in one year favoring legalizing marijuana or same-sex marriage, but 35 percent of fourty-year-olds in favor ten years later. Notice that this is the same cohort of people—those who were thirty ten years ago are now fourty. Such changes are called *intracohort changes*.

The survey data for attitudes about both same-sex marriage and marijuana legalization show such intracohort changes. People became more receptive to both causes, and these effects occurred across many social categories—among males and females, those who were more and less religious, in all geographic regions, and so on. Across the population, attitudes toward legalizing marijuana and same-sex marriage became more liberal. Neither age effects nor cohort effects can explain this.

So why did these changes occur? Claimsmakers have been calling for legalizing both marijuana and same-sex marriage for decades. What seems to have changed are the ways the issues were framed. In the case of marijuana, the news media increasingly adopted a medical—as opposed to a criminal justice—frame. In state after state, campaigns to legalize marijuana for medical purposes led to new laws; these campaigns relied heavily on typifying examples of patients with various ailments insisting that marijuana was the most effective drug in making their suffering more manageable. This frame focused on the drug's pharmacological effects, as opposed to the criminality of those using the marijuana. This in turn led several states to pass popular referenda approving of recreational uses of marijuana. While counterclaimsmakers continue to warn about the drug's dangers, the early evidence does not seem to show that legalizing recreational use has caused widespread harms, which doubtless encourages more people to alter their opinions.

Something similar seems to have occurred with same-sex marriage. While we tend to think of marriage in emotional or religious terms, it is also a legal status: married individuals benefit from favorable tax laws, rights to make medical decisions on each other's behalf, and countless other legal protections. Courts became increasingly receptive to claims that denying same-sex couples the right to marriage also denied them equal protections under the law. Coupled with a growing number of typifying examples of sympathetic same-sex partnerships, these claims shifted public opinion. Not surprisingly, as the momentum in public opinion shifted, it became increasingly easy to contemplate changing social policies. Finding effective claimsmaking rhetoric can influence public opinion as measured by surveys.

QUESTIONS

1. This chapter treats surveys as one way of assessing public reactions. What are surveys' advantages, and what are their limitations?

2. Social media seem to give a sense of public opinion. Compared to surveys, what are social media's advantages and disadvantages?

3. Surveys also reveal a long-term decline in racial prejudice. What should we conclude from this evidence?

7

Policymaking

Most claimsmakers hope to do more than simply draw attention to a troubling condition; they also want to change things, to improve social arrangements so that the problem can be, if not eliminated, at least made better. Toward this end, claimsmakers seek to change social policies, to alter how the society deals with the troubling condition; and this means that their claims must reach those who have the power to make policy changes—the **policymakers**.

The most obvious way to change policy is through the law. Laws define what is and is not legitimate within a particular jurisdiction; they specify what is required, what is permissible, and what is forbidden. So the study of policymaking turns first to the study of legislative bodies—Congress, state legislatures, city councils, and so on—that not only pass laws but also allocate funds and issue guidelines to the various official agencies that administer those laws.

We are used to seeing media coverage about legislative debates over proposed new laws; such debates can be a high-visibility arena for policymaking. Votes on controversial legislation—to fund or cancel a program, to criminalize or decriminalize a behavior, and so on—are dramatic, visible policymaking moments. But much policymaking is less visible. Many new laws attract little attention, and once passed by legislators, those laws must be implemented, which creates further opportunities for behind-the-scenes policy-making. All manner of government agencies enforce and implement laws. Though our thoughts may turn first to law enforcement agencies (such as the FBI or local police forces), we must recognize that all sorts of administrative agencies oversee how particular laws are applied (for example, the Environmental Protection Agency is charged with administering many federal environmental policies). Even local governments have specialized officials responsible for enforcing health ordinances and other local laws. And because laws usually cannot spell out how they should be applied in every possible circumstance, much of the work of interpreting how the law should be applied falls to such agencies, which therefore find themselves making policy.

In addition, in the United States, court rulings have the power to shape the law. Appellate courts, for example, can rule that legislators have exceeded their authority by passing laws that are unconstitutional, or they can rule that the way a particular law is being applied or enforced is not legal. In dramatic cases (such as the *Roe v. Wade* ruling, which dictated that states could not restrict a woman's access to abortion during the first trimester of pregnancy), Supreme Court rulings can shift fundamental perceptions of what is considered legal. Thus, sometimes government agencies and courts also act as policymakers.

However, we should not equate policy with law. A wide range of organized nongovernmental bodies—think of corporations, churches, professions, charities, and so on—set their own rules or policies. When a homeless shelter announces rules regarding who is qualified to seek admission or how people must behave if they are to be allowed to remain in the shelter, this, too, is a form of poli-cymaking. Although this chapter will tend to concentrate on how legislatures and other government bodies establish laws, we should not forget that policymaking occurs in many different settings.

POLICY DOMAINS

One way sociologists think about how legislators and other policymakers organize policymaking revolves around the concept of **policy domains** (Burstein, 1991). A policy domain is that part of the political system that focuses on a particular social issue, such as family problems, criminal justice, or health policy. A given domain includes many people who are especially concerned with the issue addressed by that domain, including legislators, other officials, and people outside the government. For example, Congress has committees that deal with health issues; various federal agencies, such as the Centers for Disease Control and Prevention and the National Institutes of Health, address those issues; and outside the government, there are interest groups, think tanks, medical professionals, and other experts especially concerned with health policy. In general, health policy is likely to be formulated by those who belong to that policy domain; after all, these are the people most knowledgeable about—and most willing to devote time and energy to—health policy issues. Although Congress as a whole must vote on health-related legislation, the legislation itself is shaped within the health policy domain.

The concept of a policy domain is akin to but not the same as the concept of an arena (see Chapter 5). An *arena* is a setting where claims can be presented (a congressional committee's hearings might be an example). A *policy domain* is a network of people who share an interest in a particular policy issue; those people may oversee several arenas in which claims about that issue can be presented (such as different committees' hearings, specialized newsletters, and so on).

We can begin thinking about policy domains by considering the social circumstances of legislators. Although analysts usually focus on the federal Congress, we can assume that similar considerations affect state and local legislative bodies. Imagine a social problems claim that has been attracting attention: the media have been covering the story, public opinion polls may indicate that people are expressing concern about this troubling condition, and claimsmakers and constituents may contact legislators and ask them to take action. These circumstances might lead to a new law—to policymaking—but then again, they might not.

A new policy is by no means an automatic outcome. After all, there are lots of people who want legislators to do lots of different things, and legislators cannot possibly respond to all of these demands; there are simply too many calls for action. It would cost too much to implement them all, and many of them call for legislators to take contradictory actions. Moreover, legislators may have their own ideas about what ought to be done. Although some claims about valence issues enjoy nearly unanimous agreement (see Chapter 2), people disagree about many position issues, so there may be both people who favor and people who oppose passing a particular law. How can legislators sort out all of these demands?

Recall that Chapter 5 spoke of the media's role in agenda setting. It helps to think of legislators as having an agenda—a prioritized list of things they want to address. The list of demands they face is impossibly long; legislators don't have enough time or enough money to do everything that they are asked to do, so they need to establish priorities, to decide which things really need to be addressed now.

Once again, we see the competitive nature of claimsmaking. Just as claimsmakers must compete for media coverage and public attention, they also must compete for places on legislators' agendas. During this process, claimsmakers may wait years until they finally get legislators to address their concerns. Because laws touch on virtually all aspects of social life, there is terrific competition for legislators' attention among people calling for new laws or changes in existing laws. One result is the establishment of lobbyists, professionals responsible for knowing the ins and outs of the legislative process, who maintain networks of contacts with legislators and their staff members, and who understand how to effectively package claims so as to attract legislators' interest and support. Most industries, professions, and other well-established interest groups maintain permanent lobbying operations to try to influence lawmaking.

Recall the discussion of ownership in Chapter 3—how some claimsmakers become the established authorities on an issue, and how other people turn to those claimsmakers when questions arise regarding their issues. One way to maintain ownership of an issue is to establish a lobbying operation so that someone is always ready to convey your views to those assembling legislation.

Attempting to influence policymaking can require patience. The political scientist John W. Kingdon (1984) offers one model for understanding how particular policies arrive at the top of Congress's legislative agenda. He describes three streams: (1) the problem recognition stream, (2) the policy proposal stream, and (3) the political stream. Each stream is constantly flowing, but the three streams often have minimal contact with one another. On occasion, however, they seem to converge, and when they do, Congress is more likely to act. While Kingdon's focus was Congress, his three-stream model has implications for other policymakers (see Box 7.1).

The Problem Recognition Stream

What Kingdon calls the **problem recognition stream** is already familiar; it has been the focus of the preceding chapters. In the process of problem recognition, claimsmakers identify troubling conditions, name those conditions, devise compelling rhetoric to persuade others to become concerned about those conditions, and campaign to bring those conditions to the notice of the press, the public, and policymakers. These claimsmakers' efforts can receive a boost from current events—an attention-grabbing news story about a terrible crime or a natural disaster can catapult an issue into prominence. But most claimsmakers who hope to influence policy need to work

Box 7.1 Why Animal Welfare Policies Are Hard to Develop

The policy streams model can help us think about local policy issues. Krcatovich and Reese (2018) use the three-stream model to understand why Detroit—a city facing major economic challenges—has had difficulty developing a coherent policy for dogs, let alone for animal welfare more generally.

The city's problem recognition stream has been unable to define the nature of Detroit's dog problem. Instead, people identify three very different troubling conditions concerning dogs: There are concerns that the city's animal shelters euthanize too many dogs too quickly; claims that focus on pit bulls as a particularly dangerous breed; and calls to do more to halt dogfighting. All of these claims have reappeared at different times, and while each might be seen as part of a broader animal welfare issue, there is no effort to consolidate concerns about dogs—or animals in general.

Given these diverse claims, it should be no surprise that the policy proposal stream receives a variety of specific proposals based on some narrow definition of what is wrong, and that these proposals usually attract brief, temporary attention without actually leading to policymaking.

The political stream is constrained by Detroit's larger economic and social problems; it is a city that has been experiencing a long-term financial crisis. However much people in Detroit may care about animals, calls to do something about animal welfare must compete with all manner of other pressures to devise new policies. When studying policymaking, it is easy to assume that making policy is natural, somehow inevitable. But Detroit's failure to make much progress on policies for canine welfare is a reminder that it can take a long time before the necessary streams converge.

to keep their constructions visible, interesting, fresh, and compelling so that they can maintain continual pressure for policymakers to act; thus, the claimsmakers' particular views are readily accessible, should the policymakers' attention begin to turn toward their issues.

The Policy Proposal Stream

Kingdon's second stream—the **policy proposal stream**—consists of more specialized constructions, those that offer specific proposals for new legislation. Such proposals may be fairly general, in that they sketch broad ideological approaches toward a new policy; for example, at any given time, there are probably advocates calling for the government to create new programs to help the poor, as well as other advocates arguing that existing antipoverty programs are misguided and ought to be cut back. Other policy proposals may be quite elaborate and specific; advocates may design detailed plans for action or even draft suggested legislation for consideration.

All sorts of people work at devising policy proposals: in addition to the various experts, think tanks, and officials discussed in Chapter 4 who may develop proposals as part of their claims-making, there are lobbyists, as well as legislators and their staff members. Whereas outsider claimsmakers tend to concentrate their activities in the problem recognition stream, the policy proposal stream features far more insiders, those members of the polity who populate particular policy domains. Just as claims compete for public recognition, policy proposals compete for policymakers' attention. Again, patience is required: policy advocates must continually test the waters, constantly revise and repackage their proposals, and wait for a moment when those proposals can get a hearing (see Box 7.2).

The Political Stream

Finally, what Kingdon calls the **political stream** refers to what we might think of as the current political situation. Who has been elected, what ideologies do they hold, and what interests do they tend to represent? A new president or a new Congress may favor particular approaches to government (such as being relatively sympathetic or unsympathetic toward government regulation). Any legislature's activities reflect its composition: Does one party have

Box 7.2 Waiting for the Next Policy Wave

The political scientist John W. Kingdon (1984) quotes an analyst for a Washington interest group:

> When you lobby for something, what you have to do is put together your coalition, you have to gear up, you have to get your political forces in line, and then you sit there and wait for the fortuitous event. For example, people who were trying to do something about regulation of railroads tried to ride the environment for a while, but that wave didn't wash them in to shore. So they grabbed their surfboards and they tried to ride something else, but that didn't do the job. The Penn Central collapse was the big wave that brought them in. As I see it, people who are trying to advocate change are like surfers waiting for the big wave. You get out there, you have to be ready to go, you have to be ready to paddle. If you're not ready to paddle when the big wave comes along, you're not going to ride it in. (p. 173)

The competition for space on policymakers' agendas is intense, and not all claims can succeed. This quote suggests that advocates need to be persistent, prepared, and flexible enough to take advantage of shifts in the policymaking environment. There may be various ways to frame an issue in order to advance the desired policies.

a dominant majority? Do the legislature and the chief executive come from the same party? What other issues are competing for the politicians' attention? Is the economy fairly robust, or are budgets tight? Such factors shape the degree to which legislators believe they have a free hand. Politicians also track public opinion, and they may respond to perceived shifts in what the public favors. The political situation is constantly evolving, affecting what legislation might receive consideration—let alone pass—at any given time.

The Policy Stream Model:
Convergence of the Three Streams

Kingdon's policy stream model (Figure 7.1) illustrates how these three streams come together and assumes that, at any given moment, people are actively promoting the recognition of different problems, the adoption of different policies, and assorted political opportunities. All of these people are competing for attention and influence over the policymaking process. This intense competition ensures that most of these efforts will fail; it is just too hard to gain a place near the top of the agenda. However, sometimes the streams converge, with each reinforcing the others' influences. Sometimes a particular construction of a troubling condition complements a particular policy proposal that, in turn, coincides with the current political alignments. In those cases, proposals for new policies stand a much better chance of being enacted.

The competitive world of policymaking, with its cacophony of diverse claims demanding attention, helps explain why policy domains are so important. Policymakers cannot hope to master all of the issues, to stay on top of every topic. Instead, people specialize; they become familiar with one or two domains. Legislatures, for example, assign their members to committees (and often those committees are divided into more specialized subcommittees) charged with overseeing particular sorts of legislative proposals, and many committees can be seen as belonging to particular policy domains. These committees are much smaller than the larger legislative body, and they offer individual legislators opportunities to become relatively familiar with the issues within a specific policy domain. Policy domains bring knowledgeable people together: lobbyists, officials from related agencies, and legislative staff members often specialize in particular policy domains, and they focus their attention on the committees most concerned with that domain. This greater familiarity with a domain's issues translates into influence; committees' recommendations often influence the larger legislative body. After

Figure 7.1 Kingdon's Policy Stream Model

Problem Recognition Stream
(Claimsmakers' constructions of problems, media coverage of claims, and public response to claimsmaking draw attention to different issues.)

Policy Proposal Stream
(Policy community [officials, interest groups, think tanks, experts, etc.] devises various proposals for policy changes.)

Political Stream
(Party affiliations of officials, political alliances, and public opinion regarding satisfaction with government create the current political environment.)

Confluence
(When streams merge, opportunities are greatest to actually change social policies.)

Source: Kingdon, 1984, pp. 92–94.

all, these committee members are the people most knowledgeable about the issue.

In advancing policies, legislators can draw on a repertoire of tactics. Once they decide to emphasize particular issues (rather than any of the multitude of other possible issues they might promote) and choose to endorse specific policy proposals (among the broad array of available choices), legislators can adopt a public posture to promote their chosen policies: they can make speeches, publish their thoughts, appear on television programs, and generally seek to draw attention to their proposals. Others work backstage. Whether their efforts are public or relatively private, legislators must try to muster allies among their colleagues; they must find others who share their concerns and are willing to join the cause.

Legislators' committee positions serve as an important resource; legislators can use their committee positions to hold hearings to draw attention to the issue they're promoting. They can invite people to testify at these hearings, to present their views. Note that the power to control these invitations, to decide who will speak at these hearings, allows legislators to ensure that the hearings will highlight particular positions or proposals. Again, hearings vary in the degree to which they seek publicity. Sometimes witnesses are chosen for their ability to draw media coverage; hearings featuring show business celebrities, sympathetic victims who can recount their sufferings, or figures who have been implicated in scandalous events are more likely to become subjects of media reporting. Well-orchestrated hearings—that is, those that attract heavy media coverage and involve dramatic presentations by witnesses—can help increase an issue's visibility and can give a cause the momentum needed to get legislation passed.

Sometimes this process results in what seems to be a significant, sudden policy change: the passage of a pathbreaking law. However, when we step back from the legislature's final vote and examine the streams leading up to the shift, we may recognize that the legislators' change of heart was preceded by social changes, particularly in problem recognition—in how claimsmakers, the media, and the public constructed the troubling conditions. There also may have been a long series of policy proposals appearing to be headed nowhere, before someone devised what proved to be a winning package. And often the political situation will have changed as well, making available the necessary votes. In other words, dramatic new legislation tends to emerge only when the three policy streams converge. For example, although earlier laws treated adolescent runaways as delinquents, subject to incarceration in juvenile facilities, by the 1970s Congress had shifted to a new policy affirming that running away was not a criminal matter and funding shelters to protect—not detain or return—runaways (Staller, 2006).

More often, however, legislative reform is incremental rather than sudden. A first bill may create a tentative, exploratory program, with advocates settling for a modest compromise measure that can be implemented. They hope this new policy will be a foot in the door—that once they have gained this initial level of acceptance, it will be possible to press for further policy measures. Passage of a first, relatively minor law may be followed by a series of additional laws over the next few years that expand and further institutionalize the policy shift. For example, the initial federal hate crime law was the Hate Crimes Statistics Act (1990), which merely required that the FBI begin keeping records of reported hate crimes (Jenness & Grattet, 2001). The Hate Crimes Sentencing Enhancement Act, which followed in 1994, allowed federal judges to impose harsher sentences on those convicted of some hate crimes. In the meantime, most state legislatures passed their own hate crime statutes, and in many cases they passed additional laws that expanded the definition of hate crimes or increased the penalties for those convicted. Over time, then, the domain of hate crime policy expanded.

Although policymaking is obviously a key stage in the social problems process, it has largely been taken for granted by sociologists (political scientists have tended to be the social scientists most interested in policy formation). The remainder of this chapter will try to suggest some sociological dimensions for analyzing the policymaking process; it will look at social organization and the pressures on policymakers before turning to policies as social constructions, to the rhetoric of policymaking.

PRESSURES ON POLICYMAKERS

We have already noted that policymakers operate under constraints. Lots of people insist that they take action, yet policymakers have limited resources at their disposal. Hence, they must set priorities and establish an agenda. But the effect of these constraints varies among policymakers—and among the issues they are asked to resolve (see Box 7.3).

We tend to think first of the most visible, most contentious policy issues. For example, consider abortion: This issue can be easily understood by most people; it leads different people to have sharply opposing views about what policy ought to be, so policymakers cannot possibly satisfy everyone; and those conflicting opinions sometimes are expressed with great passion. Topics related to abortion policy—legislative action, court decisions, and so on—receive considerable media coverage, and however policymakers act regarding abortion is likely to become widely known and is sure to anger at least some people.

However, hot-button issues like abortion are atypical. Much policymaking is almost invisible. We can presume that an agency in the federal government sets standards for, say, the composition of the concrete used in federal highways. This is basically a technical matter: most of us don't know anything about the chemical and physical properties of concrete. We probably prefer that the government build the best-quality highways (so that the roads won't

Box 7.3 Prioritizing Diseases

The National Institutes of Health (NIH) is the federal agency that supports medical research. It has a budget—that is, it has finite available resources—and there are many people trying to influence how it allocates its money. There are scientists calling for more funds to support basic research that may have significant payoffs in the long run but which is less likely to have immediate direct effects on people's health. There are members of Congress who complain that disproportionate amounts of NIH funding go to major research centers (which tend to be concentrated in particular geographic locales), while little finds its way to researchers in their constituencies. And, increasingly, there are advocates for specific diseases who argue that more money ought to go toward addressing Disease X because it kills lots of people or leads to widespread suffering or has been overlooked in the past. How should the NIH weigh these competing demands? Should it prioritize based on health effects (such as reducing mortality)? Should it focus on short-run or long-term benefits? Obviously, there are good arguments to support all of these claims, and reasonable people can disagree about how to prioritize research on different diseases, but given the NIH's limited budget, policymakers will be forced to make decisions. Note that there is also inertia: funding decisions made in one year are not likely to be suddenly overturned in the next.

The ideal solution to these dilemmas is for more money to become available. In the late 1990s, a coalition of advocates—all of whom wanted more money for something—called for doubling the NIH budget over a five-year period, and presidents and Congress complied. During this period, funds for studying many diseases increased, and many advocates believed that their campaigns had worked—until the Great Recession caused the budget to tighten again.

Source: R. K. Best, 2019.

deteriorate quickly) at the lowest possible cost, but we have no idea what sort of concrete composition is required, and we expect somebody else—presumably experts in that agency—to handle the matter. On the other hand, we might imagine that the people who manufacture concrete—who doubtless view the federal government as a major customer—will have strong opinions about concrete policy: they probably want to encourage concrete consumption, but they don't want those policies to cut into their profits. Probably the industry employs lobbyists to work with legislators and officials in the various agencies that determine concrete-related policies. This sort of insider claimsmaking leads to policies being made almost entirely out of the public view.

This is why policy domains are so important. Each domain contains the people who are most interested in—and most knowledgeable about—a particular set of issues. Although we might agree that, as taxpayers, we all have an interest in whether the government buys the best concrete at the lowest possible price, few taxpayers have the time or energy to pay attention to that policy domain, let alone to play an active part in that policymaking process. This means that, within some domains, policymakers have a relatively free hand: they aren't closely watched, and they aren't subjected to strong, competing pressures.

Policymakers respond to this freedom in different ways. At least sometimes, policymakers adopt relatively activist stances to take advantage of their powers. For example, when Congress passed the Rehabilitation Act of 1973, the law contained a section prohibiting discrimination against "handicapped" persons (Pettinicchio, 2019). This was a minor provision in a much larger, apparently routine bill designed to renew a federal vocational rehabilitation program; the antidiscrimination section attracted little notice while the bill was being considered in Congress.

However, officials at the Department of Health, Education, and Welfare's Office of Civil Rights (OCR) took an active role in interpreting the new law's provisions very broadly. They argued that the law's antidiscrimination section required altering a wide range of social arrangements previously taken for granted, such as modifying curbs and other physical barriers to wheelchair access. The OCR found allies in the emerging disability rights movement, and the agency's broad interpretation led to far-reaching changes, such as requirements that public buildings be refurbished to be accessible to the disabled. It is quite possible that without the OCR's decision to promote an expansive interpretation of the new law, disability policy would not have changed as dramatically or as quickly as it did. In contrast, we can imagine occasions when agencies might choose to turn away from potential policymaking opportunities and decide simply to continue administering ongoing policies.

Of course, there is always the possibility that officials will suddenly find that what in most years would be routine, virtually invisible decisions are suddenly subjected to the glare of publicity. How a state's wildlife agency manages, say, its river otter population, is not ordinarily a major public issue, but under the right circumstances, it can become a contentious topic, with people who enjoy fishing arguing that otters are pests and need to be eliminated, while environmentalists demand that otters be protected (Goedeke, 2005). In such cases, policies that usually might be shaped by insider claimsmaking may be subjected to countervailing demands by all sorts of insiders and outsiders, the policymaking process now made visible through media coverage.

It is also not certain how policymakers will respond to such conflicting demands. Although at first glance it might seem obvious that officials are influenced by lobbying efforts, the evidence on this score is relatively weak and, perhaps contrary to popular belief, a fair amount of evidence suggests that legislators are responsive to public opinion. We might suspect that insider claimsmaking is most likely to be effective when policymaking is not especially visible. This does not mean that policies are necessarily made in secret or that the process is always corrupt, but simply that much poli-cymaking occurs outside the spotlight of media coverage. When policymaking attracts more media attention, policymakers prob-ably become more responsive to public opinion (Burstein, 2014).

Note, too, that policymaking on an issue can occur in multiple arenas. More than one congressional committee may be involved with legislation related to a particular policy domain; proponents can launch proposals before each committee and then, depending on how the different committees respond, choose to concentrate their efforts in those arenas that seem to offer the best prospects. In addition, policymaking arenas may be found at both the state and federal levels. Advocates can press for new policies at both levels: success at the federal level can provide momentum for fur-ther state-level campaigns; on the other hand, a successful state campaign or two may help persuade federal officials that they need to act. Similarly, those dissatisfied with the laws that are passed can press agency officials for interpretations that will shape policy implementation in particular directions; or if the agencies aren't responsive, it may be possible to appeal either the law's content or its implementation through various courts. Many doors offer open-ings to policymaking, so there are multiple opportunities for modest beginnings that get an issue's foot in the door and might lead to greater policy changes.

Although we tend to equate policymakers with government officials, remember that policymaking also can occur in the private sector. Corporations, churches, or other organizations can devise their own responses to claims about troubling conditions. Unlike government officials, who may be subject to countervailing pres-sures, private policymakers are less accountable to those outside their organizations. Foundations, for example, may donate money to encourage certain social policies (Silver, 2006).

As private entities, foundations have considerable latitude in choosing which projects to support; and they are flexible, able to make decisions and even shift their priorities relatively quickly. In earlier decades, major foundations sometimes worked in partnership with the federal government: foundations funded experimental social programs, and then evidence that those programs had been effective was used to justify establishing federal social policies based on similar models, much as examples of successful state or local government programs can be used to promote federal legislation (Silver, 2006). In recent years, however, the federal government has tried to reduce its involvement in social programs by arguing that private, "faith-based" (that is, church-sponsored) programs can provide social services more efficiently or effectively than government agencies can. Thus, today's private efforts seem less likely to inspire larger public programs.

As we have seen, myriad organizational considerations can shape the direction of policymaking. Particular instances of policymaking will depend on the constellation of parties—claimsmakers, legislative committees, interest groups, official agencies, and so on—who are willing to weigh in on a particular issue. These actors become elements in Kingdon's (1984) policy proposal and political streams. But we should never forget that policymaking also depends on the problem recognition stream, on how social problems and their proposed policy solutions are constructed.

SYMBOLIC POLITICS AND THE RHETORIC OF POLICYMAKING

Policymakers must explain and justify their actions; that is, they must convince others that their policies are wise and appropriate. Such persuasion necessarily involves rhetoric—efforts to convince others that the new policies are the best courses of action (see Box 7.4). Why is this policy needed? What problem is it intended to solve? Why is this particular policy the most appropriate means for addressing the problem? To the degree that policymaking is

Box 7.4 Party Vocabularies

Political parties often disagree about social policies. Among policy-makers, party differences may involve very different constructions of the troubling condition being addressed, different enough that members of different parties may adopt different words to name what is at issue.

In recent decades, Republicans have been more critical of unauthorized immigration than Democrats. (While this difference may seem obvious, it is worth noting that these positions reverse those taken by the parties in the decades following World War II, when Democrats were calling for tougher border enforcement, and Republicans tended to be more lenient.) What should the people who embody this troubling condition be called? An analysis of comments made on the floor of the U.S. Senate reveal the different vocabularies adopted by senators from the two major parties.

About 90 percent of the time, Republicans used one of two terms: *illegal aliens* (which used to be a fairly standard way to refer to those crossing the border without permission, but has increasingly fallen out of favor because it is now seen as combining two negative terms); or, more than twice as frequently, *illegal immigrants*. Both of these terms, obviously, emphasize that these people are not in the country legally. Democrats occasionally used those terms or *unauthorized immigrants*, but 75 percent of the time they spoke of *undocumented immigrants*. Notice how this shifts the focus from legality (or authorization) to what seems to be a more bureaucratic matter—whether the person's documents are in order. (In part, this may have been a reaction to a campaign urging journalists and politicians to "Drop the I-Word," referring to the term "illegal.") This example reminds us that the vocabulary used to construct troubling conditions can make a difference, even during policymaking.

Source: Haynes, Merolla, & Ramakrishnan, 2016.

a public act, policymakers need to anticipate and address such questions. This task requires yet another reconstruction, one that highlights certain aspects of the troubling condition and explains how and why a particular policy will solve the problem.

The political scientist Deborah A. Stone (1989) argues that policymaking involves the construction of **causal stories**. After all, a policy solution is most likely to be effective in solving a problem if it reflects an understanding of what causes that problem. Causal stories classify troubling conditions into familiar categories according to the nature of their causes. Different categories of causes invite different policy remedies. For example, a troubling condition might be depicted as having an accidental cause (which is to say that neither the events leading to the troubling condition nor their consequences were intentional). Put simply, accidents cannot be helped, so no one is blamed for them.

Other causal stories have other implications. Another popular explanation depicts social situations as caused by intentional action; this is, for example, how we think of most crimes—that people know they are supposed to obey the law, but sometimes they deliberately break laws. A third causal story emphasizes inadvertent causes: people do things intentionally, but their actions have unintended consequences.

It is possible to devise competing constructions of the same troubling condition using all three types of causal stories. Consider Hurricane Katrina, in 2005, which broke the levees in New Orleans and resulted in catastrophic flood damage. It is possible to construct the effects of the hurricane as an accident (the storm just happened to strike the city); or as a product of inadvertent causes (officials built the city's flood control system to withstand less severe storms because strong levees would have been much more costly, and it seemed unlikely that such a powerful storm would directly strike the city); or even as intentional (such stories might involve human intent [politicians willingly constructed levees that left the city's poorest districts at grave risk] or divine will [God was deliberately punishing New Orleans for its sinful ways]). Different causal stories carry different policy implications: Should the city be rebuilt? If so, who should pay for the rebuilding? Should anyone be blamed for the disaster?

Note that the choice of a causal story also affects the characterization of the people affected by the troubling condition—the policy's **target population**—in very different ways (Schneider & Ingram, 1993, 2005). Some causal stories depict troubling conditions as affecting vulnerable but morally worthy people—victims who deserve the policymakers' help and support. At the other extreme, stories can characterize target populations as villains— individuals who embody the troubling condition, and whose bad behavior needs to be controlled through the new policy's implementation. Note that different causal stories can construct the same target population in various ways, so, for example, drug addicts might be depicted either as villains (people who knowingly break the law) or as victims (whose hopeless lives lead to despair that causes them to turn to drugs).

Target populations can be relatively powerful (that is, politically influential), or relatively weak, and their status shapes policymakers' constructions. Contrast the differences in the ways politicians talk about Social Security (a program that benefits older citizens— one of the population segments most likely to vote) and welfare programs (which benefit poorer people, who vote less often): whereas Social Security recipients are generally described as having a right to expect that their benefits will be protected, when it comes to welfare some politicians express skepticism that welfare recipients actually need—or deserve to receive—their benefits (see Box 7.5).

It is important to appreciate that there is nothing inevitable about these constructions; the same troubling condition could lead policymakers to devise very different causal stories and characterize the target population in very different ways. A causal story that is widely accepted and is taken for granted at one time may fall out of favor, pushed aside by a rival construction that might have once been unthinkable but now has wide acceptance.

When new constructions take hold, people throughout the social problems process may begin to rework their positions to fit the

Box 7.5 Who Bears the Burden of a New Policy?

Whether a new policy emerges during the social problems process is only part of the story. There are additional issues about the form the policy takes that can shape its impact.

Most policies involve administrative burdens. Most of us have experience filing our taxes, applying for credit cards or admission to college, and so on. In some cases, policies are designed to minimize the burdens on those who hope to benefit. Social Security is a good example. Once you sign up for Social Security (itself a relatively easy process), there are few other burdens: the Social Security system keeps track of all your payments into the system and makes eventually signing up to start receiving benefits another simple process.

In other cases, policies are designed so that individuals who might benefit from the policy will bear much of the administrative burden. For example, individuals applying for asylum in the United States are required to complete an elaborate, twelve-page application that usually calls for considerable documentation to be attached (successful applications are often two inches thick) and necessitates the assistance of a lawyer or some other person who understands the process. We can suspect that this discourages many would-be applicants.

Policymakers choose to design policies that involve greater or fewer burdens as a way of encouraging or discouraging individuals to take advantage of them, and there are often debates among policymakers about whether it should be easier or more difficult to vote, to receive an abortion, and so on. Often hidden from notice, the administrative burdens associated with policies shape those policies' impact.

Source: Herd & Moynihan, 2018.

new story. Prior to the environmental movement's rise, for instance, pesticide manufacturers marketed products under tough, militaristic brand names, such as Arsenal or Torpedo (Kiel & Nownes, 1994). However, once policymakers began to respond to claims about the dangers posed by pesticides and the need for tighter regulation of the industry, the companies began describing their products as "crop protection chemicals," and devised less threatening brand names, such as Accord or Green Mountain. The rise of a new causal story can force many parties to adapt.

Not all causal stories and their associated policies are equally attractive, equally compelling. Ideally a causal story needs to be easily understood. That is, a good causal story should be easy to tell, simple enough to be conveyed by the media (which—as described in Chapter 5—prefer stories that can be converted into relatively straightforward secondary claims), and easy for audiences to follow. It also helps if the problem can be presented as having a straightforward, easily understood solution, and if that solution can be promised to be economical. Policymakers would prefer to construct their policies as effective and inexpensive: "this should solve the problem once and for all." Of course, such policy claims create expectations among the policymakers' audiences.

Policymakers typically emphasize the *instrumental* purposes of their policies. That is, they claim that the policy is intended to make a difference, to correct or improve a particular troubling condition in society. Of course, such claims make sense. The content of policymakers' claims—the causal stories, the definitions of the target populations, and so on—depict the troubling condition as having particular sorts of features, and also present the policy as the appropriate measure needed to address the troubling condition's causes, the target population's needs, and other aspects of the policymakers' constructions.

However, analysts often argue that policies can serve *symbolic* purposes as well. That is, policies embody values, serving to promote particular constructions of the world. Consider drug laws. The historical record is filled with examples of efforts to ban the distribution and use of illegal drugs, and most of those efforts have failed. The classic example is the United States' experiment with Prohibition, the period when alcohol was treated as an illegal drug. During Prohibition, an illegal trade in alcohol flourished; it created new opportunities for organized crime and led to considerable corruption. After about a dozen years, policymakers reversed course, legalized alcohol, and sought to regulate drinking through various liquor control laws limiting the conditions under which alcohol could be sold and consumed. Of course, alcohol problems did not disappear; alcoholism remains a major health problem and drunk drivers continue to kill people, but most policymakers consider the problems associated with legalized alcohol to be less troubling than those that might emerge if alcohol again became a target of prohibition.

It is easy to make parallel arguments about the problems associated with laws against other illegal drugs (MacCoun & Reuter, 2001). However, many policymakers insist that legalizing drugs is unthinkable. Legalization might be interpreted as constituting approval of drug use; it would "send the wrong message"—that is, it would seem to endorse the wrong values. Maintaining a strong commitment to the prohibition of drugs may not have particularly positive instrumental effects; experts disagree, but it is at least possible to argue that the effects of legalizing drugs would be no worse than the consequences of our current prohibitionist policy. However, antidrug laws also serve important symbolic purposes: they affirm society's commitment to sobriety and other moral principles.

Symbolic considerations are important, particularly when policymakers are elected officials. Topics that become contentious public issues—alcohol in the decades leading to Prohibition, or such contemporary topics as abortion, drugs, and welfare—encourage policymakers to adopt positions that play well as symbolic politics. Such policies affirm that one is standing up for the right values, and policymakers can assert that, at least in principle, these policies should work (even when their track record suggests that, in practice, such policies do not work as anticipated).

The notion of symbolic politics reminds us that policymaking is also a form of rhetoric, that it can be intended to persuade audiences—a category that can include the media, the public, and even claimsmakers (whom the policymakers may hope to placate, so they will stop calling for further policy changes)—that the policymakers have done the right things for the right reasons. We need to be alert to the dramatic nature of policymaking, to watch for the ways that policymakers—particularly elected officials—put policymaking to symbolic uses.

The competition for policymakers' attention and the policymakers' own desire to get favorable publicity for their activities encourages dramatizing the creation of new policies. Thus, policymakers often announce new policies with considerable fanfare; for instance, the new policy may be given a distinctive name in order to convey the sense that this policy represents a dramatic change from past practices. For example, American political leaders have a fondness for "declaring war" on social problems; there have been heavily publicized wars on poverty, cancer, drugs, and most recently, of course, terrorism (J. Best, 1999). War rhetoric conveys a sense of widespread commitment to eradicating a social problem; calling a particular policy a "war" serves symbolic, not instrumental, ends.

The problem with this sort of war rhetoric is that it creates very high expectations. Americans tend to think of wars as relatively brief struggles that are supposed to end in total victory (for example, U.S. involvement in World War II lasted less than four years, and the Axis powers all surrendered). Our history is characterized by a series of short, generally successful wars; it is not marked by a Thirty Years' War or a Hundred Years' War. In fact, military conflicts that seem unlikely to be resolved quickly—Vietnam, Iraq, and Afghanistan are obvious examples—quickly become unpopular.

Of course, social problems are not clearly identifiable enemies that can be defeated and driven to public surrender. There isn't one form of cancer; there are dozens. Curing cancer would actually require many different cures. Similarly, people are poor for lots of different reasons, and no single policy is likely to address all of those causes; eliminating poverty is likely to require attacking many different causes over a long period. Solving social problems usually takes time and often occurs piecemeal (see Box 7.6).

Box 7.6 The Undeclared War on Traffic Fatalities

In 1966, 50,894 Americans died in traffic accidents; in 2017, there were only 37,806 such deaths. In fact, the decline has been much more dramatic than those numbers suggest: Deaths fell even as the population grew by almost 65 percent, the number of drivers more than doubled, and the miles driven more than tripled. The number of traffic fatalities per 100 million miles driven dropped from 5.5 in 1966 to 1.2 in 2017 (National Highway Traffic Safety Administration, 2018).

Numerous apparently mundane policy changes account for this improvement, including the following:

- *Better cars.* Various safety features (such as seat belts, padded dashboards, electric turn signals, and air bags) became mandatory.
- *Better roads.* Various road improvements were made, including additional lanes, controlled-access highways, broader shoulders, and better signs.
- *Better drivers.* Tougher limits were imposed on alcohol consumption, and licensing was both delayed and made a graduated process for beginning drivers.

No one declared war on traffic fatalities, and no single policy change can account for the declining death toll. Rather, lots of minor policy changes nibbled away at the problem, but the cumulative effect is impressive.

This example serves as a reminder that often social policies are effective because of the combined effect of many small improvements, rather than dramatic policy pronouncements—such as heavily promoted wars on social problems—designed to get politicians favorable headlines.

Because successful policies often proceed gradually, their contributions may go almost unnoticed, although they can transform society's face over time. Consider the impact of childhood vaccination programs, stricter fire codes, or mandatory educational requirements—all policies that we take for granted. Such policies do not result in dramatic year-to-year changes, but over decades they can produce profound transformations. A look back in time can produce surprising revelations: in 1900, measles was one of the ten leading fatal diseases (U.S. Census Bureau, 1975, p. 58); today, of course, measles has virtually been eliminated. It is a shock to realize that this disease—now easily managed through childhood vaccinations—was once a serious threat to life. The policy's success is simply taken for granted.

Compare such quietly effective policies with the noisy announce-ments heralding many new policies. The announcement of a new war on a particular social problem raises expectations and thereby creates opportunities for prospective critics. After four or five years— roughly as long, remember, as Americans expect a war should last— it will be possible for critics to point to evidence that poverty or drug use or whatever the current pressing issue is continues to exist, and to argue that the new policy has failed. In other words, policies enacted with an eye toward symbolic politics are often vulnerable to critiques that are themselves grounded in symbolic arguments.

In summary, policymaking has important sociological dimen-sions (see Figure 7.2). Policies emerge only under favorable social conditions, and they involve yet another reconstruction of the trou-bling conditions—this time by policymakers who must devise a plausible causal story, depict a suitable target population, and so on. Nor is this the end of the matter. We have already noted that the tendency to herald new policies in dramatic terms, as the means by which a troubling condition can be defeated or eliminated, sets the stage for future critics. We will have more to say about the process of evaluating social policies in Chapter 9. Before examining the construction of those critiques, however, we need to explore how policies are implemented through social problems work—the topic of the next chapter.

Figure 7.2   POLICYMAKING IN THE SOCIAL ⬛⬛⬛EMS PROCESS

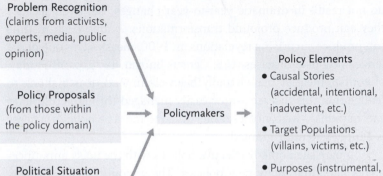

Problem Recognition
(claims from activists, experts, media, public opinion)

Policy Proposals
(from those within the policy domain)

Political Situation
(officeholders, party affiliations, ideologies, etc.)

Policymakers

Policy Elements
- Causal Stories (accidental, intentional, inadvertent, etc.)
- Target Populations (villains, victims, etc.)
- Purposes (instrumental, symbolic, etc.)
- Other

MAKING CONNECTIONS

- *Activists compete for attention from policymakers. Chapter 3 describes how these outsider claimsmakers try to influence the policymaking process.*

- *Policy changes frequently result from a shift in how the public or the media construct a troubling condition. See Chapter 6 for more on the role of public reactions in the social problems process.*

- *After policymakers ratify a new policy, it still must be implemented. The next chapter explores how social problems workers put a policy into action.*

CASE STUDY
Popular Hazards and Policymaking

Popular hazards are troubling conditions that both (a) are very popular (that is, they involve many people—perhaps tens or even hundreds of millions) and (b) harm some people (J. Best, 2018). There are many examples, including automobiles, alcohol, firearms, gambling, cigarettes, bicycles, credit cards, marijuana, and pornography. Notice that different popular hazards inspire very different social policies: some are legal and treated as a normal part of everyday life (although there are often legal restrictions on the minimum age for being involved, so that very young people cannot drink, drive, or buy cigarettes); others may be banned (and there are examples, such as gambling or pornography, of formerly banned hazards that are now legal). Popular hazards often become the focus of intense policy debates, such as the current range of policies concerning marijuana, which is classified as an illegal drug in some states (and under federal law), and legally available as a medical treatment in others, while still others have legalized its recreational use. Similarly, there are sharp differences in how states regulate firearms.

When we examine statistics on the popularity and harms related to different popular hazards, we discover a clear pattern: people who use or enjoy a particular popular hazard vastly outnumber those who are harmed by it. For instance, more than 200 million Americans are licensed drivers, whereas there are over thirty thousand traffic fatalities each year (this works out to just over one death for every 100 million miles driven). Predictably, claims from those who favor popular hazards tend to emphasize their popularity, while opponents tend to emphasize their harms.

Conversations about social policies tend to address one particular policy, so that today people debate what ought to be done about marijuana, and then turn their attention to, say, guns tomorrow. Each issue is viewed as distinct, and people rarely compare the challenges popular hazards present, or acknowledge the parallels in the debates over different polices. Still, it may help to think about what apparently very different popular hazards have in common. They all pose the same challenge: how to balance a widespread demand for something against the clear risk that some people will be harmed.

When automobiles were a novelty, people quickly realized that there would be accidents, even fatal ones, involving cars. An automobile might strike and kill a child playing in the street. Appreciate that in those days, cars were expensive, so many drivers were wealthy young men; also realize that many children who played in the streets did so because they were poor and lived in areas with few other recreational facilities, so many of these accidents had a subtext of class. Still, it is startling to learn that many of the early motorists who killed child pedestrians blamed the children for getting in their way and the parents who had allowed their children to play in the streets (Vardi, 2014).

More than a century later, we understand both the advantages and the hazards of cars far better, and policymakers have developed an elaborate regulatory apparatus to allow widespread use of motor vehicles while simultaneously reducing risks. We require that manufacturers build cars that meet ever-stricter safety standards and inspect individual vehicles to ensure that they are roadworthy. We require drivers to qualify for drivers' licenses, and we restrict access to drivers who are either very young or very old or who have compiled records that suggest they don't drive safely. We have also tried to design roads and signage to minimize the chances that accidents will occur. All of these measure work: over time, the rate of traffic fatalities has fallen dramatically (see also Box 7.6).

Many other popular hazards involve analogous policies that seek to minimize harms. Setting age limits is particularly common, but there are often other restrictions on when and where popular hazards are available. People used to be free to smoke cigarettes in most settings; however, as secondhand smoke became defined as a serious health hazard, there have been more and more policies restricting where smoking is allowed (Wolfson, 2001). Today, smoking is banned in most workplaces, and it has become increasingly inconvenient to find locations—usually outdoors—where one can legally smoke.

Policymaking about popular hazards is often contentious. These debates almost always focus on the particular popular hazard in question, and ignore the similarities with other popular hazards. Thus, campaigns to reduce restrictions on some popular hazard (to, say, make it easier to use marijuana or gamble) typically emphasize its popularity and downplay the risks, while their opponents highlight the dangers. So, advocates for legal recreational marijuana insist that the drug is likely to be less harmful than alcohol (which is already legal), or that gambling is for most people simply a form of entertainment that has minimal consequences for their lives. To contrast, those opposed to reducing restrictions emphasize possible harms, particularly to the young, who are society's most vulnerable members; they worry that heavy marijuana use while young can damage still-developing brains, or that the families of people who become compulsive gamblers will suffer. Each of these debates asks policymakers to weigh a trade-off: maintaining existing restrictions limits the freedom of the many people who would like to enjoy the popular hazard (and may involve other costs, such as the disrupted lives of people arrested for using marijuana), in return for some reduction in harm.

Note that few people adopt consistent positions across popular hazards. Many liberals favor legalizing marijuana for recreational use (that is, they view this as an issue in which popularity ought to outweigh risks), even as they support tougher restrictions on firearms (because they believe that policymakers should place more weight on the risks than on the popularity of guns). Similarly, many conservatives argue for minimizing restrictions on guns but favor maintaining laws against marijuana. And many policymakers reflect these views. Although rhetoric tends to emphasize lofty theoretical principles—that individuals should be free to smoke tobacco or marijuana, or to own firearms, or that government has a responsibility to protect its citizens from harms—translating those principles into policy often involves arguments that in this case popularity should outweigh risks, while in some other case risks should outweigh popularity. These are political judgments and policymaking rhetoric seeks to justify particular stands.

Notice that popular hazards need not involve bitter disputes. There are lots of cases where some sort of generally accepted balance has been struck. Few people argue that the state has no right to license drivers and vehicles (and to take licenses away when risks seem too great). We could dramatically reduce traffic fatalities by, say, instituting a national 25-mile-per-hour speed limit, but we accept thirty-some-thousand deaths per year as a fair trade-off for the convenience of being able to move reasonably quickly from place to place. Presumably, any popular hazard could lead to similar compromises that acknowledge the importance of both respecting popularity while minimizing harms.

QUESTIONS

1. Identify two additional popular hazards. How do people construct their popularity and harms?

2. Policy debates over popular hazards often have long histories. Why is it so difficult to settle these disputes once and for all?

3. Policymaking for popular hazards sometimes begins with court rulings or state referenda, after legislatures have proven reluctant to act. What accounts for this pattern?

8

Social Problems Work

The previous chapters explored the initial stages of the social problems process: claimsmaking, media coverage, public reaction, and policymaking. At each of these stages, people construct and reconstruct social problems: claimsmakers first draw attention to troubling conditions; the media then transform the claimsmakers' primary claims into secondary claims; next the public adds its own interpretations; and finally policymakers reframe issues in ways that can be addressed by new social policies.

This chapter concerns social problems work—the next stage in the social problems process. In this stage, too, people reconstruct the meaning of the troubling condition—but with a difference. The earlier constructions—during the stages from claimsmaking through policymaking—tended to characterize social problems in fairly abstract, general terms as widespread, even society-wide, problems. For instance, claimsmaking about the problem of poor people without medical insurance is likely to discuss the numbers of the uninsured poor, whether those numbers are rising or falling, how much caring for the uninsured costs, and so on. These claims may feature a typifying example or two, but the focus tends to be broad—on the implications of the troubling condition for the larger society. That is, claimsmaking, media coverage, and policymaking tend to take what sociologists call a **macrosociological** approach.

In social problems work, the focus narrows. *Social problems work* consists of applying constructions of social problems or social policies to their immediate, practical situations (Holstein & Miller, 2003; Miller & Holstein, 1997). Instead of discussing, say, crime, in the abstract, people doing social problems work construct specific events as instances of crime, even as they conclude that other events should not be treated as crimes. Social problems work is how people apply constructions of social problems in their everyday lives.

Most obviously, people engage in social problems work when their jobs require that they implement social policies. For example, medical professionals such as doctors and nurses will encounter sick people who don't have medical insurance, and they must decide what to do in such cases—whether to provide care or turn the ill away. Such social problems work is where "the rubber meets the road"—occasions when general, theoretical constructions about social problems or social policies must be applied to real-world situations. Although some sociologists define social problems work more broadly, to encompass any occasion when people apply their constructions of social problems (for instance, in everyday conversations), this chapter will emphasize the social problems work done by "street-level bureaucrats" (Lipsky, 1980): people who work as police officers, teachers, social workers, doctors and nurses, counselors, and so on—those who have to implement whatever policies have been devised for dealing with troubling conditions.

Social problems work often occurs in face-to-face interactions—for example, when a doctor examines a patient, a teacher instructs a student, or a police officer questions a suspect. To describe the participants in these interacting pairs, we will refer to **social problems workers** (that is, the doctors, teachers, and others whose jobs involve carrying out social policies) and their **subjects** (the people—variously called *addicts, clients, defendants, offenders, patients, suspects,* *victims*, and so on—who in some way embody a socially constructed social problem). Therefore, parts of this chapter will adopt a more **microsociological** perspective, focusing on the dynamics of these interactions between individual social problems workers and particular subjects. To understand these face-to-face encounters, however, we must also consider the larger social context within which these interactions develop. This chapter will begin by considering this context and, in particular, the nature of the jobs that social problems workers do. Then, after exploring the nature of interactions between social problems workers and their subjects, we will expand our focus to consider the sorts of social problems work that occur in everyday life.

ON THE JOB

Social problems workers find themselves squeezed between great expectations and mundane reality. The expectations travel from the top down; they are imposed on social problems workers by the larger society, by policymakers, and particularly by those who directly supervise what social problems workers do. At the grandest level, these expectations come from the larger culture's understanding of social problems work. In general, we expect doctors to heal the sick, teachers to help their students learn, police to fight crime by enforcing the law, and so on. These expectations are reaffirmed by popular culture. Think of all those television series featuring dedicated doctors and nurses, cops and prosecutors, and teachers. In general, these heroic figures confront and solve instances of social problems in each episode: patients are healed, criminals are brought to justice, or whatever. Because most of us have fairly limited real-world contacts with social problems workers, these idealized images may shape how we think of social problems work; we may imagine that social problems work is as straightforward and effective as these melodramas imply.

Further, social problems workers operate within broad-based institutions—such as medicine or the legal system—that state both general principles and specific rules that should govern the social problems workers' actions. Police, for example, enforce the criminal laws that define not just the nature of various crimes, but also boundaries for legal police conduct. The activities of different social problems workers are governed by various institutional sets of rules—professional codes of conduct, standards for appropriate behavior, and so on. These rules provide another layer of expectations that constrain how social problems workers should act.

Finally, most social problems workers belong to particular organizations—a police force, hospital, or welfare agency—that have bureaucratic hierarchies, including supervisory personnel who have their own expectations for their subordinates. Organizations vary in the importance they place on implementing particular policies; for instance, some police departments assign a much higher priority to enforcing hate crime laws than other departments do (Jenness & Grattet, 2005). A police chief may decide that traffic offenses are becoming a problem in the community and order the department's officers to be especially vigilant about ticketing traffic offenses, or a hospital administrator may discourage medical personnel from ordering expensive tests. In these examples, officers who fail to issue tickets and doctors who continue to require lots of tests may become targets of their supervisors' disapproval. Obviously such organizational expectations act as further constraints on social problems workers (see Box 8.1).

The combination of cultural, institutional, and organizational expectations may be thought of as pressing social problems workers from above; these are all ways in which the larger society tries to shape how social problems work is conducted (see Figure 8.1). At the same time, social problems workers find themselves confronting the realities of the particular people and situations they encounter. Police officers observe minor traffic violations, or see a group of youths congregating on a street corner or an intoxicated

Box 8.1 Local Standards in Policing

Over decades, there have been efforts to standardize much social problems work. For instance, there have been efforts to professionalize police work by increasing formal training, clarifying what constitutes legal police work, and so on. Still, local variations occur.

Blueville is a blue-collar city in Ontario (Canada's largest province) that has experienced an economic downturn. The members of its police department argue that their policing practices—the "Blueville Way"—differ from the standardized policing methods promoted by provincial authorities. Blueville officers see themselves as using more efficient, more expedient methods, rather than always "going by the book." They value toughness. Because the city is built around blue-collar factory workers, officers have a sense that Blueville's citizens expect their police to behave in the manner they do, that policing is different here.

Officers report that the provincial Police College, attended by recruits from all of Ontario's departments, reinforces Blueville's distinctiveness. They recall attending classes where instructors, in the process of explaining the standardized expectations for the province's police, made a point of mentioning that things were done differently in Blueville.

All of this is a matter of emphasis; Blueville police sometimes pay less attention to standardized rules than other departments in the region, but the department is not so far out of line that provincial authorities see it as necessary to interfere. However, this example reminds us that police officers, like other social problems workers, are constrained to some degree by both their organization (in this case, Blueville's department) and standards imposed by higher authorities (the province).

Source: Campeau, 2018.

person shambling down the sidewalk, or answer a call about a domestic dispute. These are all occasions when the officers face choices: Should they ignore what they see? Should they investigate

Figure 8.1 SOCIAL PROBLEMS WORKERS IN THE MIDDLE

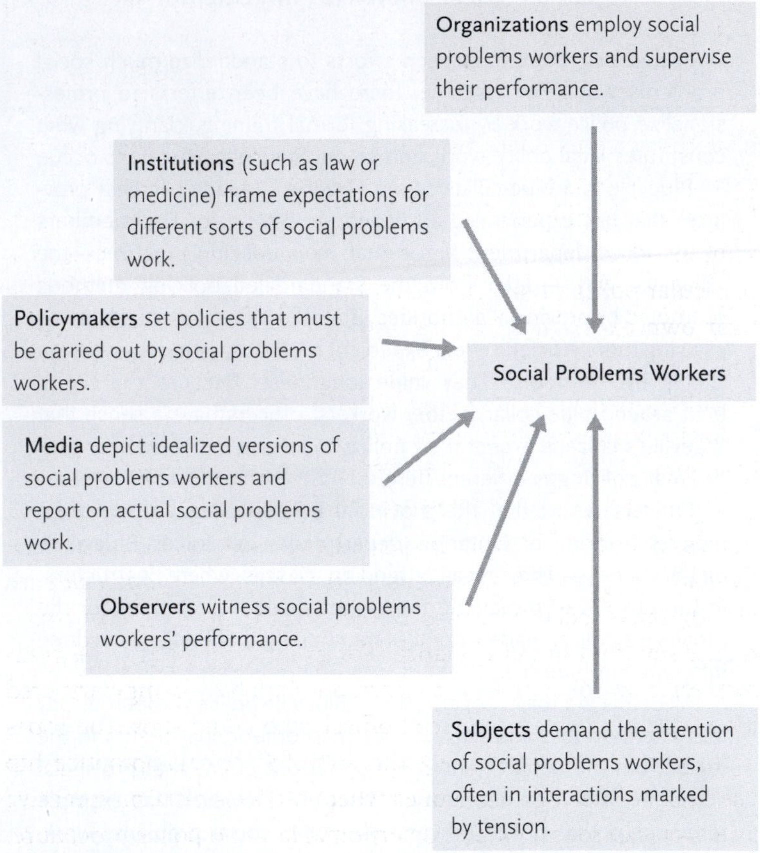

Organizations employ social problems workers and supervise their performance.

Institutions (such as law or medicine) frame expectations for different sorts of social problems work.

Policymakers set policies that must be carried out by social problems workers.

Social Problems Workers

Media depict idealized versions of social problems workers and report on actual social problems work.

Observers witness social problems workers' performance.

Subjects demand the attention of social problems workers, often in interactions marked by tension.

further by speaking to the individuals involved? Or should they take official action, such as issuing a ticket or making an arrest? During any day on the job in social problems work, lots of decisions of this sort will need to be made.

All this means that most social problems workers have considerable discretion. Their supervisors cannot oversee all of their actions, and on many occasions a social problems worker may conclude that "going by the book"—following the institutional and organizational rules—isn't the wisest, or best, course. Society tends to idealize social problems work, but social problems workers recognize that what they do must be practical. They may have reservations about the wisdom of the policies that they are expected to execute—those policies may seem too idealistic to fit the gritty, practical world that the social problems workers confront—and they may choose when to invoke, and when to ignore, particular policies (Åkerström, 2006). In short, they must draw on their own experiences, as well as their conversations with other social problems workers about how best to do their jobs, in order to decide what to do in any given instance.

Social problems workers vary in the amount of decision-making discretion they have; the lone police officer on patrol is harder to supervise than a social welfare caseworker whose supervisor's desk is only a few feet away. In general, the historical trend has been for institutions and organizations to try to reduce the independence of individual social problems workers in the name of ensuring a higher standard of performance. For example, it used to be common for new police officers to learn on the job by being partnered for a time with an experienced officer who could show the ropes to the newcomer; increasingly, this sort of informal apprenticeship has been replaced by academies where officers-in-training receive weeks of classroom training on criminal law and police procedure.

Similarly, medicine changed during the early twentieth century: medical schools began being accredited, states established procedures for licensing physicians, and there were other formal developments designed to ensure that all doctors would have at least a minimum set of qualifications and be able to provide at least a minimum standard of care (Starr, 1982). In much the same way, recent efforts by the federal government to use standardized testing to measure the performance of students in the nation's schools are an effort to improve the caliber of instruction in individual classrooms.

In other words, the discretion of social problems workers can itself be constructed as a social problem in that it can lead to inconsistent work that may be, among other things, corrupt or incompetent. Therefore, reformers devise policies to press social problems workers to be more consistent and to meet higher standards of performance. Such reforms emphasize professionalism; they encourage social problems workers to think of themselves as having special training and qualifications, and to aspire to meet their professions' high standards (Freidson, 1986). These reforms often require paperwork: social problems workers are required to provide records of their actions, or even to apply for approval to proceed—measures intended to give supervisors more control over the individual social problems worker's performance. Still, there is an inherent problem: grand principles, whether they are laws or professional standards, must be translated into practical actions. The social problems worker remains the front-line figure, the person who has to have some discretion to assess particular situations involving particular subjects and decide what ought to be done.

The tendency toward the professionalization of social problems work has other consequences. Our discussion of claimsmakers (particularly in Chapter 3) noted that claimsmaking campaigns often originate with activists who may have personal experiences with a particular troubling condition, or who may hold ideologies that help them frame critiques of existing social arrangements. Such activists invest time and energy in claimsmaking because they feel strongly that this issue is important and must be addressed. In some cases, activists may even engage in private policymaking by establishing their own grassroots programs to address troubling conditions. For example, after some members of the hippie community became concerned about the vulnerability of adolescent runaways, they established shelters to provide runaways with food, shelter, and other basic necessities (Staller, 2006); similarly, early feminists created centers for rape counseling and shelters for battered women.

Such grassroots operations tend to be staffed by volunteers and equipped through donations, but it is difficult to maintain them on that basis. The need for stable funding—to cover salaries and other costs—eventually leads these agencies to request government support. But this support usually comes at a cost; the agency may be expected to demonstrate that it is a professional operation, staffed by social problems workers who hold the appropriate credentials (rather than sharing the ideological positions of those who started the grassroots operation) and who can be counted on to abide by whatever legal constraints come with government funding (see Box 8.2).

There are exceptions to this pattern of professionalization. The obvious example is Alcoholics Anonymous (and the other twelve-step programs modeled on AA) that consist solely of people "in recovery." AA is an all-volunteer organization that refuses to acknowledge the relevance of professional credentials; its members turn to one another for support because AA's ideology insists that only those who have experienced alcoholism and recovery are qualified to guide those with drinking problems toward sobriety (Rudy, 1986). Even here, however, the emergence of health insurance provisions to cover alcohol and drug rehabilitation treatment has led to the creation of careers in alcohol and drug counseling, in which individuals who have themselves passed through the recovery process can become "professional ex-s" employed by rehabilitation centers to lead AA-like groups (J. D. Brown, 1991). Thus, the practical problems of maintaining the funding needed to support a stable program of social problems work tend to foster at least a sort of professionalism among social problems workers.

All this means that social problems workers have difficulty maintaining the ideological and emotional edge that helps motivate primary claimsmakers. At earlier stages in the social problems process, troubling conditions have been constructed and reconstructed, often in melodramatic terms, to make claims as persuasive as possible.

Box 8.2 Victim Advocates' Roles Vary across Organizations

Most social problems workers belong to organizations that have expectations for how the workers should do their jobs. Even jobs that bear the same title can involve very different organizational demands. For example, some people called *victim advocates* work for government agencies, while others work for nonprofit organizations, and the ways these two groups approach their work are very different.

Publicly employed victim advocates tend to be part of a prosecutor's office. Prosecutors pursue criminal cases, and they use victim advocates to explain the legal proceedings and ensure that the victim is prepared to offer testimony should the case come to trial. The victim advocate, then, is expected to be part of a team that has the purpose of convicting criminals.

In contrast, the nonprofit agencies that employ victim advocates tend to have been started by activists, either feminists concerned with violence against women or those involved in the movement for all crime victims' rights. These agencies tend to have a much broader definition of what victims need and the services victim advocates should provide. Advocates working in these agencies are, for instance, more likely to provide counseling, emotional support, and other sorts of aid victims want (including helping victims contact and communicate with people in the criminal justice system).

The agencies that employ victim advocates, then, vary in how they construct victims and how they define the appropriate ways their employees should interact with the victims who are their subjects.

Source: Globokar & Erez, 2019.

In the construction of new crime problems, the crimes tend to be depicted as terribly harmful, and the criminals who commit those crimes tend to be characterized as callous, brutal, terrible people. Similarly, other troubling conditions, such as poverty, tend to be characterized as grave threats that inflict harm on innocent, good

victims. Most claimsmaking portrays a melodramatic world popu-
lated by evil villains and innocent victims.

In contrast, the people whom social problems workers actually
meet on the job present more variety, complexity, and ambiguity
than most social problems constructions promise. Police officers
find themselves dealing with lawbreakers who may be hurt, frustrated, angry, sick, drunk, desperate, and so on—in other words,
very different sorts of people from the melodramatic evildoers
who must be brought to justice by, or the sympathetic victims
who require the protection of, television's heroic cops. Similarly,
other social problems workers meet people who are less admirable,
less noble, and less innocent than the victims portrayed in many
claims. Social problems work is not so clear-cut, so unambiguous,
as claimsmakers and policymakers imply it will be.

CONSTRUCTING CASES

Typically, social problems work entails dealing with a series of
individuals, subjects who require attention. On a given shift, a
police officer encounters any number of people; the officer may
stop some of them, others may hail the officer, or the dispatcher
may send the officer to a place where someone thinks the police
are needed. Similarly, a physician deals with a series of patients
who feel sick, a social worker meets with various clients who may
need assistance, and so on.

Each contact with a subject requires the social problems worker to
assess the nature of the encounter: the police officer needs to decide
whether a law has been broken and, if so, what the specific violation
was (this was a robbery, that was an illegal turn); the doctor needs
to decide whether the patient is actually ill, what the illness might
be, and how best to treat it; and so on. Note that social problems
workers may decide that there is really nothing wrong, or at least
that there isn't anything wrong enough to require official action: the

police officer may simply warn the person to stay out of trouble; the doctor may decide that further treatment is unnecessary.

A central theme in social problems work is the construction of **cases**; that is, social problems workers must decide whether particular subjects represent *instances* of a previously constructed troubling condition that requires attention through the application of an appropriate policy. Thanks to institutional and organizational expectations, social problems workers have an array of categories or labels that they might apply to the subjects who become their cases, as well as procedures for dealing with those cases (Chambliss, 1996). But first, subjects must be classified as cases; that is, individual people's practical problems must be translated into the categories (crimes, diseases, and so on) used by the social problems workers (see Box 8.3). Studies of social problems workers find that they consider a wide range of factors in making these assessments, asking questions such as:

- **What seems to be the problem?** Most obviously, social problems workers must label their subjects by categorizing their troubles. Such assessment involves yet another process of social construction. Consider a physician. Doctors are trained to recognize different diseases; a doctor who meets a new patient will ask questions designed to identify a familiar pattern of symptoms, such that the doctor can, with some confidence, declare that the patient suffers from a particular disease. Labeling the patient's disease will, in turn, allow the doctor to prescribe the appropriate treatment for that illness. Just as doctors construct individual patients as having particular maladies, other social problems workers classify their subjects into familiar categories: police officers must decide whether a crime has been committed (and if so, which crime) and whether there is sufficient evidence to make an arrest; educators must determine which students are having trouble learning, and then seek to identify the source of the difficulty (perhaps by diagnosing a particular learning disability); and so on.

Box 8.3 Using Social Media to Identify Welfare Fraud

Federal law requires that state agencies check on the eligibility of individuals receiving benefits from the Supplemental Nutrition Assistance Program (SNAP—"food stamps") or Temporary Assistance for Needy Families (TANF—the principal "welfare" program). Individuals must qualify for these programs, and those discovered to have misrepresented their qualifications can lose benefits for having committed welfare fraud.

The social problems workers responsible for investigating potential welfare fraud gather evidence from the beneficiaries' social contacts. In some cases, those receiving benefits may be on bad terms with people who reach out to the investigators to draw attention to what they consider fraud. But in other cases, the social problems workers contact neighbors to check the accuracy of the information on an application to receive benefits (for example, asking who lives next door may reveal the presence of a husband or other breadwinner who was not reported on the application—information that would have disqualified the application).

In still other cases, investigators may examine benefit recipients' posts on Facebook and other social media. These posts may reveal evidence (for instance, that the family has taken expensive vacations) that seems inconsistent with qualifications for benefits depicted in the application. Like prospective employers who check the social media accounts of job applicants, the investigators take advantage of potentially discrediting information that individuals willingly share with their social media contacts even as they hope to conceal it from those they are approaching for a job or other assistance. Contemporary social networks connect people, but sometimes in unexpected and consequential ways.

Source: Headworth, 2019.

Often a social problems worker is able to conclude that a particular subject does not meet the standards to become a case, or that the subject represents a sort of case that a different kind of social problems worker handles. Such rejections or referrals may frustrate both subjects and social problems workers. If a physician proves unable to classify a patient's symptoms, the patient is likely to be dissatisfied with the doctor (and the doctor may conclude that there is nothing really wrong—that the patient is just a hypochondriac, someone who complains without a valid medical reason).

- *Which aspects of the case are relevant?* The need to classify each case into a familiar category leads social problems workers to focus on those features of the cases that are relevant for purposes of classification or treatment. For example, a doctor trying to diagnose an illness will be interested in particular symptoms that can help distinguish among different possible diagnoses, but may be uninterested in hearing about other symptoms that can't help with the diagnosis. These narrowly focused concerns may produce tension between the social problems worker and the subject: the social problems worker may dismiss some of the subject's concerns as irrelevant (which may frustrate the subject), and the social problems worker may in turn be frustrated by the subject's failure to grasp which information needs to be reported.

- *Does this seem to be a serious matter?* (For example, has someone been seriously injured?) Obviously, the more serious the problem, the more likely it is to be pursued—and to be assigned a higher priority—by the social problems worker. Differences regarding these judgments also can lead to tension between subjects and social problems workers. People may try to convince police officers, for example, that a fight was just a minor misunderstanding, that everyone has calmed down and that there's no need to make an arrest; on other hand, patients may insist that their symptoms are serious, and that the doctor needs to take action.

- *What is the nature of the subject?* Social problems workers may classify subjects by race, gender, social class, age, education, or any of the other status categories commonly used to locate individuals within their larger social context. Often, cultural expectations dictate that different kinds of people should be treated differently—most people would doubtless agree that a police officer ought to treat a child of six differently from someone who is sixteen, or sixty-six for that matter. In other instances, subjects may suspect that the social problems worker is unjustly focusing on race or class; for example, an African American motorist who has been stopped may suspect that the police officer has engaged in racial profiling. Subjects and social problems workers may disagree about the relevance of the subject's characteristics for doing social problems work; for instance, subjects may complain that people of their status receive more—or less—attention from social problems workers than the circumstances of their cases warrant.

Social problems workers often are more concerned with other, nondemographic aspects of their subjects. For instance, an individual's demeanor may affect the social problems worker's actions. Is the person calm or upset? Is the social problems worker being treated respectfully? Those who challenge the authority of police officers are more likely to wind up arrested than those who remain calm and respectful. Another consideration is the individual's career as a subject. Some subjects come to the attention of social problems workers again and again; they become the equivalents of students repeatedly sent to the vice principal's office. Social problems workers often become frustrated with such repeaters, particularly if those subjects seem to have ignored earlier advice or admonitions.

- *Are other people watching?* The knowledge that there is an audience observing the social problems worker's interactions with a subject can make things more complicated for both parties. During a conversation between a police officer and a teenager, the presence of other youths may make it harder for either party to back down. In particular, audiences may make social problems workers more careful, so as to avoid criticism of their conduct. Here, too, both parties may become frustrated because the other is, in a sense, playing to the gallery.

- *Are there work-related considerations?* Is the social problems worker's shift about to end? No one is eager to spend after-hours time filling out paperwork. Has the social problems worker's boss encouraged—or discouraged—particular practices? All manner of organizational and individual considerations can shape social problems work.

In particular, a social problems worker's job is often complicated by a heavy caseload. For example, doctors may be expected to deal with many different patients, just as social workers or public defenders are assigned many clients. There may be a constant influx of new cases—new patients, new arrests, and so on—that need to be addressed by social problems workers. A social problems worker can ill afford to devote too much time to any one case, lest the flow of new cases creates an unmanageable backlog, a queue of other people needing that worker's services. This pressure to deal with cases in an efficient, expeditious manner encourages social problems workers to focus on just the professionally relevant features of each case. But, of course, this narrowing of focus creates yet another source of tension: subjects may feel that their cases are not receiving the careful, individualized attention they deserve.

In short, social problems work is complicated; many factors can influence how social problems workers decide to deal with particular cases. At the same time, they usually find themselves under pressure to be efficient, to deal with cases as quickly as possible, so as not to get backlogged. Social problems workers typically resolve this dilemma by devising *routines*, standard practices that allow them to sort through cases, classify them, do what needs to be done, and then move on to the next case. For example, both prosecutors and defense attorneys learn to deal with their heavy criminal court caseloads by negotiating guilty pleas (so that many cases can be handled in a relatively short amount of time). Lawyers on both sides must review the record to identify the key relevant features of each case; this evaluation allows them to classify these cases not just in terms of which law was violated, but also in terms of the seriousness of the defendant's particular offense, which in turn enables them to figure out reasonable terms for negotiating an appropriate guilty plea.

In the course of dealing with many cases, social problems workers may become aware of deficiencies in the policies they are charged with implementing. Perhaps a policy's language is ambiguous; perhaps it fails to address particular sorts of cases; perhaps social problems workers realize that the policy isn't producing the desired results—there are all sorts of possible problems. As the people with the most firsthand experience with these issues, social problems workers may devise practices that modify the policy in hopes of making their work more effective, so the boundary between policy implementation and policymaking may blur.

THE SUBJECT'S VIEW

As the preceding discussion has made clear, social problems workers are encouraged to view the people they deal with as cases, as instances of a particular disease, crime, or other troubling condition, rather than as unique individuals. But, of course, the people who constitute those cases—those who, depending on the particular kind of social problems work, are termed *patients*, *complainants*, *defendants*, *students*, *clients*, and so on—do not see things that way. These subjects tend to view their experiences as special, unique. They want to discuss their particular symptoms, the reasons they had for making particular choices or taking particular actions, the specific series of events that led them to the social problems worker.

A person who feels sick and goes to the doctor experiences illness as a personal, unique series of events and wants the doctor to return his or her body to good health. People's perspectives as subjects within the medical system—or with any other form of social problems work—are personal, individualistic. We would prefer not to be treated as "just another case." It can therefore be shocking to discover that, among themselves, social problems workers may refer to their subjects not as individuals but as types of cases. For example, hospital personnel may speak of "that stomach ulcer in Room 313"; such depersonalization violates the subject's expectations for individualized social problems work (Chambliss, 1996).

We have already noted that tensions may arise because social problems workers and their subjects are likely to view their interaction in very different ways. The differences in the perspectives of the social problems worker who needs to classify subjects into cases of familiar categories, and the subjects who want to have social problems workers acknowledge them as individuals with unique problems create another, familiar tension. Subjects often criticize social problems workers for being uncaring or insensitive, even as social problems workers complain that subjects expect individualized treatment for what, in the social problems workers' view, are common, routine problems (see Box 8.4).

Often, then, social problems work requires guiding subjects to redefine both their selves and their problems. An individual whose drinking has led to difficulties at work or at home is likely to explain those difficulties in idiosyncratic terms: if only my boss weren't so unreasonable, if only my spouse were more understanding, if only people could recognize that sometimes I need a drink; oh, maybe sometimes I drink a little too much, but it doesn't really hurt anyone else; and so on. The individual subject is likely to present a unique, autobiographical account of the circumstances that brought him or her to the social problems worker's attention: if only people would try to understand my point of view, they would recognize that what I did was reasonable.

Box 8.4 Veterinary Death Work

When a sick man or woman consults a physician, the patient (the person who needs the doctor's help) and the client (the one who will pay for the service) are one and the same. This is not true for all medical professions: pediatricians, for instance, treat the child but expect to be paid by the parent. Veterinarians face a similar situation: they treat animals but work for those animals' owners. This can create tensions, particularly involving decisions about whether to treat or euthanize a pet.

In some cases, veterinarians may feel that an animal should be treated: perhaps it may be possible to cure the pet, or at least to prolong its life. But some pet owners/clients may be unwilling to follow these recommendations: perhaps the treatment will be expensive, with costs projected at thousands of dollars; perhaps the result will be imperfect, for instance, the animal will be unable to control its bladder. In such cases, clients may reject the proposed treatment and request euthanasia. Veterinarians may be frustrated by these reactions, by the clients' refusal to remain committed to the animal. In other cases, a client may insist on keeping an animal alive, even after the veterinarian believes that euthanasia is warranted. If the animal's condition will only deteriorate, and treatments can only prolong and perhaps increase its pain, the veterinarian may consider the client's refusal to euthanize the pet as wrong.

In both sorts of cases, veterinarians find themselves negotiating with clients, trying to convince them that the appropriate course is to delay death, or to hasten it.

Source: P. Morris, 2012.

The social problems worker's task is to help the subject rework that idiosyncratic account into a more general construction. The subject needs to reinterpret whatever unique combination of events led to the encounter with the social problems worker, to learn to construct those events as instances of a larger troubling condition—excessive drinking, family violence, criminal activity, or whatever. Ideally, the subject will adopt the new identity offered by the social problems worker: "I am an alcoholic"; "I am a battered wife, and my husband is an abuser"; and so on.

Twelve-step programs, for example, demand that subjects undertake this sort of redefinition of self: Alcoholics Anonymous meetings begin with participants identifying themselves as alcoholics, and the program's first step is to admit to being powerless over alcohol. In other words, subjects are urged to identify themselves as instances of a general type of problem (so that they say, in effect, "I am an alcoholic, and my personal troubles are just one instance of the larger problem of alcoholism"). The subjects are helped to understand that what once seemed to them to be their personal, unique circumstances can be understood—and are understood by the social problems workers and others—as just another case of a general problem.

Social problems workers not only find it necessary to convert individual subjects into cases in order to do their jobs effectively, but they also may believe that subjects need to identify themselves as cases if they are to benefit from the process. Some social problems work is based on force, or *coercion*: people who are arrested by police, brought to trial by prosecutors before judges, and sentenced to prison or probation are usually reluctant participants in the process; most would prefer to avoid the social problems workers' attentions. Even so, coercive social problems workers try to gain their subjects' cooperation using a combination of sticks ("You don't want to make this any harder on yourself") and carrots ("Be cooperative, and you may get a break"). Subjects who constantly offer maximum resistance make the social problems worker's job difficult; it is usually preferable to convince subjects to go along with the process, at least to the extent of accepting being defined and treated as a case.

Of course, not all social problems work is coercive; many social problems workers offer desired *services* to subjects who seek them out, providing different sorts of aid, assistance, or therapy (see Box 8.5). For example, physicians, social welfare workers, drug counselors, and

Box 8.5 How Status Complicates Social Problems Work

Social problems workers commonly have higher status and more power in their interactions with their subjects; patients usually defer to their doctors' expertise, and citizens recognize that police officers have the power to arrest. But some sorts of social problems work involve subjects with higher status than the social problems workers.

For instance, the IT helpers who provide computer services at a medical school find that many of their subjects are professors of medicine—individuals who hold positions of very high status both in the school and in society at large, yet who need assistance in making their computers work. These professors are used to receiving a great deal of deference based on their expertise in medicine, but their knowledge does not necessarily extend to knowing how to make their computers work properly, which means they need to turn to the helpers (who, of course, hold jobs of much lower prestige). The interactions between these high-status subjects and the lower-status social problems workers often prove to be difficult, with the professors treating the helpers imperiously. In general, the higher the professor's status, the less he or she seems concerned about behaving civilly toward the helpers. The helpers resent not being treated more respectfully, but recognize that there is little they can do to require better behavior, let alone to change the medical school's status system.

This example reminds us that the interactions between social problems workers and their subjects are also shaped by each individual's place in the larger social system. People's status is affected by their age, education, race, and social class, as well as by whatever formal position they may hold as a social problems worker (or a social problems worker's subject).

Source: Seeley, 2019.

so on see themselves—and are probably seen by their subjects—as helping the subjects deal with their difficulties. Yet again, a key to these services is persuading the subject to accept the social problems worker's construction of the case, first to concede that the social problems worker has correctly defined the problem and to adopt the suggested identity ("Okay, you're right, I'm an alcoholic"); and second, to follow the social problems worker's recommendations for addressing the problem. Following the prescribed program often involves adopting the social problems worker's construction of the situation, so subjects ideally acquire a new view that is supposed to help reduce or even solve their personal difficulties.

This process of subjects accepting the social problems workers' constructions is not always smooth. The social problems workers' redefinitions may be resisted by some subjects who insist on alternative interpretations. In general, subjects who have more resources (more money, more education, more social support, and so on) find it easier to resist whatever pressures the social problems workers apply, but even subjects with limited resources may be able to resist. A homeless person may insist on living on the street and refuse to enter a shelter, or someone arrested for violence against an abortion clinic may insist that it was a moral act in accordance with God's law (a view that even many abortion opponents would reject). Note that these subjects' acts of resistance may have different degrees of social support: on the one hand, for example, a homeless person may be unable to explain the decision to live on the streets in terms that make sense to anyone else; on the other, some abortion opponents may endorse the morality of antiabortion violence.

Much resistance, though, is less active, less visible. Doctors advise countless patients to eat less, stop smoking, drink in moderation, and get more exercise. To the doctors' frustration, many patients fail to follow this sensible advice and continue to suffer deteriorating health. Most forms of social problems work have these sorts of repeat subjects: most people who go through drug treatment programs return to drug use, most inmates released from prisons wind up back in prison, and so on. Often, of course, it is possible to construct these repeaters in sympathetic terms, as victims of larger social forces (for example, not only do ex-inmates retain the disadvantages [such as limited education and job prospects] that initially encouraged their involvement in crime, but having been imprisoned usually further reduces their options, making recidivism more likely). Still, many social problems workers place much of the blame on the subjects, arguing that if only the subjects had been sincere, determined, and otherwise virtuous, they might have avoided becoming repeaters.

In general, social problems workers prefer their subjects to be compliant, willing to adopt the workers' constructions, so that their interaction with the subjects can be cooperative and the social problems work effective. However, at least some social problems workers anticipate resistance and noncooperation; the police, for example, have the power to arrest and restrain suspects, regardless of whether those subjects acknowledge the officers' authority. Other subjects may choose to go through the motions, viewing temporary submission to the social problems workers' authority as a necessary annoyance. Social problems workers, in turn, may watch for—and insist on—evidence of the subject's genuine cooperation. For instance, a drug court that offers clients the possibility of avoiding imprisonment by participating in therapeutic programs may expel clients who fail to participate fully in the program, sending them back into the penal system. Because so many tensions are built into the relationships between social problems workers and their subjects, the social problems workers are often disappointed, and it is not surprising that they may develop a certain cynicism about their work.

LOOKING OVER THEIR SHOULDERS

Social problems workers face an additional consideration: they know that they may be held accountable for their performance. Figure 8.1 illustrated how social problems workers find themselves in the middle, experiencing pressures from many directions. In particular, individual workers have supervisors, bosses who oversee how social problems work is done. These supervisors have expectations: they probably expect social problems workers to be productive (that is, to deal with their cases quickly and efficiently so that the agency's work doesn't back up); they may assign priorities, telling their workers to treat some cases as more important, deserving more careful attention than others; they want their workers to avoid mistakes or other actions that might result in critical attention being focused on the agency; and so on. Most social problems workers understand their supervisors' expectations, and they usually try to avoid displeasing their bosses.

Similarly, supervisors have others looking over their shoulders, and not just their own superiors within their organization's hierarchy (very large agencies may have several levels of authority between the agency head and the lowly, street-level social problems workers who actually deal directly with the agency's subjects). But agencies operate within a larger environment: most depend on a legislative body or other outsiders for their funding; there may be professional bodies that oversee professionals' conduct (such as state boards that license physicians); and an agency may become the subject of media coverage, or even a target of claimsmakers' criticisms. It is very easy for attention to turn to criticism, and for criticism to lead policymakers to begin interfering with an agency's operations (see Box 8.6).

Therefore, everyone involved at all levels of social problems work—for example, from the police chief to the cop on the beat—must consider not just how best to deal with the subjects of social problems work, but also how those dealings might be regarded by others. The responses of social problems workers to these considerations revolve around two central principles.

First, social problems workers try to control the flow of information about their activities. They generally prefer that others learn about the work they do directly from them. Thus, agencies issue formal reports summarizing their activities, and they may employ public relations specialists to help guide media coverage of the agen-

Box 8.6 Constructing Irredeemable Offenders

Social problems work can involve more than getting subjects to redefine their activities and situations; in some cases, social problems workers seek to get third parties to define the subject in particular ways.

In Texas, after a defendant has been convicted of a capital crime, the trial enters the penalty phase, where the prosecutor seeks to persuade the jury that the defendant should receive the death penalty. Basically, this requires establishing that the defendant remains a threat to society, and that the defendant's circumstances do not involve some mitigating circumstance that would warrant a sentence of life imprisonment. For prosecutors, this means it is necessary to construct the defendant as irredeemable, as someone who deserves to die. Transcripts of prosecutors' presentations emphasize a variety of themes: that the offender committed an especially gruesome crime against an undeserving victim, whose loss affects the victim's friends and relatives; that the crime was callous—planned in advance, undertaken deliberately, for terrible motives; and that, whatever the defendant's personal history (for example, having experienced abuse as a child), it cannot excuse the horrific crime. The offender is not only portrayed as a villain but is equated with the terrible crime, so that such a crime is necessarily the act of an irredeemable criminal. In this way, the defendant is constructed as the sort of person who warrants the death penalty under the law. (Of course, the defense attorneys—also performing roles as social problems workers—are offering an alternative construction that emphasizes the mitigating factors that might convince jurors that the defendant is not so evil as to deserve being executed.)

Source: Colomy & Phillips, 2018.

cy's activities. Having control over information means that social problems workers may try to choose what they report; they may even try to cover up some information, to keep it secret. Not surprisingly, social problems workers may seek to release information that portrays their activities in the best possible light, even if doing so requires distorting what they report. This sets the stage for an ongoing struggle between various levels of supervisors who want to know what social problems workers do so that they can be held accountable, and the social problems workers who seek to manage what others learn about their work.

The second principle is that social problems workers try to limit outsiders' authority over their activities. Here, their argument is that only social problems workers can truly understand the nature of their work and the pressures under which they operate. To the degree possible, they want their performance judged by others who share their views of the job—that is, colleagues, fellow social problems workers who can be expected to sympathize with their position and endorse their actions. For example, teachers' unions often object to outsiders' proposals to award teachers merit pay on the basis of their students' test performance (the teachers argue that test results reflect too many things the teachers can't control), just as police often resist reforms that would create review boards with civilian (nonpolice) members overseeing complaints of police misconduct (on the grounds that outsiders cannot understand the real-world pressures that police face). Social problems workers object to such proposals because they give outsiders a measure of power over social problems work.

Social problems workers vary in their ability to control information and ward off outsider interference with their activities. In general, the more resources the subjects of social problems work command, the more likely it is that social problems workers will be scrutinized by outsiders and the more carefully they need to monitor any behavior that might be observed. For example, whereas police in an upper-middle-class suburb may view themselves as providing services to the community's residents and strive to maintain good relations with the local press and with the community generally, police in lower-class urban neighborhoods may have a freer hand because their work tends to be more hidden from public view.

When social problems work—such as health care, teaching, or policing—is directed toward subjects who are relatively poor and powerless, what happens is far less likely to attract public attention and concern than when comparable services for wealthier subjects are seen as failing. Moreover, poorer populations tend to have more problems that require more services, so social problems workers who deal with poorer subjects often find themselves swamped with work compared with those working with better off, less needy subjects. At the same time, policymakers tend to be more responsive to middle-class demands for improved social problems work, so resources tend to flow to those social problems workers who need them relatively less. All this ensures that the quality of social problems work suffers—particularly work directed at less advantaged subjects—so social problems workers feel an even greater need to manage information. The result is a cycle of disappointment and fresh complaints about failing schools, unprofessional policing, and so on.

EVERYDAY SOCIAL PROBLEMS WORK

This chapter has focused on police, social workers, and other people who do social problems work for a living, carrying out the formal policies enacted to address claimsmaking about troubling conditions. However, we should recognize that we all sometimes become amateur social problems workers. Chapter 6 noted that the public reconstructs social problems claims in their everyday conversations. Similarly, ordinary individuals become aware of shifting constructions of troubling conditions, particularly via media coverage of claimsmaking and policymaking, and they find countless occasions to apply these constructions in their everyday lives.

Consider, for example, changing expectations regarding race and gender. The everyday world has become less segregated. Discrimination can take many forms; the southern states' legalized systems of racial segregation that were the targets of the civil rights movement (that is, laws that segregated everything from schools and hospitals to drinking fountains) are only the most obvious example; other forms are less blatant. For instance, prior to the emergence of the women's movement, women made up only a small minority of admissions to medical schools and law schools. Things have changed; most careers—like most neighborhoods, most schools, and most other settings—are more open to people of different races and both sexes. This is not to imply that there is absolute equality everywhere we turn. There is not. But expectations—and complaints—have shifted; for example, where activists once campaigned to open business schools to women students, they now complain that women in business confront a "glass ceiling" that makes it hard for women to move into the upper reaches of corporate leadership.

Everyday life is filled with occasions when people's behavior reflects changes in the larger culture, such as increasingly widespread assumptions about racial and sexual etiquette—the growing sense, for example, that blacks or women deserve to be treated with respect. Such changing manners, regarding how people respond to all sorts of differences—homosexuality, disabilities, unmarried couples cohabitating, and on and on—may be seen as one of the most common forms of social problems work, even if much of it has come to be taken for granted as simply the way people think they ought to act. Of course, managing such reactions may be quite conscious, as when women having abortions must decide how to think—and feel—about their experience.

One form of everyday social problems work, then, is to smooth over what once might have been awkward occasions. Close personal relationships—ties between friends or family members—may offer the most extreme examples. Here, people know one another well; each person is understood to be a unique individual, with his or her own character and patterns of behavior. Such relationships can be seen as the opposite of the efforts of professional social problems workers to classify their subjects into cases belonging to particular categories (see Box 8.7).

Box 8.7 Moms Manage Toxic Exposure

Many people do everyday social problems work. While there are various government regulations regarding food labeling, many environmental organizations argue that people are exposed to dangerous toxic chemicals in the food, personal care products (e.g., shampoo), and furniture they buy. Some consumers who find these claims persuasive seek to minimize toxic exposure through various forms of precautionary consumption, minimizing the threat by purchasing products with labels that seem to promise their contents are safe, or by shopping in stores that declare they stock safer goods.

Most of this social problems work is done by mothers. Concerns about the special vulnerability of children, of the need to protect the fetus during pregnancy as well as small children too young to protect themselves, lead many women to try to control the products with which their families will come into contact. Women invest different amounts of time and energy in this project: some may occasionally buy a food that is labeled organic on the grounds that it is a small step in the right direction; others may devote a good deal of time to educating themselves about various toxic threats so that they can make systematic efforts to minimize their children's exposure. Obviously, precautionary consumerism can be very time-consuming, and products judged safer are often more expensive, so that the women who are able to pursue this goal most intently tend to be upper-middle class.

Professional social problems workers' responsibilities are limited by social policy (such as the laws regulating how food is labeled). Policies are compromises; industries fight regulation as unnecessarily restrictive, even as claimsmakers argue that those policies should be expanded, and individuals who subscribe to the latter claims may be able to take actions tailored to protect themselves or those around them. In this way, anyone can do social problems work.

Source: MacKendrick, 2018.

A consequence of such highly personalized understanding of one another is that families and friends are often slow to construct those they know well as instances of larger troubling conditions. Cousin Joe may get drunk a lot and even hit his wife, and Jane next door may often get moody, but it is possible for those who know Joe and Jane to tell themselves that these are just personal quirks: "Joe's under a lot of strain"; "That's just how Jane is." It often takes time for friends and family to begin to use the larger culture's vocabulary of social problems—to speak of alcoholism, or domestic violence, or depression.

The media offer guidance for such everyday social problems work: many television talk show episodes are designed to help viewers reinterpret interpersonal problems as instances of larger social problems, and to offer advice—where to seek help, and so on. For example, friends, family members, and coworkers may be urged to stage an "intervention" to pressure an individual to acknowledge and do something about his or her drinking problem. In this way, ordinary people are encouraged to think that they, too, can assist professional social problems work, that they can recognize things that happen as instances of troubling conditions and respond appropriately, by guiding the subject toward professional social problems workers.

Social problems work, then, is a key stage in the social problems process because it connects general discussions of macrosociological social problems with the practical realities of individuals' lives. At one time or another, all of us experience troubling conditions, either personally or through our contacts with other people, and we all come into at least occasional contact with professional social problems workers. On these occasions, the currently available constructions of troubling conditions can affect us in many ways—through media messages, through the policies interpreted by social problems workers, and so on. What happens to us, what happens to those around us, and how we understand what's happening when we become involved with social problems work are all part of the social problems process. And, in turn, people's experiences with social problems work can lead to various reactions, which will be addressed in the next chapter.

MAKING CONNECTIONS

- *Through their jobs, social problems workers transform the meaning of a social problem from an abstract, general condition to a specific or immediate situation.*

- *The measurement of social problems workers' success will be discussed in the next chapter, on policy outcomes.*

- *Social problems workers frequently become targets themselves of claims by activists and experts and are subjected to new policies to address repackaged social problems. Chapters 3 and 4 explain how claimsmakers frame troubling conditions.*

CASE STUDY
CAMPUSES DEAL WITH SEXUAL
ASSAULT COMPLAINTS

Arguing that they had an *in loco parentis* responsibility (that is, they had an obligation to supervise young people in place of their parents), colleges and universities have long tried to supervise their students' sexual behavior. When most institutions became coeducational, they established separate male and female dormitories (often located at some distance from one another), as well as elaborate rules regulating when males could visit women's dorms. For the most part these arrangements have vanished, and administrators acknowledge that many students will be sexually active. At the same time, the dominant sexual script—the widely shared expectations for how sexual relationships will develop—has changed, from a dating script that presumed a couple would spend some time becoming acquainted during which they might become increasingly intimate, to a hooking-up script that accepts that couples who may not know each other well may have sexual encounters (Bogle, 2008).

If sexual freedom is one product of the feminist movement, so is concern about sexual assault. Surveys of college women reveal that a substantial proportion have had some troubling sexual experience, although they may have difficulty labeling what happened to them, as suggested by the title of one early study—*I Never Called It Rape* (Warshaw, 1988). On many campuses, first-year students attend presentations intended to emphasize that sex needs to be mutually consensual, and to offer guidelines for what this means. Since some students may not have a lot of experience with sex or alcohol consumption, there is an attempt to clarify individuals' rights and responsibilities. Still, there are inevitably complaints about sexual encounters gone wrong, and some of these are brought before campus authorities. These cases can prove difficult to handle: often the two parties were alone when the events in question occurred, with one or both under the influence of alcohol or drugs. If they had very different accounts of what had happened, it was hard to judge these cases. Moreover, this social problems work was often being done by student review boards.

Women's advocates were frustrated that many complaints did not get resolved in the woman's favor. They also emphasized that victims were traumatized by both the assaults and the administrative process for dealing with their complaints. They argued that this was yet another instance of institutional sexism, and often issued broader critiques (of, for example, sexually exploitative fraternity culture) (Sloan & Fisher, 2011). In 2011, the Obama administration responded to these complaints by announcing and publicizing new federal guidelines for campuses responding to sexual assault complaints aimed at better protecting the rights of victims. It warned that failure to follow these guidelines might put colleges in noncompliance of Title IX—the federal law prohibiting sexual discrimination at federally funded institutions. Virtually all colleges and universities receive federal funding of some sort; for instance, a very large share of students receive federal student loans or Pell grants. The Department of Education released a lengthy list of institutions under investigation for noncompliance with Title IX. Many colleges responded to this threat by establishing special administrative offices intended to handle complaints about sexual misconduct.

The Obama administration justified its action by constructing the campus sexual assault problem in particular ways. It argued that this was a large problem and presented statistics to suggest that victimization was common. It further argued that a substantial part of the problem was caused by serial offenders, males who were able to get away with sexually victimizing large numbers of women precisely because colleges were failing to give women's complaints the serious attention they deserved. In order to correct these failings, colleges were urged to devise new standards, to "start by believing" the person making a complaint, and by avoiding procedures that might traumatize victims. In practice, this meant that those against whom complaints were lodged might be unable to confront their accuser or even examine the evidence that would be the basis for deciding the case against them.

Most social problems work is shaped by rules that govern it, such as the guidelines for the college administrators who were increasingly making decisions about sexual assault complaints. Social problems vary in terms of how much autonomy these rules allow. In some cases, the rules constrain social problems workers and protect their subjects from some sorts of abuses. For instance, the Constitution and the body of criminal law constrain operation of the criminal justice system and protect those accused of crimes from various potential abuses: defendants have the right to be represented by counsel, to examine the evidence against them, and so on. While it is certainly possible to argue that the authorities retain substantial advantages in pursuing criminal convictions, when we compare U.S. courts to the ways justice is dispensed in totalitarian regimes, it is clear that the law imposes real constraints on social problems workers.

The effect of the Obama administration recommendations for college sexual assault proceedings was to change the rules to make it much easier to find in favor of the people complaining they had been assaulted. These changes soon attracted critics, who noted that the new arrangements did not give the accused students rights that would be taken for granted in ordinary criminal trials—the right to examine the evidence or to question the complainant or witnesses (K. C. Johnson & Taylor, 2017; Kipnis, 2017). In some cases, students who had been charged with assault received serious penalties, such as being expelled from the institutions where they had been studying. Hundreds of these students sued their schools in federal or state courts, arguing that their rights had been violated because they had not received the sorts of protections given defendants in criminal cases. Some of them began receiving judgments against their colleges or universities.

In response, the Trump administration's Department of Education rescinded the Obama administration's recommendations on sexual assault, and proposed new regulations: "Schools would now be required to employ a presumption of innocence, explain the specific allegations to both the complaining and accused parties, and give both parties access to all the evidence directly related to the allegations. . . . The new regulations would require that the person who investigates the facts be different from the person who makes the decision and that the parties have the opportunity to be heard and to hear each other in front of the decision-maker" (Gersen,

2019). These proposals in turn inspired a round of criticism that they would make it easier for offenders to get away with sexual assault.

Even what might seem to be mundane aspects of social problems work, then, can become a central element in claims and counterclaims. In the case of campus sexual assault, claimsmakers argued that higher education was failing to protect its students by not taking charges seriously enough, and the Obama administration pushed institutions to address these claims. However, the new arrangements themselves came under criticism for failing to protect the students who had been accused, and the Trump administration rescinded the Obama-era standard and proposed new arrangements to address those counterclaims. This debate over how these social problems workers should operate is unlikely to disappear.

QUESTIONS

1. Does all social problems work involve balancing competing interests (as in the case of a complainant and the accused)?

2. Are there other reasons for adjusting the rules governing social problems work?

3. Does it make a difference whether a debate over social problems work attracts considerable media attention?

9

Policy Outcomes

The social problems process can be lengthy. In its typical form, as described in earlier chapters, claims lead to media coverage, public reaction, and policymaking, and the resulting policies shape social problems work. At each stage in this process, actors reconstruct the troubling condition: just as media workers repackage the primary claims of activists and experts into secondary claims that fit the media's requirements for suitable news or entertainment, social problems workers must figure out how to bring the idealized generalities that inspired the social policies to bear on the gritty, practical situations they confront. At every stage in the social problems process, there are likely to be shifts in how the troubling condition is understood, as it is constructed and reconstructed by different people.

This chapter concerns what we can view as the final stage in the process: its *policy outcomes*, reactions to the way that social problems workers have implemented policies. There is a broad range of possible outcomes. At one extreme, we can imagine everyone agreeing that a particular policy solves the problem; perhaps all interested parties smile, dust off their hands, and turn their attention to something else. The Nineteenth Amendment to the Constitution, which granted women the vote throughout the United States, might be an example; women's right to vote became a part of the political landscape that is now simply taken for granted. However, this sort of complete satisfaction with social policy is probably rare. At the other extreme, a policy may be completely rejected, perhaps because it is seen as having failed to work, or even as having made things worse. For instance, the Eighteenth Amendment, which established prohibition of alcohol as the law of the land, was quickly found unsatisfactory and repealed (via the Twenty-First Amendment). Most policies fall between these extremes and are seen as flawed—satisfactory in some respects, but unsatisfactory in others.

In most cases, policies fail to make the troubling conditions that they are intended to address vanish. This should not come as a surprise. Crime, racism, poverty, and most other troubling conditions are unlikely to disappear simply because a particular policy has been implemented. These conditions tend to have multiple causes—consider all of the various things that might lead someone to commit a crime—and it is unlikely that any one policy can address them all. It is almost certain that more will remain to be done. This helps explain why so few social policies are regarded as completely successful.

It is significant that our culture speaks of social *problems*. The very term implies that there must be a solution; after all, schoolchildren learn to *solve* arithmetic *problems*. We might use other terms to characterize society's troubling conditions. We might call them **social conditions**, an expression that does not seem to imply the same confidence that there must be a solution; or **social issues**, a term that draws attention to disagreements or debates without necessarily raising expectations that they can be resolved. But because we think in terms of social *problems*, people often judge social policies as falling short if they don't solve everything; they tend to criticize policies that don't work, construct interpretations for those policies' shortcomings, and make recommendations regarding what ought to be done differently.

This chapter will focus on such critiques—what we will call *policy outcomes*. As we will see, the range of such outcomes is very broad. Even when people agree that a policy is flawed, they may have very different interpretations about what the flaws are, what causes those flaws, and how the flaws might be repaired. This chapter cannot possibly explore all of the many ways that people respond to social policies; it can only sketch some key features about policy outcomes. The discussion will begin by considering how policy outcomes can evolve into new claims, and then turn to the types of people who participate in constructing policy outcomes, as well as the rhetoric they tend to favor.

NEW CLAIMS BASED ON POLICY EVALUATION

As suggested already, general acceptance of a social policy's success may be relatively rare. Certainly our attention is drawn to cases of vocal critical reactions, in which people charge that the policy is somehow imperfect. These reactions can be viewed as new claims, claims that the flawed social policy itself now constitutes a troubling condition that needs to be addressed. Although such claims about policies' flaws can take many forms, we can identify three general types of critiques about social policies.

Critique #1: The Policy Is Insufficient

The first critique is that the policy is *insufficient*. Here, critics argue that the policy was a step in the right direction, but that it doesn't do enough and, as a result, has fallen short of what is needed to eliminate the troubling condition that it was intended to address (see Box 9.1). For example, critics might argue that an antipoverty program, although it may help some poor people, is insufficient to end poverty; or that a civil rights law does not do enough to

Box 9.1 The Ironic Consequences of Border Enforcement

In 1965, the United States set limits on immigration from the Western Hemisphere and canceled a long-standing guest worker program that had allowed Mexicans attracted by higher wages to enter the United States to perform seasonal work in agriculture. The workers continued to cross the border even though they no longer had legal standing, but at first this remained circular migration, in that the vast majority of these workers returned to Mexico carrying the earnings they had saved.

By the 1970s, policymakers began warning that illegal immigration was a threat, and they began increasing border security to try and halt the flow of undocumented workers. Initially these efforts focused on the areas around El Paso and San Diego (the largest border cities, which had been the routes taken by most migrants), so migrants began crossing the border in more remote locations. This led to the United States pouring more resources into border enforcement, and a pattern of escalation began.

While it was impossible to keep undocumented workers from crossing the border, tighter enforcement could make it harder and therefore more costly. Rather than returning to Mexico each year and running the risks of being caught the following year, immigrants began to settle in the United States. The undocumented population increased and their presence, in turn, led to more calls for tougher measures to halt illegal immigration, and the cycle continued.

The debate on immigration policy has continued for decades. Claimsmakers continue to argue that even tougher border enforcement policies are needed, but other advocates argue that such tough policies have the ironic consequence of making the problem worse and call for reforms that would allow workers to come and go legally.

Source: Massey, Durand, & Pren, 2016.

eradicate the legacy of racism. An insufficient policy, according to its critics, does too little.

The critique of insufficiency is often promoted by those who supported the original claims that led to implementation of the social policy. Having identified a particular troubling condition and having successfully urged policymakers to act, they now claim that the policy just isn't enough, that the policy needs to be extended or expanded to better deal with the troubling condition. Often these new claims are part of a broader strategy. After all, when claimsmakers first draw attention to a troubling condition, they may anticipate considerable resistance from the press, public, and policymakers who find the claims too unfamiliar or the claims-makers' proposals too radical. Although they may privately think that eliminating the troubling condition will require extensive—and expensive—policy changes, claimsmakers may fear that it will be impossible—at least at first—to convince the public and policy-makers to buy into such far-reaching changes. It's better to call for specific, narrower—and cheaper—policies; that is, it's better to ask for something that others might be willing to give. And, as discussed in Chapter 7, policymakers may adopt a similar approach, settling for a modest initial program in hopes that it will be a foot in the door. Once many people accept the need to do something about the troubling condition, it may be possible to mount a new campaign, arguing that the original policy is insufficient and that more needs to be done.

Critique #2: The Policy Is Excessive

The second critique, which is the opposite of the first, states that the policy is *excessive*. The argument is that the policy goes too far, that it does too much and needs to be rolled back. For example, some critics argue that laws protecting endangered species are too broad (in that they block economic progress in order to protect minor, unimportant species), too cumbersome (in that there are too many bureaucratic steps required to demonstrate compliance with the laws), and not in society's best interest (in that the requirement to protect endangered species impedes society from achieving other important goals). These, too, are claims—claims that policies have an inappropriate, damaging impact.

Those who present claims about excessive policies are likely to have resisted those policies in the first place. They may have seen the proposed policy as threatening their interests or their values, yet failed to block the policymaking process. Now they have returned to argue that the policy has, in fact, proved to be excessive, and they may seek to cut it back. In particular, they may try to convince media workers, members of the public, and policymakers who supported the initial policy that they made a mistake, that it is time to backtrack and undo the damage.

Critique #3: The Policy Is Misguided

Finally, policies may be critiqued as *misguided*. Once again, these evaluations are claims that the policy has led to a troubling condition, but in this case the claim is not so much that the policy goes too far or not far enough, but that it heads in the wrong direction. There are various bases for making such claims. For example, the critics can argue that the *construction of the troubling condition* that led to the original policy was mistaken, that the problem needs to be understood in completely different terms (see Box 9.2).

Such claims often offer alternative definitions of the troubling condition that are grounded in a different underlying ideology. For example, concerns about the spread of sexually transmitted diseases among adolescents and about teenage pregnancy have led liberals to advocate policies for sex education and for providing youths better access to contraception and abortion (Irvine, 2002). In effect, such programs of reproductive health services define the troubling condition as caused by society's failure to deal effectively with the reality of widespread adolescent sexual behavior. These programs

Box 9.2 Constraining the Discussions about Low-Birth-Rate Policies in Japan

Since 1990, Japanese policymakers have been concerned that the country's total fertility rate (the average number of births per woman over her lifetime) is below the replacement level. Unless this changes, Japan's population will begin to shrink, and there will not be enough young people joining the workforce to pay for the growing population of elderly who receive social benefits. There have been periodic debates about the need to devise social policies to promote more births.

Feminists and policymakers construct this as a problem of work–life balance. They argue that there need to be more supports—especially more nursery schools—for mothers in two-income families. Critics argue that the problem might be more effectively addressed through other means, such as paying all parents a monthly child allowance to help cover the costs of raising children (a policy that would benefit all parents, including those in single-income families who do not use nursery schools), and encouraging earlier marriages. However, there has been considerable resistance to such proposals, and officials have repeatedly reaffirmed their constructions of the work–life balance problem and the solutions in providing better supports for working mothers. In the meantime, Japan's total fertility rate (like those of virtually all Western European countries) has remained below the replacement level.

This example reminds us that policy outcome discussions do not occur in a vacuum. Policymakers and their critics seek to evaluate policies from their own perspectives; they find it easiest to support critiques that match their own assumptions, and resist ideas that contradict their assumptions about how the world does—and should—work.

Source: Akagawa, 2019.

had long met resistance from—and were sometimes blocked by—conservatives who worried that sex education and reproductive health services might promote adolescent sexual activity.

However, the emergence of HIV/AIDS as a major health risk led many schools and communities to adopt expanded new programs. After the programs were in place, some conservatives presented an alternative construction of the troubling condition by arguing that it was the liberals' policies that were promoting sexual activity among the young; the conservatives' counterclaims argued instead for abstinence-based programs designed to discourage premarital sexual behavior. There are many similar examples, cases in which critics argue that the assumptions behind social policies—such as those dealing with poverty or homelessness—are mistaken, and that only by reinterpreting the nature and causes of the troubling condition can effective policies be designed and implemented.

Other critiques may generally accept the initial construction of the troubling condition, yet argue that the *policies* that emerged were in some way misguided. For example, Lipsky and Smith (1989) argue that constructing social problems as emergencies often wastes resources. Emergencies are defined as short-term challenges for which policymakers tend to adopt short-term solutions, but it often might make more sense to establish long-term arrangements to deal with such conditions. For instance, instead of viewing homelessness as an emergency that requires short-term shelter and other assistance, it might be less costly and more helpful in the long run to establish programs to make stable, low-cost housing available for longer periods. Just because people agree about the nature of a social problem doesn't mean they won't disagree about how best to deal with it.

One important theme in critiques about misguided policies is that the policies actually make things worse, that they exacerbate the troubling conditions they are designed to eliminate. That is, these claims often describe policies as having *ironic* consequences.

For instance, critics argue that antidrug policies actually encourage the spread of illicit drugs (for example, they might argue that arresting drug dealers increases the risks of dealing and reduces the supply of drugs, leading to higher drug prices, which in turn attract more people to the now even more lucrative business of drug dealing), or that programs designed to lift people out of poverty actually increase the numbers of poor people (here the argument might be that the more generous social welfare programs become, the more likely it is that people will choose to remain dependent on welfare rather than working) (MacCoun & Reuter, 2001; Murray, 1994). Note that the former critique tends to be favored by liberals, while the latter usually is presented by conservatives; claims that policies have ironic consequences are not limited to particular ideologies. Such claims often describe a vicious cycle: a troubling condition leads to a policy that makes the condition worse; in response, the policy is expanded (because that's how people have agreed to address this issue), which in turn causes the condition to get even worse, and so on. Critics insist that the only way to break this cycle is to devise completely different policies that approach the problem from a fresh direction.

A somewhat different critique of misguided policies argues that the implementation of the policy—the *social problems work*—violates the policy's true intent or purpose. Here, critics claim that the initial construction of the problem and policy—perhaps what was intended by its advocates to be a supportive, generous plan to help the afflicted—is being subverted by social problems workers. Such critiques may contrast the public face of a policy with its hidden workings, arguing that, for example, job training programs usually do not help their clients find good jobs so much as steer them into low-paying, dead-end jobs (Lafer, 2002). Alternatively, the critics may argue that the social problems workers are abusing their positions, wasting resources, or paying too little attention to the needs of those the policy is meant to help. Claims about police brutality or police corruption, for instance, are less about flawed laws than about problems with the ways the laws are enforced.

Such policy outcome debates can seem intractable, with Claim A leading to Policy A, then Critique B inspires Policy B, which in turn invites Critique C that produces Policy C, and on and on. Federal student loan policy has inspired a series of claims, each constructing the troubling condition along new lines that lead to new policy that in turn proves vulnerable to a different critique (J. Best & Best, 2014). Thus, the initial federal loans were intended to guarantee that any qualified young person could get access to funds needed to pay for higher education. But critics soon charged that too many loan recipients were failing to pay off their loans on time, leading to tougher policies on repayment. More recent criticism has focused on students' debts being excessive, and there are calls for loan forgiveness and other remedies. When troubling conditions are complex, it may be extremely difficult to devise a policy that stands above criticism.

In short, there are various ways to construct the workings of social policies as imperfect—as troubling conditions in their own right. The social problems process does not usually come to an end after a particular social policy has been implemented. Rather, new social policies often provide the raw material for launching yet another social problems process, one in which critics construct claims that the policy is doing too little, too much, or the wrong thing; that this in itself is a troubling condition; and that something ought to be done about it. In fact, dissatisfaction with the operation of current social policy is an element in most claimsmakers' rhetoric. A glance back at the examples in earlier chapters will reveal that many of the claimsmaking campaigns we have discussed throughout this book have focused, at least to some degree, on the deficiencies of existing social policies. This means that social problems processes can be linked through time: when one runs its course, it often inspires one or more new claimsmaking campaigns, as illustrated in Figure 9.1.

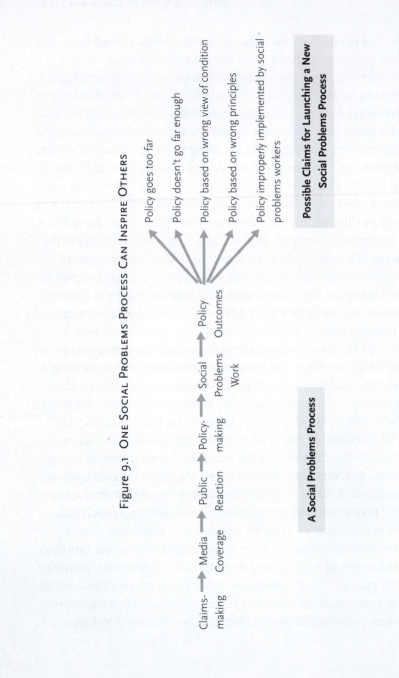

FIGURE 9.1 ONE SOCIAL PROBLEMS PROCESS CAN INSPIRE OTHERS

Claims- → Media → Public → Policy- → Social → Policy
making   Coverage   Reaction   making   Problems   Outcomes
                                          Work

A Social Problems Process

Policy goes too far

Policy doesn't go far enough

Policy based on wrong view of condition

Policy based on wrong principles

Policy improperly implemented by social problems workers

Possible Claims for Launching a New Social Problems Process

ACTORS, EVIDENCE, AND EVALUATION

The previous section described several ways to criticize the workings of social policies. But who presents these critiques? And what sorts of rhetoric do they use to make their claims convincing? This section considers some of the actors who play prominent roles in constructing outcomes to the social problems process, as well as the sorts of evidence that they are likely to feature in their claims (see Box 9.3).

Most obviously, *social problems workers* can become critics. As noted in Chapter 8, it is not unusual for social problems workers to be ambivalent about the policies that they must implement. Moreover, they have a good sense of what is—and isn't—working. Social problems workers often have to report to their supervisors about what they have been doing. Because most social problems workers keep records, they have two important advantages in debates over social policy outcomes: they understand how social problems work is actually practiced, and they have access to those records. Again, Chapter 8 noted that social problems workers seek to control information about their work, and this desire shapes their claims. They have an interest in convincing other people that they're doing a good job and, perhaps, that they would be able to do an even better job if only they had more resources—more personnel, a bigger budget, and so on. Thus, social problems workers may be reluctant to challenge either the basic policies that they are supposed to implement, or the manner in which they actually implement those policies, unless they can, in the process, advocate receiving additional resources for their agencies.

Because they control their agencies' records, social problems workers are particularly likely to support their claims with evidence of organizational activity—that is, measures of how much work they do. It is relatively easy for them to compile this information: police departments can tally the number of arrests made during the previous year, hospitals can count the number of

Box 9.3   Evaluating Swedish Social Workers

Public constructions of the effectiveness of social policies and the social problems workers who implement them are shaped by media coverage, which in turn tends to be driven by dramatic typifying examples. For instance, Sweden's press gave extensive coverage to the case of Yara, an eight-year-old refugee who was murdered by her relatives after social workers failed to remove her from the home. The case became a touchstone for coverage that sought to assess its meaning and the larger significance of this case.

Most stories present social services as in crisis, with social problems workers struggling under difficult working conditions, such as inadequate staffing to deal with an overwhelming caseload, making it impossible to do their jobs as well as they ought to be done. Other accounts are more critical and point to the children who wind up being abused by the system that is intended to protect them; these reports seek to identify particular points at which the system failed. Blame for these shortcomings can be directed at the social problems workers who made what in retrospect seem to have been bad decisions, at the administrators who failed to adequately supervise those social problems workers, or even at the politicians who are supposed to oversee those administrators. Obviously, these differing interpretations choose to emphasize different facts: are social problems workers doing the best they can under admittedly difficult circumstances, or are they failing to live up to the expectations for people in their jobs? Not surprisingly, there are also stories that call for taking action, for all of the parties—from social problems workers to politicians—to work together to address policy shortcomings. The media often become a forum in which the effectiveness of social policies can be debated.

Source: Blomberg, 2019.

patients, and so on. Social problems workers can use these data to demonstrate that they have been busy doing what they are supposed to do, and they often argue that the fact that they are busy is evidence that they need bigger budgets and additional personnel to handle the demand for their services. In other words, social problems workers are particularly likely to use measures of organizational activity to support claims that existing policies are insufficient, and that they need to be expanded to give social problems workers more resources.

Sometimes the social problems workers' *subjects*—the people whose lives constitute the troubling condition that the policy is supposed to address—offer their own evaluations. For example, poor people may criticize antipoverty programs for not doing enough to help poor people, just as both people who have been arrested and crime victims may complain about mistreatment at the hands of the criminal justice system. Again, as noted in Chapter 8, subjects often are frustrated in their dealings with social problems workers, and they may be dissatisfied with the actual implementation of social policies.

Like social problems workers, subjects have the advantage of firsthand experience with how policies work, and they are most likely to draw on these experiences for evidence to support their claims. Thus, they tend to favor anecdotal accounts—this is how the policy failed to work in our particular cases, or in the cases of people we know—which then serve as typifying examples for what are constructed as larger policy failings. (Recall a lesson from Chapter 2: typifying examples are rarely typical; they are chosen because they offer compelling illustrations of claims.)

Whereas social problems workers usually argue that policies are insufficient, subjects' critiques can be more varied. Subjects, too, may claim that the policy is insufficient; for example, they might argue that there are long waiting lines and other delays because there aren't enough social problems workers to aid the subjects who need services. Or they may warn that policies are excessive; for instance, they may charge that people who commit minor criminal offenses may suffer unreasonably harsh, life-damaging penalties. Or subjects may insist that the policies are misguided; for example, they may claim that social problems workers ought to help their subjects, rather than coerce them. Properly chosen typifying examples can support any of these critiques.

Compared with social problems workers, subjects tend to have significant disadvantages when critiquing policies. To the degree that subjects draw on their own personal experiences to document the policy's shortcomings, audiences may dismiss the subjects' claims as self-interested. High-status subjects' claims may receive careful attention. But the subjects of many kinds of social problems work have relatively few resources (that is, they have limited money, education, and social status), and the very fact that they are subjects can be stigmatizing (in that they may have been labeled as criminals, mentally ill, and so on). Although it is not impossible for low-status or stigmatized subjects to devise claims criticizing how a particular social policy operates, these disadvantages can make it much harder to get the media, policymakers, and other audiences to attend to the subjects' claims.

The prospects are better for a third set of critics, those whose claims launched the initial social problems process—the *original activists and experts* who first drew attention to the troubling condition and the need to do something about it. These people may already have the advantage of ownership; that is, the media and policymakers may be used to listening to what these claimsmakers have to say about this troubling condition. In particular, experts' critiques may seem more credible because they have professional credentials, and these experts may be seen as offering authoritative assessments. Claimsmakers' criticisms that the policy they promoted has somehow failed to deal effectively with the problem, then, stand a somewhat better chance of being heard than do critiques from other people.

In fact, such dissatisfaction from claimsmakers may be expected. As noted in Chapter 7, policymakers may have altered the claimsmakers' original proposals; social policies often are products of compromise, as policymakers try to placate both claimsmakers who are calling for action and opponents who want to do nothing, or as little as possible, or perhaps something very different. To the degree that a policy was a compromise measure, everyone may anticipate that the initial claimsmakers will still be dissatisfied and want more, that they are likely to argue that the policy was insufficient and call for further reforms.

Activist and expert claimsmakers alike may draw on both anecdotes and measures of social problems workers' activity to document their claims that policies are insufficient. Like subjects, they can use typifying examples to show that the policy doesn't do enough to help those affected by the troubling condition. Expanding the policy may require nothing more than increasing resources (bigger budget allocations and so on), but it may also involve domain expansion (see Chapter 2). Here the claimsmakers argue that the policy defines the troubling condition too narrowly, that a broader definition is needed so that a larger share of those affected can be helped.

Alternatively, like social problems workers, claimsmakers can point to statistical evidence (perhaps collected by social problems workers) to demonstrate that there is a growing problem requiring further action. After social policies are established to deal with previously neglected troubling conditions, social problems workers' statistics often display a marked jump. For example, the campaign to draw attention to child abuse led to laws requiring that doctors, teachers, and others report instances of suspected abuse; not surprisingly, the number of reported cases increased dramatically. But child abuse claimsmakers could then use these statistics to argue that the increased numbers of reports proved that child abuse was a growing problem, that current policy responses were insufficient, and that additional resources were needed to fight child abuse.

Policies may be critiqued not only by the claimsmakers whose efforts led to policymaking, but also by *rival activists and experts*. These are people who opposed the original claims and the resulting policy, whose counterclaims proved unsuccessful during the social problems process. They are, of course, predisposed to be critical; and they are particularly likely to argue either that the policy is excessive, or that it is misguided. In their view, the policy was a failed experiment: it didn't work, and it may even have made things worse. These rival claimsmakers call on policymakers to undo the damage, and they warn that expanding the policy will only exacerbate matters.

These rival claimsmakers also can draw on both anecdotal and statistical evidence. Their typifying examples point to subjects whose lives have been harmed by their contacts with social problems workers implementing the policy (for instance, a nice middle-class college student who suddenly faces felony charges for possessing a small amount of drugs, or a welfare recipient who is discouraged from finding work by a system of benefits that encourages dependency). Similarly, they can interpret the available statistical evidence as showing that the policy is having negative effects (that, say, the war on drugs has imprisoned large numbers of people, and a disproportionate share of these are African Americans; or that people are remaining welfare recipients for longer periods of time than under the preceding policy). Note that just as initial claimsmaking campaigns can be mounted by either liberals or conservatives, these critiques by rival claimsmakers who opposed those campaigns are not restricted to one ideology: both liberal and conservative claimsmakers can frame parallel critiques of policies that each opposed (see Box 9.4).

Thus far, we have examined policy critiques by four different groups: (1) social problems workers, (2) subjects, (3) the initial claimsmakers whose activities led to the policies, and (4) opposition claimsmakers who stood opposed to the original claims. Each group tends to favor particular arguments and to rely on particular sorts of evidence. Although some successful policies can lead to social problems work that attracts minimal criticism, other, more contentious issues inspire prolonged, visible debates. Topics such as abor-

Box 9.4 Broken Windows' Breakage

"Broken windows" policing refers to the strategy of aggressively policing minor offenses as a way of signaling that the law will be enforced, thereby deterring people from committing more serious crimes. It was adopted in New York City and its proponents insist that it caused the city's crime rate to fall, but critics argue that it has led to other, less positive consequences.

Although the policy generated thousands of additional arrests that brought people into the criminal justice system, a majority of those cases did not lead to court decisions of guilt or innocence. Instead, a system emerged to manage the increased flow of cases by postponing trials or sentencing. People who had been arrested found their trials being postponed and re-postponed; they might be required to show up in court and then told to stay out of trouble and come back for another appearance in a couple months. This was a system of procedural hassles that drew out the legal process while officials could evaluate the performance of the accused. Individuals who stayed out of trouble might then find their cases dismissed without having a criminal conviction on their record.

The people who find themselves caught up in this system are often poor; they can't afford to hire private defense attorneys, and they are therefore more or less at the mercy of the court's social problems workers. The court cannot afford to convict and jail all the offenders the police are arresting, so it tries to sort defendants into those who can stay out of trouble and those who seem to keep getting into trouble, reserving conviction and incarceration for the latter. It is a way of dealing with all the arrests broken windows policing produces, but it also basically creates an extra-legal system of justice.

Source: Kohler-Hausmann, 2018.

tion, gun control, drug law enforcement, environmental regulation, health care, and welfare policy are widely known to be issues about which people have disagreed in the past, disagree at the present, and in all probability will continue to disagree in the future. Such contentious policies attract many critics—sometimes from all four groups—but often their critiques tend to be discounted because each group is widely understood to have a vested interest in a by now predictable position in the debate, and therefore cannot be counted on to be an impartial judge of a policy's effectiveness. Is there no way to develop accurate, objective assessments of how social policies work?

THE SEARCH FOR IMPARTIAL EVALUATIONS

Doubts about whether interested parties can be trusted sometimes lead to efforts to solicit impartial evaluations of how well policies work. The most obvious of such efforts take the form of **evaluation research** (Rossi, Lipsey, & Freeman, 2004). Evaluation research usually involves some sort of social scientific assessment of a policy's effectiveness; the hallmarks of such research are efforts to create objective measures of a policy's costs, benefits, and outcomes. Often the evaluators are outsiders, chosen because they do not come from within the ranks of social problems workers, although such evaluations also can be done by insiders. The real issue is not who does the evaluation, but whether the methods used to produce the evaluation can lead to information that others will find convincing.

In theory, the most compelling evidence would come from careful experiments to assess the policy's effectiveness. At a minimum, two matched groups of subjects would be compared: social problems workers would apply the policy to the experimental, or treatment, group; and the control group would experience something else (usually whatever social problems workers did before the policy was implemented). In practice, experimental designs are often more elaborate: there may be several treatment and control groups that undergo slightly different conditions. Well-designed experiments can provide fairly convincing evidence regarding whether a policy works better than whatever preceded it.

There are, however, significant problems with experiments. One problem is that experimental research tends to be time-consuming, in part because designing the research, carrying it out, and then analyzing the results can take a long time. But experiments also take time because the evaluators may want to wait to follow up with the subjects who experience the policy. It may take time for the policy's effects to be felt, or a policy's early effects on the subjects' lives may wear off over time; since it takes a while for either of those consequences to become apparent, researchers may prefer to make their final measurements years after the subjects' contacts with social problems workers end. In addition, experimental designs, because they can be elaborate and take years to complete, are often costly. As a practical matter, people engaged in policy debates are often too impatient to wait for experimental results that may not be available for years, as well as unwilling to pay for such expensive research.

Therefore, evaluation research usually winds up using less compelling, nonexperimental methods to study policy effectiveness. Often such studies consist of two sorts of comparisons. The first is across time: the evaluators compare a particular measure of the old and new policies' effectiveness (for instance, under our old policing policy the crime rate was X, whereas under our new policy it is Y). Second, evaluators may compare different places (other cities, states, or countries) to see whether our policy seems to be more effective than those used elsewhere.

The evidence produced through such comparisons is weaker than the findings of experiments because the differences between the old and new policies may actually have been caused by another factor (such as the economy booming or declining), or perhaps the other places used for comparison aren't really comparable (for instance, City A's agencies are known to be corrupt, City B has a very different ethnic composition, and so on). Such comparisons pose complicated problems for researchers: both the troubling conditions that the policies are designed to address and the policies themselves are likely to vary from time to time and place to place; in addition, policymakers, social problems workers, and others may insist that they already know whether and why a policy works, so the evaluators' findings may not be welcome.

There is another problem: to hold down costs, nonexperimental research often winds up measuring policy effectiveness using whatever data have already been collected. In practice, this usually means using the records kept by the social problems workers— the measures of organizational activity discussed earlier, such as the number of arrests or the average amount of time that clients continue to receive welfare benefits. This information may be suggestive, but it often doesn't answer the key questions: Do lots of arrests mean that crime is under—or out of—control? Do clients stop receiving welfare benefits because they have been helped out of poverty, or because they have become frustrated with the policy and have given up?

Since it is difficult to produce high-quality, inexpensive data quickly, evaluation research rarely provides the last word in assessing policies' effectiveness. Too many questions remain. Typically, such research depends on the records compiled by social problems workers, and those records have limitations. Imagine an effort to evaluate a new antidrug policy. Evaluation researchers might try to compare available measures of organizational activity, such as the number of drug arrests or the value of the drugs seized before and after the policy's introduction. But note that this approach raises various questions: Are those records accurate? (How, for example, is the value of the drugs seized calculated?) Were the records kept in the same way before and after the policy was introduced (or was there perhaps a more systematic effort to count every case once the policy went into effect)? And, after all, what do such measures mean? Do more drug arrests and more drugs seized mean that the policy is working (because, presumably, drug dealers and drugs are being taken out of circulation), or do they suggest that the policy is failing (because there seem to be more dealers to arrest and drugs to capture)?

In short, evaluation research tends to rely on imperfect, ambiguous data, and the correct interpretation of its results is often unclear. Depending on the assumptions that evaluators bring to their work and the choices that they make in deciding how to measure the policy outcomes, it is often possible for evaluators to come to very different conclusions. And although evaluation research is theoretically impartial, evaluators can be "hired guns," brought in to buttress a particular tale. A policy's advocates may commission research that allows them to point with pride at evidence of their policy's success, while the policy's opponents may present their own research suggesting the policy's shortcomings. Not surprisingly, then, evaluation research often fails to gain acceptance as the authoritative, impartial, last word on a policy's impact (see Box 9.5).

The knowledge that evaluators may design research that seems to affirm their prejudices sometimes leads to efforts to devise special high-status, impartial bodies to evaluate policies and issue recommendations. At the highest level, the president or Congress often appoint national **commissions**; and state or local authorities may appoint similar bodies (Zegart, 2004). The commission members tend to be visible figures known for their integrity and chosen to represent a range of interest groups (for instance, leaders from business, labor, law, the media, and religion; members from both political parties; males as well as females; individuals from different regions and ethnic groups; and so on). In other words, the commissioners are meant to represent a broad range of those concerned with the policy. Such "blue ribbon" commissions may be appointed with great fanfare with the expectation that the commission's findings will also be well publicized, accepted as authoritative, and used to guide future policy.

Box 9.5 Solving the Urban Manure Problem

Until the end of the nineteenth century, cities were completely dependent on horses for most transportation: people and goods were pulled or hauled by horses. A city like Boston had 700 horses per square mile, and each horse produced a gallon of urine and dozens of pounds of manure each day. Streets were covered with inches of "mud" (which was about two-thirds manure). Ideally much of the muck was scooped each night and loaded into (horse-drawn) wagons to be carried outside the city and used to fertilize farmers' fields, but pedestrians found it difficult to cross streets without getting their shoes and the hems of their garments filthy. Urban experts projected that cities would only grow larger, that the streets would become clogged with unimaginable, unmanageable amounts of manure, and they were unable to envision a solution.

Of course, the urban manure problem soon vanished. This did not involve some president declaring a war on manure, nor were there shrewd policies implemented to solve the problem. Rather, as internal combustion engines became cheaper and more reliable, people realized that cars and trucks could better solve their transportation needs; motor vehicles were faster, more powerful, more convenient, more comfortable, and cheaper to own and operate than horses. Within a couple decades, horses nearly disappeared from city streets, and the urban manure problem vanished with them.

Certainly, we can identify deliberate policies that eliminated social problems. Smallpox, once a major cause of death and misery, was declared eradicated *worldwide* thanks to effective vaccination programs. But it is worth noting that many social problems decline or disappear because social or technological changes inadvertently eliminate those problems' causes. No one promoted automobiles because they would remove manure from the streets, but that's how the problem was solved.

Sources: Morris, 2007; I. Weinberg, 1971.

Of course, selecting commissioners who already hold important positions and lead busy lives means that they will have difficulty devoting much time to the commission's work. The actual work tends to fall on the less well-known staff members, who assemble evidence about the policy's workings and guide the commissioners in making their recommendations. Moreover, a commission's recommendations may prove unpopular. Commissions tend to be appointed precisely because an issue is seen as divisive, so it is almost inevitable that whatever is recommended will prove controversial. Although commission recommendations sometimes receive considerable media coverage, they often fail to lead to the significant policy changes that the commission hoped to achieve.

One other category of actors who play an important role in evaluating policy outcomes deserves attention: the *appellate courts* (see also Chapter 7). Policymaking often involves creating new laws, and social problems work often leads to legal actions. In turn, the people who find themselves targeted by new social policies can appeal their cases to higher courts. These appellate courts may rule on the constitutionality of the policies, affirming some, striking down others, and clarifying still others. In turn, *legal scholars* may try to influence courts' decisions by writing law review articles that criticize the legal basis for policies (Malloy, 2010). In the United States, a bill passed by legislators and signed into law by a president (in the case of federal legislation) or a governor (in the case of state legislation) may be modified—even ruled illegal—by appellate courts. Such court rulings may reject the policy itself, or the ways in which social problems workers implement that policy. This power makes courts important players in shaping policy outcomes.

Legislators are supposed to represent the popular will (recall Chapter 7's discussion of the various pressures they face), while courts are intended to provide a check on legislative enthusiasm. This means that even the most successful claimsmaking campaigns— those that elicit media coverage, mobilize public concern, and see their claims translated into new policies—may be constrained or rejected by the courts. For example, legislators often promote laws against burning the American flag, laws that have considerable vote-getting appeal (Welch, 2000). However, the courts have tended to recognize flag burning as protest, a form of political speech, protected under the First Amendment. Similarly, courts often constrain overly broad interpretations of new policies, restricting the grounds for defining, say, hate crimes (Jenness & Grattet, 2001) or sexual harassment (Saguy, 2003). The courts' rulings, in turn, may be denounced or constructed as new troubling conditions by assorted claimsmakers, media workers, policymakers, or social problems workers.

In sum, courts, like evaluation researchers and commissions, are often seen as failing to resolve debates over policy outcomes. However much we might like to imagine that an impartial interpretation will resolve people's differences in policy debates, such solutions prove elusive. People continue to disagree about which policies best address troubling conditions.

IDEOLOGICAL PREDISPOSITIONS

As we have seen in this chapter, there are many possible bases for criticizing how social policies are being implemented, as well as many types of people who might be moved to offer such critiques. From this we might conclude that all sorts of debates over policies are theoretically possible, but in fact, many policy discussions take fairly predictable forms.

Key to many policy debates is ideology. Within contemporary America, many people—including activists, experts, media workers, members of the general public, policymakers, and social problems workers—can locate themselves on a political spectrum that is understood to run from left to right—that is, from those who have relatively liberal views to those who hold relatively conservative views. Precisely how individuals construct this ideological spectrum varies: just as conservatives may lump together people who variously think of themselves as liberals, progressives, or radicals, and who recognize these as important distinctions, liberals may not appreciate the range of positions among those on the right.

In general, however, when discussing social problems, those on the left tend to emphasize the importance of equality and worry that society discriminates too much on the basis of race, class, and gender; they favor social policies that promote equality and discourage discrimination. And in general, those on the right emphasize the importance of liberty and social order; they worry that excessive social policies may constrain liberty and, in the process, damage overall societal well-being. Of course, these are questions of emphasis: few Americans would denounce either equality or liberty, yet they may disagree about their relative importance, or the best ways to achieve these values in particular situations (see Box 9.6).

This means that debates over social policies often break down into those favoring a more liberal position opposed to those favoring a more conservative stance. Each ideological side has its own activists in social movement organizations, think tanks filled with experts, media commentators, and policymaking politicians; the same people tend to find themselves allied over a range of policy debates. In fact, when individuals thought to be associated with a particular side break ranks on an issue and agree with those they usually oppose, the split is considered remarkable, something worth mentioning. Thus, when discussions about a particular policy outcome begin, it is often possible to predict who will line up on which side of the issue.

Not all ideologies fit neatly on the familiar liberal–conservative continuum. Think of libertarianism (usually viewed as a form of conservatism, but one that leads to what are typically thought of as liberal positions on issues related to drug use or sexual behavior), various religious doctrines (which can vary a great deal, depending on the theological interpretations being advanced), or feminism

Box 9.6 Ironic Consequences of the Civil Rights Movement

The civil rights movement set out to end the system of legal racial segregation in the South, and the passage of the Civil Rights Act of 1964 and the Voting Rights Act of 1965 can be seen as evidence that the movement succeeded. However, as McAdam (2015) observed, that success had ironic consequences that reshaped the American political landscape in ways that would affect future social policy debates.

For most of the century following the Civil War, the Republican Party was considered "the party of Lincoln"; this meant both that African Americans generally voted Republican (at least until Democrat Franklin Roosevelt brought them into his New Deal coalition in the 1930s) and that southern whites voted Democratic (which produced the "solid South" represented almost entirely by Democrats who supported maintaining legal segregation). However, the civil rights movement's successes during the Democratic administrations of John Kennedy and Lyndon Johnson reinforced blacks' ties to the Democratic Party.

Sensing an opportunity, the Republican Party began to appeal to white voters in the South, which led to a new political alignment: the South is once again solid—but it is solidly Republican (except in districts that are majority African American). This new arrangement is less overtly racist, but more ideological than in the past. Many of the southern Democrats had been populists; they favored policies that supported the poor—or at least poor whites. Their Republican successors tend to be more uniformly suspicious of spending on government programs to benefit the disadvantaged. Thus, the civil rights movement continues to shape partisan debates about social policy.

(which is centrally concerned with improving women's place in society). In addition, there are professional ideologies; professions have distinctive views of troubling conditions and how these conditions ought to be addressed. For example, recall Chapter 4's discussion of medicalization: medical authorities tend to favor constructing troubling conditions as medical problems that ought to be solved through medical solutions.

Ideologies are not unrelated to *interests*. Ideologies allow individuals to appeal to principles, such as equality, liberty, or women's rights, to argue that these values *should* guide how society responds to troubling conditions (for example, a liberal might criticize a particular social policy because it fails to alleviate the inequalities at the root of the troubling condition, and a conservative policy critique might focus on how the policy unreasonably constrains people's liberty). In other words, ideologies allow their adherents to construct principled arguments, to claim that this is the right thing to do because it is consistent with a particular value. At the same time, people frequently adopt ideologies that support their interests (for example, a large share of feminists are women whose interests the ideology advances, just as medical authorities often stand to benefit from medicalizing troubling conditions). The link between ideology and interest creates rhetorical opportunities for those who oppose a particular ideology: they can charge that proponents of a particular claim may be motivated less by a principled sense of what is right than by their self-interest, by the advantages they stand to gain if their claims succeed.

The tendency for ideological critiques to invoke values creates a range of questions that might be addressed in policy debates. On the one hand, critics can focus on practical questions: Is the policy effective? Does it do what we want it to do? Does it work better or cost less than alternative policies? On the other hand, critics can emphasize principles: Is this policy consistent with important values? Is it morally sound? Is it the sort of thing we ought to be doing? Policy debates often conflate these two approaches, so that opponents denounce one another's practical claims as being unprincipled, while rejecting the opposition's principled claims as impractical. Of course, an inability to agree on the questions that ought to be asked virtually guarantees that people will be unable to agree on the answers.

Ideologies, then, can be seen as predisposing how people may respond to policy outcomes. When people are allied with particular ideological stances—whether of a political, professional, or other nature—it is often possible to predict how these individuals will respond to a particular social policy. Those whose ideology led them to favor the policy in the first place are likely to claim that any shortcomings are due to the policy's being insufficient, and to argue for expanding or extending the policy to make up this shortfall. In contrast, those who stood ideologically opposed to the initial policy are more likely to claim that the policy is excessive or misguided, that it needs to be cut back or redirected. Although ideologies do not control how everyone approaches policy outcomes, they often shape the responses of at least some participants in the discussions (see Box 9.7).

Once again we see the subjective nature of the social problems process. Just as claimsmakers must construct troubling conditions so that people become concerned enough to do something, and just as policymakers and social problems workers must construct practical responses to that concern, so, too, must critics devise interpretations of the workings of policies. They may decide that a policy is a great success (remember granting women the vote; no one now advocates disenfranchising women), or they may decide that it works pretty well and just needs a bit of fine-tuning (maybe we ought to install another traffic light at that dangerous intersection). Or, of course, some people may argue that the policy isn't working all that well and that we ought to do significantly more, or maybe a lot less, or perhaps something completely different. At the stage of policy outcomes, the social problems process comes to an end—unless it inspires an entirely new round of claimsmaking.

Box 9.7 Recycling's Tangled Roots

At the end of World War II, the vast majority of bottled soft drinks and beer was sold in reusable glass bottles; purchasers paid a deposit that would be refunded upon returning the empty bottle. It was more expensive for bottlers to collect, clean, and reuse the bottles than to sell beverages in disposable cans or plastic bottles. However, many people simply threw these unreturnable containers away, creating litter. Legislatures sought to pass laws to make the bottlers responsible for collecting disposables.

The beverage industry first responded to these efforts by promoting a Keep America Beautiful campaign against litter that portrayed litter's cause as thoughtless, irresponsible individuals failing to dispose of cans and bottles properly, as opposed to industry producing ever more single-use containers. Of course, those cans and bottles had to go somewhere.

The beverage industry threw its support behind recycling and encouraged municipalities to establish curbside recycling programs, in which citizens would put their waste out to be collected for processing. Note that the costs of managing the waste are then shifted to local governments; paying for dealing with the packaging that industry produces becomes the public's problem.

Waste disposal policies continue to be debated. Plastics are slow to degrade. Critics worry that there is a shortage of space for waste-disposal sites, and much waste is disposed of at sea (where giant "islands" of plastic waste are found floating in some places). There are a few campaigns to encourage producers and consumers to return to reusable packaging, but addressing waste-disposal policies and promoting alternatives are likely to continue to be debated.

Source: Jaeger, 2018.

MAKING CONNECTIONS

- Policy outcomes are reactions to policies after they have been implemented by social problems workers. However, as this chapter and Chapter 11 explain, the social problems process is cyclical, so policy outcomes become the basis for new claims.

- Social problems workers can become compelling critics of policies. As Chapter 8 explained, they understand how social problems work is actually practiced and see policy flaws firsthand.

- Both activists and experts frequently use typifying examples (discussed in Chapter 2) to make new claims that criticize policies.

CASE STUDY
WALLS, DREAMERS, AND IMMIGRATION POLICIES

American immigration policy has a long, contentious history. Whenever immigrants seem ethnically, religiously, or culturally different from the current U.S. population, immigration becomes a subject of claimsmaking. In the decades before the Civil War, immigrants from Ireland were defined as troubling; in the late nineteenth and early twentieth century, the focus of opposition shifted to the "new immigrants" from Italy and elsewhere in Southern and Eastern Europe. Since World War II, the focus has turned to those from Mexico and more recently Central America.

Beginning during World War II, the bracero program offered migrant Mexican agricultural laborers guaranteed work permits to move across the border to pick crops in U.S. fields. They would save much of what they earned, and then bring that money back to their families in Mexico after the harvest. Most had no intention of settling in the United States. However, in 1965, immigration policy changed, so that it was no longer legal for these workers to come to the United States. Nonetheless, U.S. farmers needed laborers to work in their fields, and the workers needed income, so they continued making their annual trips across the border. Some officials considered this (now illegal) activity a problem, and they called for tighter border security. This crackdown made it harder—and therefore more costly—to cross the border (Massey, Durand, & Pren, 2016—see also Box 9.1). This had the ironic consequence of convincing some immigrants to settle in the United States, rather than taking their chances crossing the border each year; increasingly, they brought their families so that they could stay together. This fostered the perception that illegal immigration was an ever-bigger problem, requiring tighter enforcement, which in turn raised the costs of crossing the border and encouraged even more migrants to settle in the United States.

Over the years, advocates have called for a variety of policy shifts. In 1986, there was an effort to deal with the growing undocumented population by (a) creating a path to citizenship for those already residing in the United States, while (b) declaring that future undocumented immigrants would be turned away (Bilderback, 1989). The latter objective was to be accomplished by still tougher border control measures, which had the effect of shifting border crossing into even more remote locations. This cycle—cracking down on the immigrants' favored routes, causing them to take more remote, less heavily policed routes (and then, once in the United States, settling down), which led to yet even tougher crackdowns—failed to resolve the problem.

As the new century began, President George W. Bush proposed a program that would have given legal status to people already in the United States, increased resources to fight illegal immigration, but allowed foreign workers to receive passes as guest workers (which basically would have reinvented the older bracero system). However, this proposal proved to be unpopular within his own party; many congressional Republicans insisted that illegal immigration needed to be halted, not encouraged, and the bill failed to pass.

During Barack Obama's presidency, the issue was partially reconstructed by focusing attention on young people, children of undocumented workers who had crossed the border with their families and been raised in the United States. In some cases, they had spent most of their lives in the United States, attending American schools, perhaps not even aware that they were undocumented. However, as they approached adulthood, they discovered that because they were not citizens, they might be blocked from jobs, further education, and so on. A campaign emphasized their sympathetic qualities, portraying them as talented young people, ready—but unable—to contribute to the country where they had been raised. They were named Dreamers (for the Development, Relief, and Education of Alien Minors Act—a name chosen to evoke the idea of the American Dream). Public opinion polls showed that there was considerable sympathy for their plight, but again there was congressional opposition (Doherty, 2018). In 2012, President Obama signed an executive order that allowed a two-year grace period from deportation in order to give Congress time to pass the bill, but this never happened, and at the time this was written in late 2019, the Dreamers' status remained uncertain.

During his 2016 presidential campaign, Donald Trump frequently promised to "build a wall" along the U.S.–Mexico border. Once he became president, he continued to warn about the threat of illegal immigration, and called for tougher measures. These included making it much more difficult for individuals to apply for refugee status, and separating undocumented immigrant parents and their children. The administration warned that the caravans of would-be refugees from Central America were marching toward the border and promised increased border security measures. This exacerbated the more enforcement–more illegal immigration–more enforcement cycle, but there was now a new factor: social media. Undocumented individuals residing in the United States could contact their friends and relatives via social media to warn that they ought to come right away, before additional border security measures would make the trip even more difficult. The political debate became increasingly acrimonious, with the president insisting there was a border crisis, and Congress refusing to spend billions for a wall.

Why has this policy issue been so difficult to resolve? Immigrants have always traveled to the United States to improve their lot, and those living in places offering few economic opportunities assume that they will be able to find work in America. In general, this is correct; many U.S. industries beyond agriculture employ large numbers of undocumented workers. While politicians often have been willing to pay for border enforcement, they have been reluctant to aggressively act to punish employers who hire workers without documentation. There are then both supply (of people who believe they can improve their lives) and demand (employers eager to hire undocumented workers) factors that guarantee there will be people hoping to cross the border.

It is worth remembering that this debate about policy outcomes has been continuing for more than half a century (the story is actually far more complicated than these few pages can summarize). Basically, there has been a prolonged debate between two critiques. The first critique argues that immigration policy has been insufficient, that undocumented people entering the country are simply breaking laws, and it calls for making law enforcement tougher—put more border enforcement officers on the job, give them a bigger budget, build larger barriers, and so on. This is very much the sort of solution people worried about other types of crime call for—more cops enforcing laws with harsher penalties. It also is the reasoning that led to war after war against drugs, with people arguing that if these efforts hadn't succeeded, they needed to be redoubled. The second critique argues that the policy is misguided and that it ignores the supply and demand factors that cause immigration, while tougher enforcement actually has the ironic quality of encouraging more people to attempt to cross the border and discouraging them from returning to their home countries. Again, this is analogous to critiques of drug wars that point to the causes that lead people to choose to use drugs, with advocates arguing that social policies should be aimed at reducing those causes, rather than simply focusing on punishing the drug use.

Such policy outcome debates are difficult to resolve because the participants construct the problem—and the effects of existing policies—in very different ways.

QUESTIONS

1. When policies don't succeed, why do proponents often insist that the fault lies in the policies being insufficient?

2. Does looking at the history of anti-immigration movements offer any lessons?

3. How should policymakers evaluate immigration policies?

10

Claims across Space and Time

The previous chapters have traced a six-stage social problems process from (1) the initial claimsmaking, through (2) media coverage, (3) public reaction, and (4) policymaking, and on to (5) the social problems work that implements the policy, followed by (6) policy outcomes. This sequence of stages should be seen as the natural history that a typical social problem might follow. To be sure, not every social problem fits the pattern exactly. Most important, many claims fail: they don't attract media attention, or they don't lead to public concern, or they don't lead to policy changes, or the policies are never implemented. The model of a six-stage sequence that has guided this book depicts a successful campaign to draw attention to a particular troubling condition and to get the larger society to try to do something about it. Other claims may follow different trajectories, but the model remains a useful framework for understanding the course taken by many of the claims that have the greatest impact.

There are, however, additional complexities that require some attention. Thus far, we have been thinking about social problems one at a time: here is how the U.S. Bureau of Narcotics constructed marijuana as a social problem in the 1930s, here is how today's authorities are constructing the crystal meth problem, and so on. Such **case studies** are useful, but it seems obvious that the marijuana and crystal meth cases might have some important features in common, even though they occurred decades apart. After all, both cases involve claims that a particular drug is harmful and ought to be prohibited. This similarity raises important questions: Are such drug problems constructed completely independently; that is, does each set of claimsmakers start from scratch in assembling its claims, and do policymakers adopt a fresh approach each time they encounter claims about a new drug problem? Or are there underlying similarities in the way drug problems and drug policies are constructed, and if so, what are they, and why do they occur? Does the history of previous claims about drugs affect current claimsmaking? Do claims about similar troubling conditions always take the same form, or are they affected by the social circumstances in which they emerge?

This chapter explores some of these issues; in particular, it considers how claims vary from place to place, and from time to time. It begins with comparative research in which analysts compare what happens when claimsmakers raise claims about the same troubling condition in different places—in different cities, or in different countries. Then it examines diffusion, the way claims spread from one place to another. The third section of the chapter asks how claims evolve over time; it explores apparently cyclical claims—issues that attract considerable attention for a time, then fade from notice, only to be revived in a new wave of claimsmaking. The chapter concludes with a discussion of progress: claimsmakers often warn that things are getting worse, but is envisioning societal decay the best framework for thinking about social problems?

COMPARISON

Usually sociologists who study the construction of social problems conduct case studies (J. Best, 2015). That is, they examine one instance, one case of the social problems process—how and why a particular problem was constructed in a given place at a given time. In fact, many studies focus on specific aspects of a particular case, so different analyses of the same case might consider, for example, just how the claims' rhetoric was assembled to make a persuasive argument, who made those claims, or how the media covered the topic.

The main advantage of the case study is that it permits a careful, detailed analysis of how one particular instance of the social problems process developed. Most of the points raised in the earlier chapters of this book are the product of sociologists' case studies, and a large share of the sources cited in this volume's references present such case studies. But case studies have a major disadvantage: there is no way of knowing whether the case being studied is fairly typical or quite unusual. Throughout this book we have been discussing things that can happen during the construction of social problems. When we first diagrammed the social problems process in Figure 1.1, the picture seemed simple and straightforward. But later chapters featured more detailed, more complicated diagrams of the various stages in the social problems process. These complications reveal that not all social problems follow exactly the same trajectory; there are important differences in how social problems can develop, so the particular case being studied may not always be all that typical.

The simplest way to study such differences is to compare two cases that we might expect to be fairly similar. For example, Cynthia Bogard (2003) examined how the problem of homelessness was constructed in two major American cities—New York City and Washington, D.C.—during the early 1980s. She found important differences. In Washington, activists—a self-styled group of "Christian anarchists"—promoted homelessness as a moral issue; they devised clever protests designed to attract media attention (in a city filled with media workers), and they sought to involve nationally prominent politicians in the issue. While acknowledging that many homeless individuals were troubled by mental illness or substance abuse, the Washington activists constructed the homeless as rational figures who would stop living on the streets if only they had access to safe, nonintrusive shelters. In contrast, in New York City the issue of homelessness centered around a struggle between city and state officials over who ought to be held responsible for the condition—and pay the costs of fixing it. The state blamed the city for encouraging gentrification that had eliminated low-cost housing units and thereby had made their former residents homeless; the city, on the other hand, insisted that many of the homeless were seriously mentally ill individuals who now found themselves on the streets after the state had closed many of its mental hospitals. In New York, the homeless were typified as incapable of caring for themselves, and as a threat to public order. In short, the two cities featured different claimsmakers, with different interests, who constructed the homelessness problem in different ways.

Bogard's study shows that, even in dealing with the same problem during the same years, the social problems process can develop along different paths—with different claims made by different claimsmakers leading to different policies. There are all sorts of possible bases for making such comparisons:

- *Geography.* Bogard compared the social problems process in two cities, but it is possible to compare other geographic entities. Most obviously, analysts can compare how the same troubling condition is addressed in two or more countries (J. Best, 2001a).

- *Time.* Many social conditions have been around for a long time, so it is possible to compare two or more efforts to construct the same social problem in the same place during different times. For example, there have been a series of anticult campaigns in American history (Jenkins, 2000).

- *Similar conditions.* Some troubling conditions are understood to belong to the same category of social problems, so the basis for comparison seems obvious. For example, there are parallels in the ways that different drugs have been constructed as social problems (Reinarman, 1994).

- *Similar constructions.* Sometimes analysts compare problems that seem to be constructed with similar claimsmaking rhetoric. For instance, freeway shootings, stalking, and other crimes characterized as "random violence" can be compared, as can how claimsmakers construct different problems that involve "victimization" (J. Best, 1999).

- *Other bases for comparison.* Analysts might compare different campaigns by the same claimsmakers (for instance, examining how feminists—or medical authorities—construct various social problems), how different media construct the same problem, and so on. The bases for comparison are limited only by the analysts' imagination.

Figure 10.1 illustrates some of these forms of comparison among social problems processes. The top of the figure displays one six-stage social problems process (for a particular problem—call it Problem X). The same process is shown in reduced size at the center of the figure, where it is surrounded by other social problems processes that suggest various bases for comparison between the construction of Problem X and the construction of other social problems. Note that it is not necessary to compare the entire sequences of stages in two social problems processes; a sociologist might focus on comparing particular, even very narrowly defined topics (such as the use of statistics in two claimsmaking campaigns).

Comparison is a powerful method of analysis because it can help us discover both underlying similarities and unexpected differences. People involved in the social problems process sometimes assume that things have to be the way they are; they take it for granted that the problem pretty much has to be constructed in the terms with which they're familiar. One of the most important lessons from comparing social problems processes is that whatever we understand about social problems is a product of people's choices, that people—claimsmakers, media workers, policymakers, social problems workers, and so on—have chosen to highlight some aspects

Figure 10.1 BASES FOR COMPARISON AMONG SOCIAL PROBLEMS PROCESSES

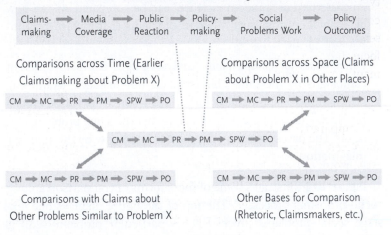

Social Problems Process Concerning Problem X

Claims-making → Media Coverage → Public Reaction → Policy-making → Social Problems Work → Policy Outcomes

Comparisons across Time (Earlier Claimsmaking about Problem X)

CM → MC → PR → PM → SPW → PO

Comparisons across Space (Claims about Problem X in Other Places)

CM → MC → PR → PM → SPW → PO

CM → MC → PR → PM → SPW → PO

CM → MC → PR → PM → SPW → PO

CM → MC → PR → PM → SPW → PO

Comparisons with Claims about Other Problems Similar to Problem X

Other Bases for Comparison (Rhetoric, Claimsmakers, etc.)

of a troubling condition while downplaying others. It can be hard to notice what those people have ignored, but comparisons often can help us recognize that choices were made, and to ask how and why those proved to be the favored choices.

Consider the issue of sexual harassment. Americans take it for granted that sexual harassment is a type of gender discrimination, and that it should be defined broadly to encompass not only demands for sexual favors but also inappropriate joking and other behaviors that create a "hostile environment" (Saguy, 2003). In France, however, sexual harassment has been defined not only more narrowly (encompassing only demands for sex), but also very differently (as sexual violence involving the abuse of hierarchical authority). These different definitions evolved through different processes: in the United States, court rulings gradually established the domain of sexual harassment; in France, courts cannot establish the law, so an act of Parliament was required—which was important because policymakers had to find a legislative consensus, and there was not enough support for a broader definition of what constituted sexual harassment. Press coverage also differed in the two countries. The American press devoted a large share of its coverage to scandals—claims implicating prominent politicians in sexual harassment. In contrast, considerable French media coverage focused on the "excesses" of *Americans'* treatment of sexual harassment; commentators argued that France should avoid copying the Americans' example. In other words, there were numerous differences in how sexual harassment was constructed in the two nations.

Comparative studies often reveal such differences in how social problems are constructed, even when we might imagine that the issue would have to be constructed in the same way (see Box 10.1). If cell phones pose a threat of exposure to radioactivity, as some claimsmakers suggest, presumably the physical processes that produce those risks ought to be the same everywhere, exposing cell phone users throughout the world to the same dangers. Yet different countries construct health risks from cell phones in very different ways (Burgess, 2004). Comparative analyses, then, can expose the social processes that underpin the construction of even physical threats. Risks of radioactivity—usually thought of as understandable in terms of physics and biology—are socially constructed, as are all other social problems. Comparative research can help make such social processes visible.

DIFFUSION

Comparative studies reveal that the social problems process can lead to different outcomes in different places: two countries may construct a given problem in much the same way; or they may construct that problem in rather—sometimes dramatically—different terms; or one country may define the troubling condition as a big

Box 10.1 Reducing the Official Crime Rate in Guangzhou, China

What might seem to be a fairly standard practice—such as police reporting crime rates—can vary from time to time and place to place. As Guangzhou (a major city in southern China) prepared to host the 2010 Asian Games, the Chinese government sought to make the city a more attractive destination for foreign tourists. There was an effort to demonstrate that the city's crime rates were falling so that the city would seem safe. The crime rate was an important quantitative performance evaluation measure used to assess local police stations, so officers were under pressure to show that they were reducing crime. As a result, police officials sought to manipulate the crime rate in various ways.

In particular, citizens were encouraged *not* to call 110 (the number used to make an official report—equivalent to calling 911 in the United States), because crimes reported through 110 calls were counted when calculating the crime rate. Instead, police urged people to call other numbers to report a crime (which would bring the problem to their attention without registering in the crime statistics). In some cases, citizens were even warned that they would be fined if they called 110 to report a crime.

The campaign worked: the official crime rate fell, even during a period when surveys that asked people whether they had been victimized by a crime showed a substantial increase in the rate of criminal victimization. The lower official crime rate did not merely help make Guangzhou appear to be a more attractive tourist destination, but it also served to legitimize the government by providing evidence that it was doing a good job of protecting and serving the citizenry, and of course those police officials whose units had produced the best numbers could expect to have their effectiveness rewarded with promotions.

Source: Xu, 2018.

deal, while the other may dismiss it as unworthy of concern (see Box 10.2). However, it is especially interesting when a problem attracts attention in different places at about the same time. Although it is possible that the social problems processes in different countries are completely independent, unrelated to one another, another possibility is that claims have spread from one country to another, and we can study this process (J. Best, 2001a).

Diffusion is the term used by social scientists to describe the spread of innovations. New things—new ideas, new inventions, and so on—emerge in particular places, but then they spread from one group to another. If one group figures out a better way to, say, make arrowheads, that group's neighbors may copy or adopt the method for their own benefit. The process of diffusion involves sources, or **transmitters**, passing the innovation along to **adopters**. Successful innovations can spread across many societies and over thousands of miles.

Diffusion can occur in the case of social problems claims. A claim may originate in a particular town, region, or country but then spread to other places. Not all claims experience diffusion, and of those that do spread, some travel farther and more widely than others. What accounts for these differences?

All social problems claims argue that a particular condition exists and that it is troubling. Successful diffusion of a claim requires that adopters accept that these basic ideas apply to the adopters' setting—their community or nation. Certainly diffusion requires accepting the notion that the condition exists; a society whose members doubt the existence of a condition is unlikely to be receptive to claims about that problem. For instance, being worried about witches requires that people believe in witches; regardless of how worried about witches a society of believers may become, they will find it hard to spread their concern to a society of nonbelievers. Similarly, the condition must be seen as troubling: a society with a traditional aristocracy might view a decline in deference as quite troubling, but their claims probably would have little appeal for

Box 10.2 Conserving Birds in Britain and Germany

The rise of ecological thinking drew attention to the importance of different species—including birds. However, birds' value could be constructed in different ways. In Germany, birds were defined primarily as a valuable agricultural resource because birds ate insects that might otherwise devastate crops. The German government funded projects to build birdhouses in agricultural regions; people had jobs protecting birds.

In contrast, the British Royal Society for the Protection of Birds (RSPB) built bird policy around play, around birding, the hobby of birdwatching. The membership of the RSPB has grown fairly steadily as increasing numbers of people have discovered they enjoy it. They've become an interest group that affects environmental policy. Birders compile lists of the species they've spotted; adding rarer species to one's list is exciting. This means that birders value species diversity, and the RSPB began campaigns to preserve areas that provided habitat for species that seemed endangered by human development. Expanding the numbers of birders meant that there were more people enjoying birds and endorsing policies that would protect birds.

As agricultural pesticides became more common, Germans shifted their emphasis. Birds no longer seemed vital to efforts to control insect populations, and there were now efforts to emulate the British model, to foster the spread of birdwatching so that policies to preserve bird habitat and protect bird populations would have broader support. As this example shows, policies that seem to share a purpose, such as protecting bird populations, may have roots in very different constructions of why this purpose is important, and how those policies should work.

Source: Bargheer, 2018.

members of democratic societies, who might agree that the condition exists but view this as a cause for celebration rather than concern.

For a claim to spread from one society to another, then, potential adopters of the claim must come from cultures and social structures that allow them to recognize both that their society has the condition about which claims are being made, and that the condition is troubling. This means that claims are less likely to spread to societies very different from those in which the claims originated. In particular, adopters need to view their society as similar to the society where the claims originated (Strang & Meyer, 1993). When similarities are harder to recognize, diffusion becomes less likely.

For example, it is easier for social problems claims to spread among countries with a common language and interwoven histories. In recent decades, many successful claimsmaking campaigns have originated in the United States and then spread to England, Australia, and Canada (for instance, concerns about satanic ritual abuse traveled from the United States to all three other English-speaking countries). In addition, claims that originated in those countries have traveled to the United States (concern about both bullying and road rage, for example, spread from Britain to the United States) (J. Best, 2001a). On the other hand, American constructions of social problems often meet resistance in France; French media tend to criticize American policies and present alternative constructions for social issues such as sexual harassment, immigration, or obesity (Benson, 2013; Saguy, 2003, 2013).

Diffusion must occur through channels; that is, there need to be links, connections between potential transmitters and prospective adopters. Theorists of diffusion make an analytic distinction between **relational channels** involving interpersonal contact between transmitters and adopters, and **nonrelational channels**, such as mass media, that do not involve personal ties (McAdam & Rucht, 1993). In practice, the diffusion of claims usually combines both relational and nonrelational channels. Through informal ties (such as acquaintanceship) and more formal ties (such as memberships in the same professional organizations), people in different countries get to know one another well enough to establish relational channels: this person got to know foreigners while attending school abroad; these folks met at international conferences for police officers, or social workers, or whatever.

At the same time, information about social problems flows through nonrelational channels—through the press and entertainment media, through books and news broadcasts and the Internet. Relational and nonrelational channels are mutually reinforcing. Once again, it should be clear that a common language makes it easier for diffusion to occur through both sorts of channels. Translating claims into another tongue takes time; claims can travel faster when transmitters and adopters share a language.

All diffusion ultimately depends on the actors in the process—the transmitters and, especially, the adopters. Transmitters may make deliberate efforts to disseminate social problems claims to other countries. Drawing attention to troubling conditions is, of course, central to social problems claimsmaking, and some claimsmakers explicitly seek to spread their message to other nations. This is particularly true when claims depict large-scale, even global problems, such as population growth, ecological degradation, or economic globalization. Such claimsmakers become missionaries, seeking to spread their message abroad, through both relational and nonrelational channels. International social movements, for example, offer a way of spreading claims about troubling conditions to countries that might be expected to resist those claims.

In other cases, transmitters are more passive; their concern may be limited to their own country, even to a particular locality; they make no effort to promote the diffusion of their claims. Still, their claims may reach other countries, particularly via such nonrelational channels as media coverage, professional publications, and the like. Nonetheless, the key actors in diffusion are adopters. Prospective adopters must define conditions in their society as being sufficiently like those depicted in the transmitters' claims before they will join in spreading those claims.

Of course, societies have differences as well as similarities. There are likely to be both cultural differences (people in the transmitting society and those in the prospective adopting society are likely to construct the world in at least somewhat different terms), as well as differences in social arrangements (such as different legal or educational systems). Such differences are potential obstacles to diffusion; they make it easier for prospective adopters to conclude that a particular claim is not really applicable to their society. For example, tobacco smoking is much more common among males in Japan than in the United States or Western Europe (Ayukawa, 2019). Whereas other countries' governments have launched vigorous public health campaigns to reduce smoking, Japan has been slower to take such actions. Why? In Japan, the government has a stake in tobacco distribution and derives considerable revenue from smokers. Also, it is hard to mobilize social movements in Japan to campaign against government interests. What is—and what is not—considered a social problem depends on a society's culture and social structure.

Therefore, diffusion is easier when claims are phrased in relatively abstract or theoretical language. **Theorization** is the presentation of claims that emphasize general, abstract principles and arguments: for instance, claimsmakers might describe sexism generally in terms of male, or patriarchal, domination rather than in terms of specific discriminatory practices; the former construction offers a general principle that might be detected at work in many different social settings, whereas the latter may seem applicable only in countries where those particular practices are common—and seen as troubling (Strang & Meyer, 1993). Theorization abstracts and simplifies. In the case of social problems claims, theorization smooths out the argument. It reduces specifics of limited, local relevance and rephrases the claim in broader, more general terms that make it more widely acceptable. The theoretical becomes significant; the practical, less important. Thus, a theorized claim is more easily spread to new societies, where it can be reformulated to take local culture and social structure into account.

As a result, claims about the same social problem often take somewhat different forms, depending on the social arrangements in different societies (see Box 10.3). In some cases, differences in social arrangements may make it hard for claims to travel successfully. In recent years, for example, British claimsmakers have focused on various types of bullying—not just bullying in schools, but also bullying in other settings, including the workplace (Furedi, 2001). The British campaign against workplace bullying received considerable support from that country's powerful trade unions. In contrast, efforts to construct workplace bullying as a problem in the United States (where unions are less influential) have been markedly less successful. The abstract—and already familiar—problem of bullying (particularly among children) spread easily, but the more specific construction of workplace bullying did not. Similarly, the abortion issue evolved differently in the United States and Britain (Lee, 2003). British law has long regarded abortion as a medical matter, subject to physicians' authority, but Americans have come to view it as a question of rights.

Contemporary commentators argue that globalization has become a central concept for understanding the world. Countries are increasingly linked through trade, rapid transportation, and essentially instantaneous communications. Money and jobs—but also ideas—flow more freely across international borders. This means that the future is likely to feature even more diffusion of social problems claims. In part, this is because some claimsmakers seek to construct global issues such as climate change or terrorism. In part, it is because some troubling conditions, such as epidemic disease, may start in one corner of the world yet spread great distances. In addition to these considerations, however, improved communications (such as through the World Wide Web) give people around the world access to claims made in distant places, and at least some of those claims will be theorized in terms that make it easier for them to spread.

Box 10.3 Polish Campaigns against Drug Addiction

From the end of World War II until 1989, Poland was a Soviet satellite. The government denied that illicit drug use occurred, or blamed it on the corrupting influence of the "capitalist West." After Poland broke free and established a democracy, it became necessary to reconstruct all manner of troubling conditions, including drug addiction.

Poland's National Bureau for Drug Prevention was established in 1993. One of its tasks was to create public information campaigns to try to discourage illicit drug use. An analysis of several of these campaigns shows that they construct the issue somewhat narrowly. The campaigns ignore the views of drug users, and argue that drugs are a mistaken choice and that participation in modern society requires people to be rational, active, and independent and to manage their irrational drives by avoiding risky situations. The choice—drugs/no drugs—is framed as clear-cut. (Similar arguments are used in campaigns warning about Internet addiction.) There is also an emphasis on communities and families uniting to prevent their youth from making bad choices.

Emerging from Soviet control meant becoming a modern, democratic state. Citizens were encouraged to think of themselves as modern—as responsible, rational, self-regulating individuals who could and would make rational choices that would prove them worthy of being part of the new, modern Poland. In contrast, antidrug campaigns in the United States tend to adopt more emotional imagery and to make decisions about drug use seem less clear-cut.

Source: Kowal-Bourgonjon & Jacobs, 2019.

CYCLES IN CLAIMSMAKING

Early in the social problems process, it is very common for claimsmaking rhetoric to describe a troubling condition as new, or at least as deserving new concern because the condition is growing much worse. After the issue begins to attract more attention and people want to know more about it, there may be an effort to trace the troubling condition's history. For instance, claims about child abuse might include brief historical accounts stating that although adults have abused children for centuries, we now know better; or a history of poverty might argue that previous efforts to eliminate poverty have been misguided, and that a totally new approach is needed. Even the most unlikely topics, such as Columbus and noise, can have elaborate histories of claimsmaking (Kubal, 2008; Schwartz, 2011). Still, claimsmakers tend to focus most intensely on the troubling condition's current manifestations, rather than on its distant past. Most claims concentrate on the present situation and pay relatively little attention to the past; to the degree they do remember an issue's history, they may simplify it.

This narrow focus is unfortunate, because careful study of the history of a social issue can often place today's claims within an illuminating context (see Box 10.4). In particular, many troubling conditions are the focus of *cycles* of concern. That is, a troubling condition may become the focus of intense claimsmaking, then slip out of the spotlight for a while before returning as the focus of renewed attention.

A cycle of concern begins when a troubling condition that has been receiving little attention becomes the subject of claimsmaking (Downs, 1972). As a result, concern increases until it reaches a peak, then interest falls off once more, until the topic is again attracting little notice. This cycle is another way of thinking about the social problems process: attention increases as claimsmakers, the media, the public, policymakers, and social problems workers become involved. But why does interest decline? Why doesn't it remain high? Why are there cycles of concern?

Part of the answer is that the social problems process values novelty. Claims that seem new or fresh compete more easily in the social problems marketplace to attract attention from the media, the public, and policymakers. This is why claimsmakers who come

Box 10.4 Reading as a Social Problem

For most of history, literacy was rare, and literate members of the elite worried that spreading literacy might destabilize existing social arrangements by exposing people to new ideas. Before the printing press, books were very rare, and clerical claimsmakers opposed allowing laypeople to read the Bible, lest their interpretations challenge the Church's teachings. Of course, printing allowed for the reproduction of many copies of, not just Bibles, but all manner of other texts, and claims shifted to warnings about the dangers of the population being corrupted by messages in this new medium. Young readers were seen as especially vulnerable to exposure to these dangerous influences.

Because we live in a society where literacy is understood to be an essential skill for everyone, these claims about the dangers posed by reading strike us as ridiculous. But notice the parallels with the sorts of claims made whenever new media for imparting information emerge. At various times, new forms of printed works, including translations of the Bible, novels, newspapers, magazines, dime novels, and comic books, have been subjects of suspicion, with claimsmakers worrying about the moral corruption they might cause. And, of course, similar claims have targeted other new media, including telephones, movies, radio, pinball games, television, video games, cell phones, the Internet, smartphones, and social media. In each case, claimsmakers have worried that the established moral order might be in danger. Often, their claims have focused on particular types of content, such as new musical styles such as jazz, rock, or hip hop, or content that features sexual or violent images, with their concern often centered on the potential harms to youth.

Source: Furedi, 2016.

to own particular issues find it necessary to constantly update and repackage their claims (as discussed in Chapter 3). But even when claimsmakers work to keep an issue visible, they find themselves at an increasing disadvantage because other, competing claims that seek to draw attention to topics that have been neglected are likely to seem more novel. The fact that a particular claim has been occupying center stage for a while begins to make other claims seem fresher, more interesting, particularly to the media, which depend so heavily on presenting novel material (see Chapter 5). In addition, as noted in Chapters 8 and 9, once the social problems process reaches the stage of social problems work, there is likely to be some disillusionment. Very often the policies touted as the solution to the problem haven't caused the problem to disappear; instead, the troubling condition endures, and people begin losing their enthusiasm for those policies.

All of this means that however successful claimsmakers have been in managing to raise concern about a particular troubling condition, that concern eventually is likely to decline, so the issue moves out of the limelight. However, that need not be the end of the matter; once enough time has passed, the previous wave of concern is likely to be forgotten, thanks to all of the competing claimsmaking campaigns that have captured the attention of the social problems marketplace in the meantime. Conditions may once more become ripe for drawing attention to what now again seems to be a neglected topic. Therefore, we should not be surprised to discover that the histories of many social problems display sequential waves of concern interspersed with periods when the topic receives relatively little attention.

For example, consider three waves of intense concern about delinquent gangs—youth gangs—in twentieth-century America. The first began in the 1920s, the second in the 1950s, and the third in the 1980s. Each period was marked by warnings that today's gangs were much worse—larger, better organized, more dangerous—than gangs in previous eras. Each wave featured claimsmaking by experts, such as sociologists, psychiatrists, and criminologists; each became the subject of both sensational news coverage and popular cultural depictions of gangs. Nor did these waves begin in the twentieth century; waves of concern about gangs date back to the 1840s in U.S. cities, and to the eighteenth century in London (Pearson, 1983).

We can spot similar sequential waves of concern regarding many other issues. The historian Philip Jenkins has described the oscillating attention given to the sexual exploitation of children (Jenkins, 1998) and to cults (Jenkins, 2000). The pattern turns up in surprising places; for example, Christian theologians periodically direct their attention to claims that there are "hidden gospels"— ancient manuscripts that were suppressed by religious authorities because they reveal that Christ's true message was antithetical to what the established church now endorses (Jenkins, 2001).

In each of these cases, a new set of claims attracts a great deal of attention for a time, but then concern begins to dissipate. When claimsmaking on the topic revives, usually people pay little attention to the previous wave of concern. The older set of claims— and the intense concern it generated—is often forgotten, as a new generation of claimsmakers reinvents the wheel. Even if the earlier claims are recalled, they tend to be dismissed: those people in the "good old days" may have thought they had a gang problem, but their gangs were nothing compared with ours.

What accounts for these waves of concern? One possibility, of course, is that the troubling conditions criticized by claimsmakers become more or less common over time, and claimsmaking merely tracks these shifts. Perhaps gang membership actually rises and falls in different historical periods. However, it is impossible to document such changes. There are probably always some gangs operating, but there is no long-term measure of such activity; in particular, in periods when gangs aren't a focus of attention, it is unlikely that anyone is charting gang involvement. When gangs attract concern, we have no way of being sure that the reason for the concern is that they have become more active.

Another possibility is that dramatic events attract media and public attention to particular social issues. For example, Jenkins (1998) notes waves of great concern over sexual crimes against children (as well as periods of much lower concern about these crimes). To be sure, during the waves of concern, heavily publicized news reports described terrible sex crimes against children; however, there were similar reports during the periods of low concern. During the waves of high concern, such crimes were depicted as *instances* of the larger problem of sexual violence against children—proof that something needed to be done. In contrast, during the periods of low concern, press coverage of such terrible crimes treated them as aberrant, exceptional behavior—not as representative of a larger phenomenon. It is difficult to make a strong case that claimsmaking activity simply rises and falls along with the increases and declines of a potentially troubling condition.

How, then, should we understand these waves of concern? One clue is that some of the same issues—gangs, cults, sexual crimes against children, even hidden gospels—appear again and again. Such recurrence might seem only sensible; it doesn't seem surprising that people would worry about these topics. But such wavelike patterns seem more striking when we realize that they occur in other societies and involve constructions that strike us as peculiar, such as waves of concern about vampires in East Africa (White, 2000). The variation in the types of concerns that are prevalent in different societies suggests that certain problems may be particularly easy to construct in particular societies—that some combination of cultural and social structural arrangements may foster such recurring claims (see Box 10.5).

It may help to think of societies as having the equivalent of fault lines—or "axes of variation" (Erikson, 1976). That is, social arrangements can create tensions between groups—between youths and older adults, between immigrants and the native-born, and on and on. Such tensions can flare into claimsmaking whenever self-identified groups find themselves competing for scarce resources,

BOX 10.5 THE NEW METHAMPHETAMINE PROBLEM—AGAIN

Emphasizing the chemical composition and biological effects of drugs ignores the social processes by which they come to be seen as problematic. Consider the history of methamphetamine and related synthetic stimulants (Parsons, 2014). Benzedrine arrived in the United States in the 1930s. It was seen as a useful stimulant, and was given to everyone from troops in World War II to enhance their performance, to tired housewives. Under various names, it would continue to be prescribed to individuals who needed to stay alert.

However, methamphetamine has also been the target of waves of claimsmaking. In the late 1960s and early 1970s, it was demonized as *speed* (as in the slogan "Speed Kills"). "Speed freaks" were often typified as hippies who had moved on from hallucinogens to more dangerous drugs. Then, in the 1980s (when concern about crack cocaine was also peaking), claimsmakers worried about ice, which they characterized as more dangerous than crack. If crack was viewed as concentrated in black neighborhoods, ice was portrayed as spreading among whites. More recently, in the late 1990s, attention turned to *crystal meth*. At first, "tweakers" were seen as primarily a rural problem, although by the year 2000 claims linking meth with Mexican immigrants helped portray the drug as a national emergency. In other words, the same drug was repeatedly revived, given a new name, and presented as affecting some new population of users.

The history of methamphetamine, then, offers an especially clear example of a social problem being repeatedly constructed within just a few decades.

or whenever one group controls another's access to such resources. Claimsmaking is particularly likely to increase during periods of relative scarcity, when the competition between groups is more intense (see Box 10.6).

Such tensions can be expressed in lots of different ways. Probably most often, people complain about specific individuals or particular actions: "He shouldn't have done that!" But sometimes

Box 10.6 Two Cities Recover from Major Disasters

Nearly a century passed after the great earthquake of 1906 destroyed much of San Francisco until Hurricane Katrina flooded a large part of New Orleans—two emblematic disasters that severely damaged major American cities. While we might assume that social conditions would have changed markedly over the ninety-nine years between the two disasters, Steve Kroll-Smith (2018) identifies some key parallels in how the two cities dealt with these crises. He argues that both cities were organized around their capitalist markets, that both featured considerable racial and class inequalities, and that both sought to restore those social arrangements.

Although there is some evidence that people rallied together to help one another deal with the immediate fires and floods caused by the disasters, social divisions quickly reemerged as a central theme in recovery. Both cities had substantial ethnic minorities—Chinese laborers packed into Chinatown in San Francisco, poor African Americans in New Orleans—that were viewed as causing various social problems. In both cities, there were exaggerated claims that in the immediate aftermath of the crisis, the minority population had experienced a breakdown in law and order, with charges of looting and other criminal behavior.

Later, recovery efforts clearly sought to restore the privileges of some citizens, while placing obstacles in the way of poorer citizens receiving aid. Officials in San Francisco spoke openly about the desirability of not rebuilding Chinatown (which had been almost completely destroyed in the fire), while their counterparts in New Orleans were barely more discreet about suggesting that it might be good if many of the poor black citizens who had been forced to flee from the flooding chose to resettle in the places where they'd sought refuge. People may be at their best during a crisis, but once the immediate crisis ends, altruism can be in short supply.

tensions can be linked to larger claims so that particular actions are understood as instances of a more general, troubling condition. At any given moment we can imagine that tensions inspire countless grievances—what we might think of as potential claims. Whether any particular grievance starts a full-scale social problems process will depend on contingencies: whether the grievance can be packaged as a rhetorically powerful claim, whether claimsmakers can mobilize sufficient resources, the nature of the other claims currently competing in the social problems marketplace, and so on.

The level of tension along societal fault lines can be understood as another contingency. Periods of higher tension probably increase the receptivity of the press, the public, and policymakers to claims. In some cases, these claims may even—at first glance—seem oblique. Late nineteenth-century America, for instance, witnessed an active claimsmaking campaign against the English sparrow, a bird that had been imported to the United States in hopes that it would eat insects that infested urban areas (Fine & Christoforides, 1991). The sparrow was widely denounced in moralistic terms: it was lazy and dirty. The intensity of the antisparrow campaign seems surprising, until it is understood as part of the period's larger anti-immigrant claimsmaking. In the late nineteenth and early twentieth centuries, the United States was experiencing one of its periodic waves of opposition to immigration, and claims about the influx of a foreign bird paralleled worries about the country's ability to accommodate human immigrants. Although complaints about bird species aren't all that common, the larger tensions of the time gave the antisparrow claims visibility.

In addition to cycles of concern regarding particular issues, we can note periods when American society seems particularly open to claimsmaking. Three major periods of intense reform activity appear in U.S. history. First, in the decades preceding the Civil War (roughly 1830–60), there was considerable social movement activity: the abolitionist campaign to abolish slavery, of course, but also intense interest in women's rights, new religions, the temperance movement against strong drink, opposition to immigration (particularly focused on anti-Irish sentiments), and so on. Second, the late nineteenth/early twentieth-century period featured a revived women's movement, further opposition to immigration (particularly from southern and eastern Europe), prohibitionist campaigns against alcohol and other drugs, and all of the other causes associated with the Progressive Era. And more recently, beginning in the 1960s and continuing to the present, there has been intense claimsmaking regarding civil rights, women's rights, a war on drugs, renewed concern about immigration (now from Latin America and Asia), and many other issues.

A comparison of these three periods shows that concerns with such fault-line topics as race, women's issues, immigration, and drug use do not just recur, but tend to emerge at roughly the same times. This concurrence suggests that conditions in some historical periods seem to foster claimsmaking. We might speculate that the impending Civil War left people unsettled and more open to the social problems claims of the first period. In the more recent period—as noted in earlier chapters—a new media environment and increasingly sophisticated claimsmaking methods have helped foster contemporary claimsmaking. Again, examining the social problems process across time reveals surprising similarities and differences that can help us better understand our contemporary arrangements for constructing social problems.

THE PROBLEM OF PROGRESS

Comparisons of claims across time raise another comparative question: Do things ever get better? That is, can we speak of social progress, or are things actually getting worse? It seems possible to make a strong case that there has been progress on many fronts: During the twentieth century, life expectancy rose markedly (a newborn male's life expectancy—fourty-six years in 1900—rose to seventy-eight in 2010, the improvement for females was even greater, and life expectancies for nonwhites grew more than those of whites). The percentage of young people graduating from high school climbed (from about 6 percent in 1900 to, according to some calculations, over 80 percent in recent years). The right to vote became more widely available (in 1900, few women, few African Americans in the South, and no one aged eighteen to twenty could vote). And the standard of living improved (so that, for instance, access to indoor plumbing, electricity, and phone service—all relatively rare in 1900—became nearly universally available) (J. Best, 2001b; for an exhaustive review of the evidence for long-term progress, see Pinker, 2018). Isn't all this progress?

Most people would say yes, but claims about troubling conditions tend to accentuate the negative. Claimsmakers' rhetoric often insists that things are worse than they seem and that they are deteriorating, that real catastrophe lies ahead, that progress is only an illusion. Claimsmakers rarely speak of progress; they seem to fear that acknowledging societal improvements may encourage complacency and discourage taking the actions needed to address troubling conditions. This worry is understandable: it is probably harder to arouse concern about a troubling condition if people are focused on how much things have improved. In addition, however, four aspects of the culture and organization of claimsmaking make it easier to downplay progress:

1. *Perfectibility.* Claimsmakers often invoke **perfectibility** as a standard. They declare that they won't settle for improving a particular troubling condition—that they are determined to eradicate the problem. As noted in Chapter 7, policymakers often "declare war" on social problems: heavily publicized wars have focused on such problems as poverty, cancer, drugs, and most recently, terrorism (J. Best, 1999). Similarly, education policy promises to "leave no child behind." But perfection is a very high standard; as long as one child is doing poorly in school, or one person is poor, there will be room for improvement—and therefore continued opportunities for claimsmaking.

2. *Proportion.* As big problems disappear, relatively smaller problems seem proportionally bigger than before. In 1900, many of the most

common causes of death were infectious diseases. Vaccinations and antibiotics caused many of these threats to virtually vanish. Still, everyone is going to die from some cause, so attention can now focus on potentially fatal diseases—such as breast cancer—that received relatively little attention when influenza, pneumonia, and diphtheria were killing far more people. Similarly, ending the worst forms of racial inequality (such as lynching and institutionalized segregation in the South) allows attention to focus on those less violent, less systematic forms of racism that remain. This means that claimsmakers need never run out of conditions that might be constructed as social problems.

3. *Proliferation.* Contemporary society encourages the proliferation of social problems claims. Chapter 5 discussed the growing number of arenas where claims can be mounted, including the increasing number of television channels and the Internet's endless reach, which have made it far easier to promote social problems claims. At the same time, most of these emerging arenas address segmented audiences, giving claimsmakers the advantage of being able to direct their rhetoric toward the homogeneous audience most likely to be receptive. Claimsmakers can therefore avoid confronting criticism and counterclaims, particularly during the early stages of a campaign, when they are seeking to mobilize support. The disadvantage, of course, is that in a world with more arenas, it is harder to gain general public attention for one's claims. For example, it has become easier to promote environmental causes by communicating in arenas filled with environmentalists, but harder to get the attention of the whole society and keep everyone focused on environmentalist concerns.

4. *Paranoia.* Finally, social progress fosters paranoia—fears of societal collapse. How can claimsmaking rhetoric be made compelling in a world characterized by social progress? One method is to warn that we are in terrible danger, that a collective catastrophe is on the horizon. Apocalyptic scenarios abound; claimsmakers warn about the threats of nuclear war, nuclear winter, climate change, overpopulation, pollution, resource depletion, epidemic disease, ethnic

conflict, globalization, economic collapse, famine, genetic engineering, nanotechnology (tiny technological devices that might outcompete the natural biological system), or robotics (machines that might develop superior intelligence and eliminate people). Moreover, all of these fears focus on troubling conditions that have *social* causes and are therefore suitable subjects for claimsmakers. They can argue that progress is a temporary illusion and warn that what seems to be progress will, in fact, lead to disaster.

In short, the experience of progress has, in some ways, made it easier to construct social problems: claimsmakers can insist that social arrangements remain imperfect; they find it easier to draw attention to previously neglected problems now that some of the big problems of the past have been resolved; they can target and reach audiences likely to be sympathetic to their claims; and they can warn that progress is illusionary, just a predecessor of far worse problems. At the same time, as people get used to social change, what once may have been constructed as an urgent problem may be normalized and no longer be the subject of alarming claims.

Given these patterns, it should not be surprising that social problems claims feature the most urgent rhetoric (see Box 10.7). Not only can claimsmakers draw attention to existing troubling conditions, but they also can predict alarming future problems. These are the secular equivalents of religious prophecies that the world will end on a particular date. It is worth noting that, in retrospect, these warnings often seem misguided. Consider alarmist warnings about AIDS in the late 1980s (in 1987, a leading television talk show host declared, "Research studies now project that . . . one in five heterosexuals could be dead from AIDS at the end of the next three years" [Fumento, 1990, p. 3]); and the furor about the Y2K problem (the concerns that the world's computers would be unable to cope when the calendar changed from 1999 to 2000, and that the resulting crisis might threaten civilization itself).

Apocalyptic rhetoric helps make claims stand out in the social problems marketplace. Every year brings a flu season, and it is

BOX 10.7   THE GOLD DIGGER MENACE

By the 1920s, gender relations were shifting in the United States: Women had just gained the right to vote throughout the country; young women were receiving more education, wearing their skirts shorter, and—it was the Prohibition era—drinking and smoking more. Moreover, state laws increasingly allowed married women to own their own property. Commentators noted with alarm that the divorce rate had increased (although divorce was still quite rare by our standards) and that courts were awarding a small minority (about 9 percent) of ex-wives alimony. All of these trends seemed unsettling to many.

Press coverage focused on gold diggers (women who were thought to try to marry rich men with a cynical plan of divorcing and receiving substantial divorce settlements). Popular novels (such as Anita Loos's *Gentlemen Prefer Blondes* [1925]), movies, and plays featured gold-digging women, and newspapers covered scandalous divorces such as fifteen-year-old Peaches Heenan's short-lived marriage to fifty-one-year-old millionaire Edward Browning that resulted in prolonged legal proceedings (eventually decided in Browning's favor).

Worried that easy divorce was encouraging gold digging, an anti-alimony movement emerged. One judge on New York's Supreme Court warned "alimony evil turns wives into parasites, liars, cheats, money grabbers, and contributors to immorality on a wholesale scale." Although the campaign had little effect on the law, it offers a reminder that rapid social change has occurred throughout American history, and these changes have often inspired claimsmakers to construct what are now forgotten social problems.

Source: Donovan, 2017.

always possible to speculate that this year's flu may turn into a devastating pandemic. Accentuating a positive record of progress rarely makes claims more competitive, whereas offering a dire forecast can help grab the attention of media workers, the general public, and policymakers. Terrible fears make for good headlines, create good conversation topics, and offer policymakers opportunities to take a stand defending society from a threatening menace.

In short, the question is not whether there is or is not evidence of social progress. The point is that the social problems process pits claims against one another, and that claimsmakers can justify pessimistic rhetoric as a competitive strategy—the most effective way of arousing concern for their issues. This is one more way that the larger societal context shapes claimsmaking.

EXTENDING OUR FOCUS ACROSS SPACE AND TIME

Although the case study is the typical method for studying the social problems process, this chapter has suggested that there is much to be gained from studying more than one case at a time. Comparisons allow us to compare and contrast social issues across space and time—to recognize that there are various ways to construct the same troubling condition, and that claims morph as they diffuse from one country to another, or as a new wave of concern breathes fresh life into a once visible issue that has since fallen out of favor.

Typically, claims emphasize troubling conditions in the here and now—and in the future. Claimsmakers warn that this is why things are bad now, and that there are reasons to worry that things might get much worse. Expanding our focus—thinking about claims more broadly, by considering how social problems were constructed in other places or during other time periods—can help us place those claims in context, to locate the social problems process within a larger framework, so that we can better understand how that process operates. Without such bases for comparisons, it is difficult to assess any particular set of claims.

MAKING CONNECTIONS

- *Although many troubling conditions follow the six stages of the social problems process, often claims fail to attract media attention (discussed in Chapter 5) or public concern (covered in Chapter 6).*

- *Comparisons across time or between places are a useful way of evaluating social problems and the choices made by social problems workers and policymakers. See Chapters 7 and 8 for more about social policy and its implementation.*

- *Looking at cycles of concern across time or between different countries reveals how conditions in some historical periods foster claimsmaking. Chapter 3 explains how activists exploit cultural opportunities when conditions are optimal for drawing attention to their claims.*

CASE STUDY

STATUES, FLAGS, AND THE RECONSTRUCTION OF HISTORICAL PROBLEMS

Flags of nations and their subdivisions (such as states in the United States) serve as symbols of the unity of the areas they represent. People often take great pains in designing flags; they choose the colors and shapes on the flag with care and imbue them with special meanings. A flag's design may be changed to reflect later developments; thus, the original American flag had thirteen stars and thirteen stripes to symbolize the original colonies that banded together. As states were added, so were new stars and stripes, until it became apparent that while the blue field could accommodate more stars, adding more stripes would become impractical, and the number of stripes was returned to the original thirteen. Flag etiquette evolved to ensure the flag was respected, and there have been various laws proposed to punish flag burning (although the Supreme Court has acknowledged this is a legitimate form of protest) (Welch 2000).

In the United States, states often designate other symbols—state birds or flowers (Dobransky & Fine, 2006). Debates over these choices can be surprisingly intense as groups with different interests promote their candidates for the best choice to symbolize the state. Statues, memorials, and other monuments add another dimension: They are built to endure, to offer a symbol that can be expected to last for generations, even centuries or longer. These are statements about what is worth remembering. But these symbols of collective memory can become controversial as attitudes change.

In recent years, debates have revolved around symbols of the Civil War Confederacy, especially the familiar Confederate battle flag and statues and monuments memorializing Confederate leaders and soldiers (Coski, 2005; Gardner, 2018). The histories of these symbols are complex. In the years immediately following the Civil War, many monuments were erected to honor the triumphant Northern leaders and soldiers. There were initially few monuments erected in the South; not only was the Southern economy still recovering from the damage caused by the war, but many Northerners viewed the rebellion to divide the Union as treasonous, not something to memorialize. Confederate memorials tended to be created, not in the immediate aftermath of the Civil War, but later, during two other periods: beginning at the very end of the nineteenth century when Reconstruction had ended and the Jim Crow segregation system was being instituted; and in the early 1960s, as the civil rights movement was gaining momentum. Although monuments to the Confederacy are sometimes presented as innocuous symbols of Southern heritage, as mere reminders of a tragic conflict that had brothers fighting brothers, it is easy to view these memorials to the Confederacy as having been promoted by white Southerners to serve as oblique expressions of white supremacy.

For example, legislatures in Alabama and South Carolina passed laws requiring that the Confederate battle flag be flown over their state capitol buildings (in 1963 and 1962, respectively), while Georgia (in 1956) and Mississippi (in 1894) adopted new state flags that incorporated the Confederate battle flag as a prominent element—all acts that expressed opposition to the federal government's promoting civil rights. By the end of the twentieth century, many found these symbols offensive, and states began to stop flying the Confederate battle flag. South Carolina moved the battle flag from its capitol building to the Confederate monument on the capitol grounds in 2000 and finally stopped flying it after 2015, when it was revealed that the white man who shot and killed nine people at a black church had posted a photo of himself posing with guns and a Confederate battle flag. When this book was being revised (in 2019), only Mississippi's state flag remained.

Opposition to other Confederate memorials also spread. This movement seems to have begun on college campuses, where statues of Confederate leaders were defaced. Campuses, and soon, cities began dismantling memorials, moving them to less prominent locations, placing them in museums, or adding plaques explaining the context behind their installation. Soon critiques about memorials spread to historical figures beyond the Confederacy. Princeton University debated the memory of Woodrow Wilson, a Princeton graduate who had gone on to be the university's president before becoming president of the United States, but who had certainly held racist views, while statues of Thomas Jefferson (a slaveholder) came under criticism at other campuses.

The current campaign largely focuses on the nation's racial history. In the early twentieth century, claims romanticizing the Confederacy as the "Lost Cause" downplayed the importance of slavery as the root cause of the Civil War and insisted that the Confederate battle flag was simply an expression of Southern pride. In contrast, current claims highlight slavery as the central issue over which the war was fought, and emphasize the flag's use as a rallying symbol for white supremacy. But note that there is nothing new about controversy over monuments and memorials. The decision to build a memorial to the veterans who served in the Vietnam conflict involved considerable controversy (Wagner-Pacifici & Schwartz, 1991). Because the war had been unpopular, and because it had ended in defeat, it was difficult to gain agreement about how the war should be remembered, and there were bitter debates about the memorial's design. More recently, there was disagreement over how the site of the 9/11 attack at the World Trade Center should be commemorated.

Monuments, statues, and other memorials are bids to give collective memories permanence. In effect, they make a claim that something is worth remembering, that it should not be forgotten, and that future generations should be confronted with its importance. But there is no guarantee that people in the future will share these judgments. After all, debates over designing memorials reveal that not everyone shares these sentiments at the time the projects are undertaken, that decisions to build a memorial to a particular memory—and to give it a particular design—are often controversial. It should not surprise us that attitudes often change in ways that later cause some memorials to be viewed in new ways.

It is not uncommon to see news that crowds have destroyed statues that tyrants had built to celebrate themselves, once these unpopular, frightening political figures have been deposed. These are dramatic examples of when a new popular sentiment rejects what authority once declared worth remembering. Parallel, albeit less dramatic, changes can occur as a culture evolves.

The debate about Confederate memorials reflects a larger shift toward an American history that is more comfortable with conflict. Our story features lots of disputes—over ethnic, religious, and class differences—disagreements that tend to have been toned down or ignored in history textbooks (which often seek to avoid offending students, parents, and school boards). Currently, there is more celebration of "diversity," and this casts past practices—slavery being the principal example—in a vastly harsher light. And these changing interpretations can reverberate in the form of critiques of memories and memorials. Columbus—long used as a key symbol of the American story—has become a controversial figure, and a number of states and cities have announced that they would celebrate Indigenous Peoples' Day instead of Columbus Day.

Collective memories are social constructions, and older ideas about what should be remembered can themselves be turned into troubling conditions.

QUESTIONS

1. Claimsmakers often draw attention to troubling conditions that have long histories. Is this different from reconstructing the past and interpreting historical events in new ways?

2. What are the arguments for destroying, say, a statue of a historical figure, for relocating it to a less prominent place, or for retaining it while adding a plaque offering more information about the person being memorialized?

3. In addition to statues and monuments, what other kinds of symbols become targets of reconstruction campaigns?

11

The Uses of the
Constructionist Stance

Most of us find ourselves discussing social problems with friends or family members from time to time. In general, these everyday conversations focus on what we've called *troubling conditions*. People argue about the scope of conditions, or about what causes them (for instance, some may insist that poverty is caused by discrimination or a lack of good jobs, while others counter that poor people are at least partly to blame for their own problems). Reports from the media may be used to buttress one position or another (perhaps someone will refer to a radio talk show or a program on television about poverty). There may be disagreements about what should be done (should the government distribute more—or less—money to the poor?). In short, these conversations tend to treat social problems as though they are conditions that have an objective existence in our society.

Of course, this book has adopted a very different stance. It has been relatively uninterested in such social conditions, and has focused instead on what people think and say about social problems. Instead of treating social problems as social conditions, it has described a *process* in which people's ideas about social problems emerge and evolve.

Chapter 1 introduced a model of a social problems process with six basic stages: claimsmaking, media coverage, public reaction, policymaking, social problems work, and policy outcomes. That model (reproduced as Figure 11.1) provided the organizational framework for the chapters that followed, which, in general, dealt with successive stages in the social problems process.

While exploring the six stages in the social problems process, this book has remained focused on the subjective nature of social problems. Remember that what all phenomena that are considered social problems have in common is not a particular objective quality, some sort of harm or damage that they inflict on society. Rather, the one characteristic that all social problems share is subjective: people define them as troubling. Social problems are not conditions; they are *concerns*.

This subjective work—people's efforts to understand and draw attention to what they define as troubling conditions—occurs at every stage in the social problems process. It begins with claimsmakers' efforts to construct claims that will convince others to share their concern about a troubling condition. And at each successive stage in the process, people—media workers, members of the public, policymakers, social problems workers, and those who evaluate and criticize policies—rework the claims that come to their attention, and reconstruct the problem again and again so that their new understanding will be appropriate for their purposes. News workers repackage primary claims into secondary claims to fit the demands and conventions of news coverage; members of the public respond by interpreting these secondary claims to correspond with their own understanding of how the larger world works; policymakers

Figure 11.1 Basic Model of the Social Problems Process

Claims- ⟶ Media ⟶ Public ⟶ Policy- ⟶ Social ⟶ Policy
making   Coverage   Reaction   making   Problems   Outcomes
                                            Work

make further alterations so that the troubling condition can be addressed through a formal policy; social problems workers try to apply abstract policies to practical situations; and various evaluators redefine what is needed according to their assessments of how well policies work.

In other words, social problems construction is not something that happens all at once, through the actions of a single set of actors at one stage in the social problems process. Instead, it is an ongoing process, in which different people work out different ways of making sense of the situations they confront. Any phenomenon can be understood in lots of different ways, and social construction is a process of making choices—of people in a particular situation choosing one perspective among all the possibilities. Each effort to construct or understand a social problem needs to meet two criteria: first, it needs to make sense to—and be useful for—whoever is producing the construction; second, it needs to be able to convince others—whoever the audience for that construction may be.

Social construction is thus an *interactive* process. People present their constructions to an audience of others (as when an activist holds a press conference, a legislator tries to convince colleagues to vote for a bill, or a caseworker tries to persuade clients that taking a particular action will be in their best interest). Those others, however, may react in different ways (perhaps no reporters bother to attend the press conference, perhaps the legislature votes unanimously in favor of the bill, perhaps some clients reject the case worker's advice while others follow it). These reactions become feedback, and on the basis of the audience's response, the people offering the construction may continue pressing their claims, modify those claims to see whether a repackaged version might elicit a better response, or even decide to abandon the claims entirely. Although we may think of a claimsmaker addressing an audience, we should not imagine that that audience is passive. Rather, audiences react to claims, and claimsmakers are likely to revise their constructions in response to those reactions.

All of this means that our initial model of the social problems process, as illustrated in Figure 11.1, oversimplifies the process in some important ways. First, the arrows between stages imply that influence is unidirectional; they ignore the role of feedback and the interactive nature of the process. Second, the actors at the different stages in the social problems process do not necessarily limit their interactions to contacts with those in the next stage. Third, and very important, interactions also occur *within* each stage. That is, activists interact with others in their social movement organization, as well as with activists in rival SMOs, and with other sorts of claimsmakers, such as experts. Similarly, media workers interact with their colleagues and follow one another's coverage, and so on.

Moreover, when we look at interactions between actors in different stages, we realize again that the basic model's depiction of actors addressing only those at the next stage in the process is too simple. For example, the model suggests that claimsmakers will focus their attention on influencing media coverage, but claimsmakers may do far more. Sometimes claimsmakers bypass the media and directly address members of the public, policymakers, social problems workers, or even those who evaluate policy outcomes. There are many possible pathways through the social problems process. Figure 11.1 can be thought of as offering a simplified, fairly typical natural history—a framework for developing this book's argument. In contrast, Figure 11.2 gives a better sense of the complicated ways in which actors in different stages of the process can interact; it suggests the range of possible connections that might shape how social problems evolve.

Examine Figure 11.2 carefully, and note the following five features:

1. The five one-way stage-to-stage arrows found in the simplified model reappear in Figure 11.2 as thicker arrows—a reminder that these are particularly important links in the social problems process.

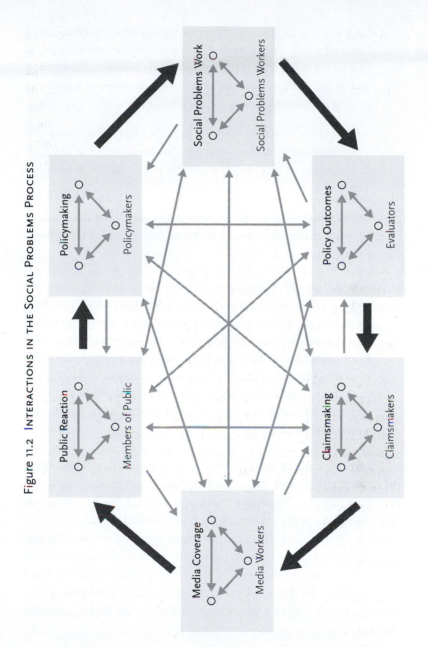

Figure 11.2 INTERACTIONS IN THE SOCIAL PROBLEMS PROCESS

Social Problems Work
Social Problems Workers

Policymaking
Policymakers

Policy Outcomes
Evaluators

Public Reaction
Members of Public

Claimsmaking
Claimsmakers

Media Coverage
Media Workers

2. Each stage in the social problems process is now represented by a box, and small circles within each box denote the various actors in that stage (that is, different claimsmakers in the claimsmaking stage, and so on). In turn, those circles are linked by two-way arrows suggesting interactions among the people at each stage.

3. Arrows connect each stage with every other stage, illustrating possible connections, in that it may be possible for actors at any stage to communicate with people anywhere else in the social problems process.

4. The arrows linking all the different stages go in both directions, to illustrate that there is always the possibility of feedback and social interaction.

5. The figure is laid out as a circle, rather than along a straight line, and there is a thick arrow between "Policy Outcomes" (which the basic model presented as the final stage in the social problems process) and "Claimsmaking" (which was, of course, the first stage). This arrow denotes how reactions to social policies often lead to new claimsmaking campaigns (as discussed in Chapter 9). The figure's roughly circular shape reminds us that the social problems process need not end—that critiques of social policies often inspire new cycles of claimsmaking.

Figure 11.2 is complex, but that is because it reflects genuine complexities—the many possible pathways through the social problems process. The entire process is an example of what sociologists call a *complex system*, with many elements that affect one another (Watts, 2011). It is important to appreciate this complexity; spend some time examining Figure 11.2. Pick one particular arrow and consider the sorts of activities it might involve. Then pick another. Do this until you are comfortable, until you understand how this complex figure depicts the overall social problems process.

These complexities become especially apparent when we compare social problems processes across space and time (the subject of Chapter 10). For example, many campaigns raise concern about dangerous drugs. Some of these efforts are remarkably successful at attracting intense media coverage, arousing great public concern, and inspiring new policies; the 1986 campaign to warn Americans about the dangers of crack cocaine is an obvious example (Reinarman & Levine, 1995). On the other hand, some campaigns flop, such as the 1989 effort to draw attention to "ice" (smokable crystal methamphetamine), although later campaigns to raise alarm about this drug had more success; or the 1993 warnings about "Cat" (methcathinone, a drug that—so far—has not aroused great concern) (Jenkins, 1999).

We can imagine a continuum of outcomes for antidrug campaigns that ranges from widespread, intense concern to indifference. Only by comparing antidrug claimsmaking campaigns—targeting different drugs, at different times, or in different places—can we begin to appreciate the many possible ways that the social problems process can unfold. And, of course, various claims about other troubling conditions—racial discrimination, ecological problems, and so on—will display similar variability in their outcomes.

In other words, our constructionist model—both the simpler version depicted in Figure 11.1 and the more complex version presented in Figure 11.2—should be understood as a tool, a framework that can be used to help us think critically about the social construction of social problems. Most days, news media present various stories that report on claimsmaking, policymaking, or social problems work; very often they also run stories about public reactions and evaluations of different policies. (And, of course, all of those stories are themselves examples of media coverage.) The constructionist model can be used to place all those stories in their broader context, to view them as parts of the larger social problems process. And that's worth doing, because we are constantly surrounded by examples of the social problems process.

IS THIS STUFF USEFUL?

As noted way back in Chapter 1, the constructionist stance for thinking about the social problems process is not the traditional approach to studying social problems. Most books about social problems have been—and continue to be—organized around a series of chapters that deal with various conditions considered to be social problems—crime, racism, and the like. Each chapter summarizes information about its problem: statistics about crime rates, theories of crime causation, and so on. This book has presented very little information of that sort.

The justification for this book's constructionist approach is that it is intellectually coherent. Rather than letting our attention drift as we examine, one at a time, crime and other specific phenomena that people consider social problems, this book has focused on the general topic of the social problems process—on the insight that the only thing the various conditions called social problems have in common is that they are socially constructed—and it has explored the ins and outs of that process.

This approach is intended to give you some tools for recognizing, thinking about, and responding to social problems claims. Ten years from now—or maybe twenty or thirty—you will encounter warnings about a terrible new social problem of some sort. There is no way of predicting exactly what the topic of those warnings will be—perhaps a new crime, or a new disease, or a new form of drug abuse. But we can be reasonably confident that you will run into such claims, because such claims have been an important part of the social landscape for a very long time, and there is no reason to expect that they will vanish—particularly not in a world where twenty-four-hour television news broadcasts, the Internet, and other forms of electronic communication make it incredibly easy to promote new claims. If anything, claims are likely to spread via ever more channels as new media evolve (consider, for example, the relatively recent emergence of Facebook pages as forums for claims, and of news bulletins transmitted to cell phones and other portable electronic devices). People who pay even minimal attention to the media can expect to spend their lives bombarded by such claims.

Moreover, the historical record is full of warnings about terrible problems that—in retrospect—seem mistaken. In the 1970s, some environmentalists warned that civilization was jeopardized by global climate change—that humans faced an impending ice age brought on by global cooling. Fifteen years later, fears about the threat of global cooling would be replaced by what seem to be their exact opposite—concerns over the danger of global warming. In another example, in the early 1990s some commentators warned that violent crime was about to spiral out of control—that a generation of "superpredators" would be coming of age. Instead, crime rates fell fairly steadily during the years that followed. These claims received plenty of respectful attention when they first appeared, even though their forecasts proved to be quite wrong.

There are many other examples of urgent claims that hindsight lets us see as exaggerated, if not silly. There is a long history of critics warning that the amusements of the young—games, toys, dances, movies, television, music, and on and on—endangered the next generation. Each successive style of rock music, for example, has been denounced as threatening the moral fabric of young people. There is an equally long history of commentators charging that the current wave of immigrants threatens the foundation of American society, that some new recreational drug is spreading out of control, and so on. Such claims often acknowledge that earlier claims about similar problems exaggerated the threat, yet the claimsmakers insist that this new problem is different—the real deal—that it presents a genuine danger that must be addressed.

At one extreme, it is possible to treat all social problems claims as correct, true, accurate. When claimsmakers warn that a particular troubling condition is this serious, affects that many people, and so on, we might simply accept those claims, even though we may realize that, in the past, many such claims have proved to be exaggerated or even false. In other words, every time we encounter a news story that warns we should be worried about a new problem, we could decide to worry. An alternative, but equally extreme stance might be to approach all claims cynically, to presume that they are wrong, false, bogus. We could suspect that claimsmakers are interested parties who are quite willing to say anything, that media workers are just trying to attract an audience, that politicians are cynically pandering to voters' concerns, and so on. Knowing that some social problems claims have been exaggerated in the past, we might simply discount and ignore any claims we encounter in the future. The first possibility encourages excessive credulity; the second fosters cynicism, apathy, and ignorance.

Obviously it would be desirable to find a middle ground between those extremes—a stance somewhere between credulousness and cynicism. That is, it would be better to approach claims thoughtfully—critically—so that we could weigh what we're told about social problems and make our own evaluations about the nature of those problems and the best ways of addressing them.

The constructionist model of the social problems process can help in this regard. Understanding that claims need to be made persuasive—that claimsmakers are competing to be heard in the social problems marketplace so that they can bring their claims to the attention of press, public, and policymakers—offers a useful foundation for thinking about social problems as a process. In particular, it can help us to think carefully about how the problem is being constructed, about the rhetoric of claimsmaking, about who is making which claims, and so on.

By adopting a constructionist stance, we can identify interesting questions that we might ask about a set of claims. Is the problem clearly defined, or are we encouraged to understand it primarily through typifying examples? Is there any reason to suspect that those typifying examples may not be all that typical? If the claims feature statistics, where do those numbers come from, and how likely is it that they are accurate? What sorts of warrants are being used to make the claims compelling? How are the media covering the issue? What sources are they drawing on, and how does what the media report differ from what the claimsmakers are saying? Are the media presenting different constructions of the problem, and what do those differences reveal?

Further questions arise at successive stages in the social problems process. Is the problem addressed in our everyday conversations? Is it a theme in stories or jokes that we hear from people we know, and if so, does the public seem to be constructing the problem in different terms from those that claimsmakers and the media are using? Which aspects of the problem do policymakers emphasize? Do their policy recommendations match their claims? Do they seem workable? How do social problems workers describe their activities and the clients with whom they work? Who criticizes social policies and why, and how do they frame their critiques?

Such questions give us tools that we can use to think critically about social problems. Note, however, that being critical sometimes does mean rejecting claims. The answers to some of the questions you ask may strike you as completely convincing; you may decide that some claims are quite correct, and you may even be moved to join some claimsmakers' causes. In other instances, though, questioning the claims might lead you to suspect that those claims are exaggerated or misguided. Thus, thinking critically can help you become a thoughtful consumer of social problems claims.

There is another way to use the constructionist approach. Studying how social problems are constructed—how some claims prove effective while others fall by the wayside—offers useful information for would-be claimsmakers. That is, constructionist research can be studied for its practical advice on how to arouse concern and mobilize action regarding whatever you might consider as troubling conditions (just as it can suggest how opposition to claims might be made more effective). Studying the social problems process offers lessons on how to assemble persuasive claimsmaking rhetoric, how to mobilize effective adherents, how to incorporate expert knowledge in campaigns, how to elicit media coverage and attract public attention, how to understand the concerns of policymakers and social problems workers, and so on. If you are inclined to take an active part in the social problems process, the constructionist stance can help you ask—and answer—very practical questions. It is a perspective that can benefit participants, as well as observers.

What constructionism cannot do is tell you which conditions ought to concern you. You have your own values, your own sense of what is or is not troubling, what needs to be changed, and what sorts of changes are needed. You may be attracted by the ideologies of liberals or conservatives, of feminists or fundamentalists. Those are choices you need to make, and the constructionist stance does not provide the grounds for preferring one choice over another. The goal of this book has not been to tell you *what* to think about various social conditions, but rather to offer guidelines for *how* to think about the social problems process. If this book advocates a moral position, it is that it is desirable for people to think critically about that process, to engage the claims they encounter.

I hope you will find these ideas useful in the years ahead. Good luck.

Glossary

abeyance A period when a social movement is relatively inactive.

activists Members of a social movement organization who make claims about social problems. Compare *experts*.

adopters The people who accept new innovations as part of the process of diffusion. Compare *transmitters*.

agenda setting Choosing which claims will receive the attention of media or policymakers.

arena A public venue where social problems claims can be presented.

audience The people whom claimsmakers seek to persuade with their claims.

audience segmentation Targeting media presentations for particular audiences.

beneficiaries People who stand to benefit from a social movement's success. Compare *constituents*.

bias A tendency for media workers' personal beliefs and views on an issue to interfere with balanced and impartial coverage.

biomedicalization The process of arguing that biological processes are the root cause of many troubling conditions.

carrying capacity The number of issues that can receive attention in an arena.

case An instance of a previously constructed troubling condition that requires attention through the application of appropriate policy.

case study An examination of a particular problem.

causal story A story that classifies a troubling condition in a familiar category according to the nature of its cause.

claim An argument that a particular troubling condition needs to be addressed.

claimsmakers People who seek to convince others that there is a troubling condition about which something ought to be done.

claimsmaking The process of making claims, of bringing a troubling condition to the attention of others.

commission A special, high-status group—often created at the national level—that evaluates policies and issues recommendations.

conclusion The part of a claim that specifies what should be done, what action should be taken to address a troubling condition.

condensing symbol A shorthand element—such as a landmark narrative, typifying example, slogan, or visual image—that evokes a package.

conscience constituents People who contribute money or even join demonstrations because they believe in a particular cause, although they do not expect to be direct beneficiaries of that cause. Compare *constituents*.

constituents People who support a social movement. Compare *beneficiaries* and *conscience constituents*.

constructionism A sociological approach that focuses on the process of social construction.

contemporary legend A story, also called an *urban legend*, spread from one person to another and believed to be true by teller and listener.

counterclaim An argument that directly opposes a particular claim.

countermovement A movement that opposes a social movement by promoting counterclaims that challenge the opponent's claims.

cultural opportunity A situation when a shift in popular ideas makes it possible to change how a particular troubling condition is addressed. Compare *political opportunity*.

cultural resources Cultural knowledge that can be incorporated in claims.

diagnostic frame A social movement's depiction of the nature of a problem. Compare *prognostic frame*.

dialog An exchange of ideas between two or more persons.

diffusion The process by which innovations spread.

domain expansion Redefining a troubling condition to encompass a broader array of cases.

economicization The process of defining a troubling condition as an economic issue.

ethnocentrism The assumption that one's culture is right or natural.

evaluation research A social scientific assessment of the effectiveness of a specific policy.

experts People—such as physicians, scientists, lawyers, and officials—who have special knowledge and claim to speak with special authority. Compare *activists*.

feedback The phenomenon in which a particular cause produces an effect that in turn affects the cause.

focus group A set of people that researchers select to discuss certain topics in order to learn what the public is thinking.

frame alignment Ways in which activists try to promote a social movement's frame to prospective members.

frame amplification Ways in which activists appeal to prospective members by arguing that a social movement's frame is consistent with popular beliefs.

frame bridging Ways in which activists appeal to prospective members thought to be already sympathetic to a social movement's frame.

frame dispute A disagreement between groups of activists about how to frame a particular troubling condition.

frame extension Ways in which activists appeal to prospective members by extending a social movement's frame to encompass the concerns of those prospective supporters.

frame transformation Ways in which activists appeal to prospective members by inviting them to reject familiar views of the world and adopt the activists' very different perspective.

framing The way in which claimsmakers construct claims about a troubling condition.

ground The portion of a claim that argues that a troubling condition exists.

ideology A system of beliefs regarding how society does and should operate.

inertia A reluctance to alter existing social arrangements.

insider claimsmakers Claimsmakers who have easy access to publicity and people in positions of power. Compare *outsider claimsmakers*.

joke cycle A set of jokes that share a form or topic and are popular for a period of time.

landmark narrative A typifying example that dominates news coverage of a troubling condition, shaping the terms in which the problem is covered and how the news audience understands the problem.

macrosociology Sociological studies concerned with whole societies. Compare *microsociology*.

master frame A broad construction that can be easily modified and applied to many troubling conditions.

media coverage Attention from mass media outlets, such as newspapers and television, that can bring claims to the attention of a wide audience.

medical model A general framework for thinking about medical matters as diseases that require treatment.

medicalization The process of defining a troubling condition as a medical matter.

microsociology Sociological studies concerned with interactions between individuals. Compare *macrosociology*.

motif A recurring thematic element in legends and jokes.

motivational frame A social movement's justification for taking action.

naming Coining a term to identify a troubling condition.

natural history A sequence of steps or stages often found in a particular process.

news work The job of locating and presenting news to the larger public.

nonrelational channel A link in diffusion that does not involve a personal connection between a transmitter and an adopter. Compare *relational channel*.

objectivism A school of thought that defines social problems in terms of objectively measurable characteristics of conditions. Compare *subjectivism*.

outsider claimsmakers People who lack easy access to publicity and to people in positions of power. Compare *insider claimsmakers*.

ownership Having one's construction of a troubling condition become widely accepted.

package A familiar construction of a particular troubling condition, including specifications of its causes and solutions.

perfectibility Using the eradication of a troubling condition—instead of its improvement—as the standard for evaluating a social policy.

pharmaceuticalization The process of defining prescription drugs as solutions to troubling conditions.

piggyback To link a new troubling condition to an already established social problem.

policy domain The part of the political system that focuses on a particular troubling condition.

policy outcome The result of how a particular social policy is implemented.

policy proposal stream A set of policy proposals that policymakers hear for addressing a troubling condition.

policymakers People who are able to establish a social policy of some kind.

policymaking The process of devising policy to address a particular troubling condition.

political opportunity A situation when a shift in power makes it possible to change how a particular troubling condition is addressed. Compare *cultural opportunity*.

political stream The current political situation recognized by policymakers in which a troubling condition might be addressed.

polity Groups and individuals who have easy access to policymakers.

popular culture Commercial entertainment.

population All those described by a statistic. Compare *representative sample*.

position issue A troubling condition about which people disagree. Compare *valence issue*.

primary claim One of the initial claims, usually presented by activists or experts, that begin the social problems process. Compare *secondary claim*.

problem recognition stream The set of claims that policymakers hear about a troubling condition.

prognostic frame A social movement's description of what needs to be done about a particular troubling condition. Compare *diagnostic frame*.

relational channel A link in diffusion that involves interpersonal contact between a transmitter and an adopter. Compare *nonrelational channel*.

representative sample A sample that accurately reflects the diversity of the population. Compare *population*.

resource Anything that can be drawn on to construct a claim.

resource mobilization Collecting and assembling money, members, and other resources needed by a social movement.

rhetoric The study of persuasion.

sample A subgroup used as a basis for statistical generalizations about a population.

sample survey A poll administered to a sample in order to generalize about opinions or other characteristics of a population.

secondary claim The media's transformation of a primary claim. Secondary claims are usually shorter and more dramatic than primary claims. Compare *primary claim.*

segmentation See *audience segmentation.*

semantic polling The use of software to classify the content of social media messages.

SMO See *social movement organization.*

social condition A social circumstance or arrangement.

social construction The process by which people continually create—or construct—meaning.

social issue A topic of social concern that is characterized by disagreement or debate.

social movement A general cause that motivates activists and social movement organizations to address a particular troubling condition.

social movement organization (SMO) A particular organization that belongs to a social movement.

social problems cluster Claimsmakers who take similar positions on similar social problems.

social problems marketplace The public forum where claims are presented and discussed.

social problems process The process through which particular troubling conditions come to be constructed as social problems.

social problems work The application of constructions of a troubling condition or a social policy to practical situations.

social problems workers People who do social problems work.

societalization The process by which claims attract national attention.

sociological imagination The ability to see private troubles in terms of larger public issues.

statistic A number that measures or characterizes a particular situation.

subjectivism A school of thought that defines social problems in terms of people's subjective sense that something is or isn't troubling. Compare *objectivism.*

subjects The people (variously called addicts, clients, defendants, offenders, patients, suspects, victims, and so on) who in some way embody a socially constructed social problem.

target population The group of people intended to be affected by a social policy.

theorization The presentation of claims using abstract principles and arguments.

topical joke cycle A joke cycle about a particular event.

transmitters The people who promote new innovations as part of the process of diffusion. Compare *adopters*.

troubling condition A condition that becomes a subject of claims.

typifying example A particular instance chosen to illustrate a troubling condition—often a dramatic, disturbing, or memorable case.

urban legend See *contemporary legend*.

valence issue A troubling condition about which there is general agreement. Compare *position issue*.

variant A version of a contemporary legend or joke.

warrant The portion of a claim that justifies doing something about a troubling condition.

References

Abraham, J. (2010). Pharmaceuticalization of society in context: Theoretical, empirical, and health. *Sociology* 44: 603–622.

Adorjan, M., Christensen, T., Kelly, B., & Pawluch, D. (2012). Stockholm Syndrome as vernacular resource. *Sociological Quarterly* 53: 454–474.

Akagawa, M. (2019). A natural history model of low birth rate issues in Japan since the 1990s. *American Sociologist* 50: 300–314.

Åkerström, M. (2006). Doing ambivalence: Embracing policy innovation—at arm's length. *Social Problems* 53: 57–74.

Alexander, J. C. (2018). The societalization of social problems: Church pedophilia, phone hacking, and the financial crisis. *American Sociological Review* 83: 1049–1078.

Alimi, E. Y., & Maney, G. M. (2018). Focusing on focusing events: Event selection, media coverage, and contentious meaning-making. *Sociological Forum* 33: 757–782.

Alterman, E. (2003). *What liberal media? The truth about bias and the news.* New York: Basic Books.

Anstead, N., & O'Loughlin, B. (2015). Social media analysis and public opinion: The 2010 UK general election. *Journal of Computer-Mediated Communication* 20: 204–220.

Appleton, L. M. (1995). Rethinking medicalization: Alcoholism and anomalies. In J. Best (Ed.), *Images of issues: Typifying contemporary social problems* (2nd ed., pp. 59–80). Hawthorne, NY: Aldine de Gruyter.

Auyero, J., Hernandez, M., & Stitt, M. E. (2019). Grassroots activism in the belly of the beast: A relational account of the campaign against urban fracking in Texas. *Social Problems* 66: 28–50.

Ayukawa, J. (2019). *Juvenile crimes and social problems in Japan: A social constructionist approach.* Kyoto, Japan: Koyo Shobo.

Bakardjieva, M., Felt, M., & Terulle, R. (2018). Framing the pipeline problem: Civic claimsmakers and social media. *Canadian Journal of Communication* 43: 147–165.

Ball, J. (2017). *Post-truth: How bullshit conquered the world.* London: Blueback.

Bargheer, S. (2018). *Moral entanglements: Conserving birds in Britain and Germany.* Chicago: University of Chicago Press.

Barnes, F. (2004, May 28). Liberal media evidence. *The Daily Standard.* Retrieved from www.weeklystandard.com.

Bartholomew, R. (2016). Clown panic! Sightings of mysterious clowns rattle nerves in South Carolina. *Skeptic.* Retrieved from https://www.skeptic.com/reading _room/south-carolina-clown-panics/.

Bartholomew, R. E., & Pérez, D. F. Z. (2018). Chasing ghosts in Cuba: Is mass psychogenic illness masquerading as an acoustical attack? *International Journal of Social Psychiatry* 64: 413–416.

Bates, V. (2018). Murderous motherhood: Munchausen syndrome by proxy in 1990s crime fiction. *Journal of Popular Culture* 51: 1113–1132.

Becker, H. S. (1995). The power of inertia. *Qualitative Sociology* 18: 301–309.

Beckett, K. (1994). Setting the public agenda: "Street crime" and drug use in American politics. *Social Problems* 41: 425–447.

Beckett, K. (1996). Culture and the politics of signification: The case of child sexual abuse. *Social Problems* 43: 57–76.

Benford, R. D. (1993). Frame disputes within the nuclear disarmament movement. *Social Forces* 71: 677–701.

Benford, R. D., & Hunt, S. A. (2003). Interactional dynamics in public problems marketplaces: Movements and the counterframing and reframing of public problems. In J. A. Holstein & G. Miller (Eds.), *Challenges and choices: Constructionist perspectives on social problems* (pp. 153–186). Hawthorne, NY: Aldine de Gruyter.

Benson, R. (2013). *Shaping immigration news: A French–American comparison.* New York: Columbia University Press.

Berger, P. L., & Luckmann, T. (1966). *The social construction of reality: A treatise in the sociology of knowledge.* Garden City, NY: Doubleday.

Berns, N. (2004). *Framing the victim: Domestic violence, media, and social problems.* Hawthorne, NY: Aldine de Gruyter.

Best, J. (1990). *Threatened children: Rhetoric and concern about child-victims.* Chicago: University of Chicago Press.

Best, J. (1999). *Random violence: How we talk about new crimes and new victims.* Berkeley: University of California Press.

Best, J. (Ed.). (2001a). *How claims spread: Cross-national diffusion of social problems.* Hawthorne, NY: Aldine de Gruyter.

Best, J. (2001b). Social progress and social problems: Toward a sociology of gloom. *Sociological Quarterly* 42: 1–12.

Best, J. (2011). If this goes on . . . : The rhetorical construction of future problems. In T. van Haaften, H. Jansen, J. de Jong, & W. Koetsenruijter (Eds.), *Bending opinion: Essays on persuasion in the public domain* (pp. 203–217). Leiden, Netherlands: Leiden University Press.

Best, J. (2013). *Damned lies and statistics: Untangling numbers from the media, politicians, and activists* (updated ed.). Berkeley: University of California Press.

Best, J. (2015). Beyond case studies: Expanding the constructionist framework for social problems research. *Qualitative Sociology Review* 11(2): 18–33.

Best, J. (2018). *American nightmares: Social problems in an anxious world.* Oakland: University of California Press.

Best, J. (2019). Knock, knock—who's scared? The knockout game as a short-lived crime problem. *Deviant Behavior* 40: 1289–1303.

Best, J., & Best, E. (2014). *The student loan mess: How good intentions created a trillion-dollar problem.* Berkeley: University of California Press.

Best, J., & Furedi, F. (2001). The evolution of road rage in Britain and the United States. In J. Best (Ed.), *How claims spread: Cross-national diffusion of social problems* (pp. 107–127). Hawthorne, NY: Aldine de Gruyter.

Best, R. K. (2019). *Common enemies: Disease campaigns in America.* New York: Oxford University Press.

Bilderback, L. (1989). "A greater threat than the Soviet Union": Mexican immigration as a social problem. In J. Best (Ed.), *Images of issues* (pp. 223–241). Hawthorne, NY: Aldine de Gruyter.

Blomberg, H. (2019). "We're not magicians!": On the use of rhetorical resources in Swedish news media narratives portraying the social services and social workers. *Qualitative Social Work* 18: 229–246.

Bloom, J. (2015). The dynamics of opportunity and insurgent practice: How black anti-colonialists compelled Truman to advocate civil rights. *American Sociological Review* 80: 391–415.

Blumer, H. (1971). Social problems as collective behavior. *Social Problems* 18: 298–306.

Bogard, C. J. (2003). *Seasons such as these: How homelessness took shape in America.* Hawthorne, NY: Aldine de Gruyter.

Bogle, K. A. (2008). *Hooking up: Sex, dating, and relationships on campus.* New York: New York University Press.

Britschgi, C. (2018, February 6). Media, legislators, activists stick by straw stats produced by 9-year-old. *Reason*. Retrieved from https://reason.com/2018/02/06/media-legislators-activists-are-all-stic/.

Bronner, S. J. (1988). Political suicide: The Budd Dwyer joke cycle and the humor of disaster. *Midwestern Folklore* 14: 81–89.

Brown, J. D. (1991). The professional ex-: An alternative for exiting the deviant career. *Sociological Quarterly* 32: 219–230.

Brown, P. (1992). Popular epidemiology and toxic waste contamination: Lay and professional ways of knowing. *Journal of Health and Social Behavior* 33: 267–281.

Brunsma, D. L. (2004). *The school uniform movement and what it tells us about American education*. Lanham, MD: Scarecrow Education.

Burgess, A. (2004). *Cellular phones, public fears, and a culture of precaution*. Cambridge, UK: Cambridge University Press.

Burstein, P. (1991). Policy domains: Organization, culture, and policy outcomes. *Annual Review of Sociology* 17: 327–350.

Burstein, P. (2014). *American public opinion, advocacy, and policy in Congress: What the public wants and what it gets*. New York: Cambridge University Press.

Cabaniss, E. (2018). Pulling back the curtain: Examining the backstage gendered dynamics of storytelling in the undocumented youth movement. *Journal of Contemporary Ethnography* 47: 199–225.

Cahill, S. E., et al. (1985). Meanwhile backstage: Public bathrooms and the interaction order. *Journal of Contemporary Ethnography* 14: 33–58.

Campeau, H. (2018). "The right way, the wrong way, and the Blueville way": Standards and cultural match in the police organization. *Sociological Quarterly* 59: 603–626.

Campion-Vincent, V. (2005). *Organ theft legends*. Jackson: University Press of Mississippi.

Carmichael, J. T., & Brulle, R. J. (2017). Elite cues, media coverage, and public concern: An integrated path analysis of public opinion on climate change, 2001–2013. *Environmental Politics* 26: 232–252.

Chambliss, D. F. (1996). *Beyond caring: Hospitals, nurses, and the social organization of ethics*. Chicago: University of Chicago Press.

Clarke, A. E., Shim, J. K., Mamo, L., Fosket, J. R., & Fishman, J. R. (2003). Biomedicalization: Technoscientific transformations of health, illness, and U.S. biomedicine. *American Sociological Review* 68: 161–194.

Colomy, P., & Phillips, S. (2018). Irremedial work and act-person merger: Constructing irredeemable selves in death penalty trials. *Sociological Forum* 33: 783–804.

Conrad, P. (2007). *The medicalization of society: On the transformation of human conditions into treatable disorders*. Baltimore: Johns Hopkins University Press.

Coski, J. M. (2005). *The Confederate battle flag: America's most embattled emblem*. Cambridge, MA: Harvard University Press.

Courtwright, D. T. (1982). *Dark paradise: A history of opiate addiction in America.* Cambridge, MA: Harvard University Press.

Daniels, J. (2009). Cloaked websites: Propaganda, cyber-racism and epistemology in the digital era. *New Media and Society* 11: 659–683.

Daniller, A. (2019, November 14). Two-thirds of Americans support marijuana legalization. *Fact Tank*, Pew Research Center. Retrieved from https://www .pewresearch.org/fact-tank/2019/11/14/americans-support-marijuana-legalization/.

Davis, A. K. (2018). Toward exclusion through inclusion: Engendering reputation with gender-inclusive facilities at college and universities in the United States, 2001–2013. *Gender and Society* 32: 321–347.

Davis, P. W. (1994). The changing meanings of spanking. In J. Best (Ed.), *Troubling children* (pp. 133–153). Hawthorne, NY: Aldine de Gruyter.

de Vaus, D. A. (1986). *Surveys in social research.* London: Allen & Unwin.

Del Rosso, J. (2015). *Talking about torture: How political discourse shapes the debate.* New York: Cambridge University Press.

Del Rosso, J. (2018). "Its own kind of torture": Denial, acknowledgement, and the debate about force feeding at Guantánamo Bay. *Sociological Forum* 33: 53–72.

Dickson, D. T. (1968). Bureaucracy and morality: An organizational perspective on a moral crusade. *Social Problems* 16: 143–156.

Dobransky, K., & Fine, G. A. (2006). The native in the garden: Floral politics and cultural entrepreneurs. *Sociological Forum* 21: 559–585.

Doering, J. (2014). A battleground of identity: Racial formation and the African American discourse on racial intermarriage. *Social Problems* 61: 559–575.

Doherty, C. (2018, June 18). Americans broadly support legal status for immigrants brought to the U.S. illegally as children. *Fact Tank*, Pew Research Center. Retrieved from https://www.pewresearch.org/fact-tank/2018/06/18/americans-broadly-support-legal-status-for-immigrants-brought-to-the-u-s-illegally -as-children/.

Donovan, B. L. (2017). Alimony panic, gold diggers, and the cultural foundations of early twentieth-century marriage reform in the United States. *Journal of Family History* 42: 111–127.

Downs, A. (1972). Up and down with ecology—The "issue-attention cycle." *Public Interest* 28: 38–50.

Dundes, A. (1987). *Cracking jokes.* Berkeley, CA: Ten Speed Press.

Dundes, A., & Pagter, C. R. (2000). *Why don't sheep shrink when it rains? A further collection of photocopier folklore.* Syracuse, NY: Syracuse University Press.

Eaton, M. (2010). Manufacturing community in an online activist organization: The rhetoric of MoveOn.org's e-mails. *Information, Communication and Society* 13: 174–192.

Elder, G. H. (1974). *Children of the Great Depression: Social change in life experience.* Chicago: University of Chicago Press.

Ellis, B. (1991). The last thing said: The *Challenger* disaster jokes and closure. *International Folklore Review* 8: 110–124.

Ellis, B. (2001). *Aliens, ghosts, and cults: Legends we live.* Jackson: University Press of Mississippi.

Ellis, B. (2003). Making a Big Apple crumble: The role of humor in constructing a global response to disaster. In P. Narváez (Ed.), *Of corpse: Death and humor in folklore and popular culture* (pp. 35–79). Logan: Utah State University Press.

Erikson, K. T. (1976). *Everything in its path: Destruction of community in the Buffalo Creek flood.* New York: Simon & Schuster.

Feder, E. K. (2014). *Making sense of intersex: Changing ethical perspectives in biomedicine.* Bloomington: Indiana University Press.

Felson, J., Adamczyk, A., & Thomas, C. (2019). How and why have attitudes about cannabis legalization changed so much? *Social Science Research* 78: 12–27.

Fine, G. A. (1992). *Manufacturing tales: Sex and money in contemporary legends.* Knoxville: University of Tennessee Press.

Fine, G. A., Campion-Vincent, V., & Heath, C. (Eds.). (2005). *Rumor mills: The social impact of rumor and legend.* New Brunswick, NJ: AldineTransaction.

Fine, G. A., & Christoforides, L. (1991). Dirty birds, filthy immigrants, and the English sparrow war: Metaphorical linkage in constructing social problems. *Symbolic Interaction* 14: 375–393.

Fine, G. A., & Turner, P. A. (2001). *Whispers on the color line: Rumor and race in America.* Berkeley: University of California Press.

Fischer, D. H. (1989). *Albion's seed: Four British folkways in America.* New York: Oxford University Press.

Fishman, J. M. (2017). *Death makes the news: How the media censor and display the dead.* New York: New York University Press.

Freidson, E. (1986). *Professional powers: A study of the institutionalization of formal knowledge.* Chicago: University of Chicago Press.

Fujiwara, L. H. (2005). Immigrant rights are human rights: The reframing of immigrant entitlement and welfare. *Social Problems* 52: 79–101.

Fumento, M. (1990). *The myth of heterosexual AIDS.* New York: Basic Books.

Furedi, F. (2001). Bullying: The British contribution to the construction of a social problem. In J. Best (Ed.), *How claims spread: Cross-national diffusion of social problems* (pp. 89–106). Hawthorne, NY: Aldine de Gruyter.

Furedi, F. (2016). Moral panic and reading: Early elite anxieties about the media effect. *Cultural Sociology* 10: 523–537.

Gamson, W. A. (1992). *Talking politics.* New York: Cambridge University Press.

Gamson, W. A., & Modigliani, A. (1989). Media discourse and public opinion on nuclear power: A constructionist approach. *American Journal of Sociology* 95: 1–37.

Gardner, S. E. (2018, February). What we talk about when we talk about Confederate monuments. *Origins: Current Events in Historical Perspective* 11. Retrieved from http://origins.osu.edu/article/what-we-talk-about-when-we-talk-about-con federate-monuments.

Gauchat, G. (2012). Politicization of science in the public sphere: A study of public trust in the United States, 1974 to 2010. *American Sociological Review* 77: 167–187.

George, R. (2009). *The big necessity: The unmentionable world of human waste and why it matters.* New York: Picador.

Gersen, J. S. (2019, February 1). Assessing Betsy DeVos's proposed rules on Title IX and sexual assault. *New Yorker.* Retrieved from: https://www.newyorker.com /news/our-columnists/assessing-betsy-devos-proposed-rules-on-title-ix-and -sexual-assault.

Gitlin, T. (1983). *Inside prime time.* New York: Pantheon.

Globokar, J., & Erez, E. (2019). Conscience and convenience: American victim work in organizational context. *International Review of Victimology* 25: 341–357.

Goedeke, T. L. (2005). Devils, angels, or animals: The social construction of otters in conflict over management. In A. Herda-Rapp & T. L. Goedeke (Eds.), *Mad about wildlife: Looking at social conflict over wildlife* (pp. 25–50). Boston: Brill.

Goldstein, D. E. (2004). *Once upon a virus: AIDS legends and vernacular risk perception.* Logan: Utah State University Press.

Gonzales, R. G. (2016). *Lives in limbo: Undocumented and coming of age in America.* Oakland: University of California Press.

Gould, D. B. (2009). *Moving politics: Emotion and ACT-UP's fights against AIDS.* Chicago: University of Chicago Press.

Griffiths, H., & Best, J. (2016). Social problems clusters as contexts for claimsmaking: Implications for the study of off-campus housing. *Sociological Spectrum* 36: 75–92.

Gusfield, J. R. (1967). Moral passage: The symbolic process in public designations of deviance. *Social Problems* 15: 175–188.

Gusfield, J. R. (1981). *The culture of public problems: Drinking-driving and the symbolic order.* Chicago: University of Chicago Press.

Haines, H. H. (1984). Black radicalism and the funding of civil rights. *Social Problems* 32: 31–43.

Hamilton, J. T. (2004). *All the news that's fit to sell: How the market transforms information into news.* Princeton, NJ: Princeton University Press.

Harris, S. R. (2010). *What is constructionism? Navigating its use in sociology.* Boulder, CO: Lynne Reinner.

Hart-Brinson, P. (2018). *The gay marriage generation: How the LGBTQ movement transformed American culture.* New York: New York University Press.

Haynes, C., Merolla, J., & Ramakrishnan, S. K. (2016). *Framing immigrants: News coverage, public opinion, and policy.* New York: Russell Sage Foundation.

Headworth, S. (2019). Getting to know you: Welfare fraud investigation and the appropriation of social ties. *American Sociological Review* 84: 171–196.

Heath, C., Bell, C., & Sternberg, E. (2001). Emotional selection in memes: The case of urban legends. *Journal of Personality and Social Psychology* 81: 1028–1041.

Hedegaard, H., Miniño, A. M., & Warner, M. (2018). Drug overdose deaths in the United States, 1999–2017. NCHS Data Brief 329. Retrieved from https://www.cdc.gov/nchs/data/databriefs/db329-h.pdf.

Herd, P., & Moynihan, D. P. (2018). *Administrative burden: Policymaking by other means.* New York: Russell Sage Foundation.

Herrman, J. (2019, March 2). Momo is as real as we've made her. *New York Times.* Retrieved from http://www.nytimes.com.

Hilgartner, S., & Bosk, C. L. (1988). The rise and fall of social problems. *American Journal of Sociology* 94: 53–78.

Holstein, J. A., & Gubrium, J. F. (Eds.). (2008). *Handbook of constructionist research.* New York: Guilford.

Holstein, J. A., & Miller, G. (2003). Social constructionism and social problems work. In J. A. Holstein & G. Miller (Eds.), *Challenges and choices: Constructionist perspectives on social problems* (pp. 70–91). Hawthorne, NY: Aldine de Gruyter.

Hoppe, T. (2018). *Punishing disease: HIV and the criminalization of sickness.* Oakland: University of California Press.

Irvine, J. M. (2002). *Talk about sex: The battles over sex education in the United States.* Berkeley: University of California Press.

Jaeger, A. B. (2018). Forging hegemony: How recycling became a popular but inadequate response to accumulating waste. *Social Problems* 65: 395–415.

Jenkins, P. (1998). *Moral panic: Changing concepts of the child molester in modern America.* New Haven, CT: Yale University Press.

Jenkins, P. (1999). *Synthetic panics: The symbolic politics of designer drugs.* New York: New York University Press.

Jenkins, P. (2000). *Mystics and messiahs: Cults and new religions in American history.* New York: Oxford University Press.

Jenkins, P. (2001). *Hidden gospels: How the search for Jesus lost its way.* New York: Oxford University Press.

Jenkins, P. (2006). *Decade of nightmares: The end of the sixties and the making of eighties America.* New York: Oxford University Press.

Jenness, V. (1993). *Making it work: The prostitutes' rights movement in perspective.* Hawthorne, NY: Aldine de Gruyter.

Jenness, V., & Grattet, R. (2001). *Making hate a crime: From social movement to law enforcement.* New York: Russell Sage Foundation.

Jenness, V., & Grattet, R. (2005). The law-in-between: The effects of organizational perviousness on the policing of hate crime. *Social Problems* 52: 227–259.

Jerolmack, C., & Walker, E. T. (2018). Please in my backyard: Quiet mobilization in support of fracking in an Appalachian community. *American Journal of Sociology* 124: 479–516.

Johnson, J. M. (1995). Horror stories and the construction of child abuse. In J. Best (Ed.), *Images of issues: Typifying contemporary social problems* (2nd ed., pp. 17–31). Hawthorne, NY: Aldine de Gruyter.

Johnson, K. C., & Taylor, S., Jr. (2017). *The campus rape frenzy: The attack on due process at America's universities*. New York: Encounter.

Johnson, T. P. (2018). Legitimacy, wicked problems, and public opinion research. *Public Opinion Quarterly* 82: 614–621.

Kavanaugh, P. R., & Biggers, Z. (2019). Competing constructions of bath salt use and risk of harm in two mediated contexts. *Crime, Media, Culture* 15: 217–237.

Kettrey, H. H. (2018). Activism without activists: News media coverage of youth as illegitimate political agents in the virginity-pledge movement and gay-straight alliances. *Mobilization* 23: 349–364.

Kiel, D. C., & Nownes, A. J. (1994). Political language, causal stories, and pesticide regulation. *American Review of Politics* 15: 491–506.

Kingdon, J. W. (1984). *Agendas, alternatives, and public policies*. New York: Harper Collins.

Kipnis, L. (2017). *Unwanted advances: Sexual paranoia comes to campus*. New York: HarperCollins.

Kirk, S. A., & Kutchins, H. (1992). *The selling of DSM: The rhetoric of science in psychiatry*. Hawthorne, NY: Aldine de Gruyter.

Kohler-Hausmann, I. (2018). *Misdemeanorland: Criminal courts and social control in an age of broken windows policing*. Princeton, NJ: Princeton University Press.

Kohm, S. A. (2020). Claims-making, child saving, and the news media. *Crime, Media, Culture* 16: in press.

Kollmeyer, C. J. (2004). Corporate interests: How the news media portray the economy. *Social Problems* 51: 432–452.

Kowal-Bourgonjon, E., & Jacobs, G. (2019). Does addiction belong in modernity? Discursive strategies of exclusion in Polish public awareness campaigns. *Discourse, Context and Media* 28: 27–34.

Krcatovich, E. M-S., & Reese, L. A. (2018). Everyone loves a dog story: Narratives of urban animal welfare policy. *Social Problems* 65: 416–437.

Kroll-Smith, S. (2018). *Recovering inequality: Hurricane Katrina, the San Francisco earthquake of 1906, and the aftermath of disaster*. Austin, TX: University of Texas Press.

Kubal, T. (2008). *Cultural movements and collective memory: Christopher Columbus and the rewriting of the national origin myth.* New York: Palgrave Macmillan.

Kurti, L. (1988). The politics of joking: Popular response to Chernobyl. *Journal of American Folklore* 101: 324–334.

Lafer, G. (2002). *The job training charade.* Ithaca, NY: Cornell University Press.

Langlois, J. (1983). The Belle Isle Bridge incident: Legend, dialectic and semiotic system in the 1943 Detroit race riots. *Journal of American Folklore* 96: 183–196.

Lee, E. (2003). *Abortion, motherhood, and mental health: Medicalizing reproduction in the United States and Great Britain.* Hawthorne, NY: Aldine de Gruyter.

Leon-Guerrero, A. (2019). *Social Problems: Community, policy, and social action* (6th ed.). Thousand Oaks, CA: Sage.

Letukas, L. (2014). *Primetime pundits: How cable news covers social issues.* Lanham, MD: Lexington.

Link, M. W., Battaglia, M. P., Frankel, M. R., Osborn, L., & Mokdad, A. H. (2007). Reaching the U.S. cell phone generation: Comparison of cell phone survey results with an ongoing landline telephone survey. *Public Opinion Quarterly* 71: 814–839.

Lipsky, M. (1980). *Street-level bureaucracy: Dilemmas of the individual in public services.* New York: Russell Sage Foundation.

Lipsky, M., & Smith, S. R. (1989). When social problems are treated as emergencies. *Social Service Review* 63: 5–25.

Lofland, J. (2003). *Demolishing a historic hotel: A sociology of preservation failure in Davis, California.* Davis, CA: Davis Research.

Lorenz, T. (2019, February 28). Momo is not trying to kill children. *Atlantic.* Retrieved from https://www.theatlantic.com/technology/archive/2019/02/momo-challenge-hoax/583825/.

Loseke, D. R. (2003). *Thinking about social problems* (2nd ed.). Hawthorne, NY: Aldine de Gruyter.

MacCoun, R. J., & Reuter, P. (2001). *Drug war heresies: Learning from other vices, times, and places.* New York: Cambridge University Press.

MacKendrick, N. (2018). *Better safe than sorry: How consumers navigate exposure to everyday toxics.* Oakland: University of California Press.

Madianou, M. (2013). Humanitarian campaigns in social media. *Journalism Studies* 14: 249–266.

Malloy, T. F. (2010). The social construction of regulation: Lessons from the war against command and control. *Buffalo Law Review* 58: 267–354.

Maratea, R. J. (2014). *The politics of the Internet: Political claimsmaking in cyberspace and its effect on modern political activism.* Lanham, MD: Lexington.

Maratea, R. J., & Monahan, B. (2016). *Social problems in popular culture.* Bristol, UK: Policy Press.

Masci, D., Brown, A., & Kiley, J. (2019, June 24). Five facts about same-sex marriage. *Fact Tank*, Pew Research Center. Retrieved from https://www.pewresearch.org/fact-tank/2017/06/26/same-sex-marriage/.

Massey, D., Durand, J., & Pren, K. A. (2016). Why border enforcement backfired. *American Journal of Sociology* 121: 1557–1600.

Maurer, D. (2002). *Vegetarianism: Movement or moment?* Philadelphia: Temple University Press.

Mazur, A. (2018). Birth and death (?) of the anti-fracking movement: Inferences from quantity of coverage theory. *Society* 55: 531–539.

McAdam, D. (1983). Tactical innovation and the pace of insurgency. *American Sociological Review* 48: 735–754.

McAdam, D. (1994). Culture and social movements. In E. Laraña, H. Johnston, & J. R. Gusfield (Eds.), *New social movements: From identity to ideology* (pp. 36–57). Philadelphia: Temple University Press.

McAdam, D. (2015). Be careful what you wish for: The ironic connection between the civil rights struggle and today's divided America. *Sociological Forum* 30: 485–508.

McAdam, D., & Rucht, D. (1993). The cross-national diffusion of movement ideas. *Annals of the American Academy of Political and Social Science* 528: 56–74.

McAlinden, A-M. (2018). *Children as "risk."* New York: Cambridge University Press.

McCarthy, J. (2017, May 18). Americans split over new LGBT protections, restroom policies. Gallup. Retrieved from https://news.gallup.com/poll/210887/americans-split-new-lgbt-protections-restroom-policies.aspx.

McCarthy, J. (2018, May 23). Two in three Americans support same-sex marriage. Gallup. Retrieved from https://news.gallup.com/poll/234866/two-three-americans-support-sex-marriage.aspx.

McCarthy, J. D., & Zald, M. N. (1977). Resource mobilization and social movements. *American Journal of Sociology* 82: 1212–1241.

McCombs, M. (2004). *Setting the agenda: The mass media and public opinion.* Cambridge, UK: Polity.

McCright, A. M., & Dunlap, R. E. (2011). The politicization of climate change and polarization in the American public's views of global warming, 2001–2010. *Sociological Quarterly* 52: 155–194.

McGreal, C. (2018). *American overdose: The opioid tragedy in three acts.* New York: PublicAffairs.

Meyer, D. S., & Rohlinger, D. A. (2012). Big books and social movements: A myth of ideas and social change. *Social Problems* 59: 136–153.

Milkman, R. (2017). A new political generation: Millennials and the post-2008 wave of protest. *American Sociological Review* 82: 1–31.

Miller, G., & Holstein, J. A. (Eds.). (1997). *Social problems in everyday life: Studies of social problems work.* Greenwich, CT: JAI Press.

Mills, C. W. (1959). *The sociological imagination.* New York: Oxford University Press.

Moloney, C., & Unnithan, N. P. (2019). Reacting to invasive species: The construction of a moral panic over Burmese pythons. *Sociological Inquiry* 89: 351–372.

Morris, E. (2007). From horse power to horsepower. *Access* 30: 2–9.

Morris, P. (2012). *Blue juice: Euthanasia in veterinary medicine.* Philadelphia: Temple University Press.

Müller, T. (2019). Cannabis, moral entrepreneurship, and stigma: Conflicting narratives on the 26 May 2016 Toronto police raid on cannabis shops. *Qualitative Sociology Review* 15: 148–171.

Murray, C. A. (1994). *Losing ground: American social policy, 1950–1980.* New York: Basic Books.

National Highway Traffic Safety Administration (2018). *2017 fatal motor vehicle crashes: Overview.* Traffic Safety Facts Research Note (DOT HS 812 603). Retrieved from https://crashstats.nhtsa.dot.gov/Api/Public/ViewPublication/812603.

Nelson, B. J. (1984). *Making an issue of child abuse: Political agenda setting for social problems.* Chicago: University of Chicago Press.

Nichols, L. T. (1997). Social problems as landmark narratives: Bank of Boston, mass media and "money laundering." *Social Problems* 44: 324–341.

Nichols, L. T. (2003). Voices of social problems: A dialogical constructionist model. *Studies in Symbolic Interaction* 26: 93–123.

Nichols, L. T., Nolan, J. J., III, & Colyer, C. J. (2008). Scorekeeping versus storytelling: Representational practices in the construction of "hate crime." *Studies in Symbolic Interaction* 30: 361–379.

Oring, E. (1987). Jokes and the discourse on disaster. *Journal of American Folklore* 100: 278–286.

Palmer, R. (2018). *Becoming the news: How ordinary people respond to the media spotlight.* New York: Columbia University Press.

Parsons, N. L. (2014). *Meth mania: A history of methamphetamine.* Boulder, CO: Lynne Rienner.

Pawluch, D. (1996). *The new pediatrics: A profession in transition.* Hawthorne, NY: Aldine de Gruyter.

Pawson, M., & Grov, C. (2018). "It's just an excuse to slut around": Gay and bisexual men's constructions of HIV pre-exposure prophylaxis (PrEP) as a social problem. *Sociology of Health and Illness* 40: 1391–1403.

Pearson, G. (1983). *Hooligan: A history of respectable fears.* London: Macmillan.

Pettinicchio, D. (2019). *Politics of empowerment: Disability rights and the cycle of American policy reform.* Stanford, CA: Stanford University Press.

Pfohl, S. J. (1977). The "discovery" of child abuse. *Social Problems* 24: 310–323.

Pielke, R. A., Jr. (2007). *The honest broker: Making sense of science in policy and politics*. New York: Cambridge University Press.

Pinker, S. (2018). *Enlightenment now: The case for reason, science, humanism, and progress*. New York: Viking.

Presser, L. (2018). *Inside story: How narratives drive mass harm*. Oakland: University of California Press.

Radford, B. (2016). *Bad clowns*. Albuquerque, NM: University of New Mexico Press.

Ravitch, D. (2003). *The language police: How pressure groups restrict what students learn*. New York: Vintage.

Reich, J. A. (2016). *Calling the shots: Why parents reject vaccines*. New York: New York University Press.

Reinarman, C. (1994). The social construction of drug scares. In P. A. Adler & P. Adler (Eds.), *Constructions of deviance* (pp. 92–104). Belmont, CA: Wadsworth.

Reinarman, C., & Levine, H. G. (1995). The crack attack: America's latest drug scare, 1986–1992. In J. Best (Ed.), *Images of issues: Typifying contemporary social problems* (2nd ed., pp. 147–186). Hawthorne, NY: Aldine de Gruyter.

Revier, K. (2017). "Once again, a meth lab exploded and somebody died": Narratives of volatility and risk in the rural drug war. *Crime, Media, Culture* 14: 467–484.

Reynolds-Stenson, H., & Earl, J. (2018). Clashes of conscience: Explaining counterdemonstrations at protests. *Mobilization* 23: 263–284.

Rosenberg, I. B. (2009). Height discrimination in employment. *Utah Law Review* 2009: 907–953.

Rossi, P. H., Lipsey, M. W., & Freeman, H. E. (2004). *Evaluation: A systematic approach* (7th ed.). Thousand Oaks, CA: Sage.

Rudy, D. R. (1986). *Becoming alcoholic: Alcoholics Anonymous and the reality of alcoholism*. Carbondale: Southern Illinois University Press.

Russell, D., Spence, N. J., & Thames, K. M. (2019). "It's so scary how common this is now": Frames in media coverage of the opioid epidemic by Ohio newspapers and themes in Facebook user reactions. *Information, Communication & Society* 22: 702–708.

Saguy, A. C. (2003). *What is sexual harassment? From Capitol Hill to the Sorbonne*. Berkeley: University of California Press.

Saguy, A. C. (2013). *What's wrong with fat?* New York: Oxford University Press.

Saguy, A. C., & Williams, J. A. (2019). Reimagining gender: Gender neutrality in the news. *Signs* 44: 465–489.

Saletan, W. (2003). *Bearing right: How the conservatives won the abortion war*. Berkeley: University of California Press.

Sanders, J., & Stryker, S. (2016). Stalled: Gender-neutral public bathrooms. *South Atlantic Quarterly* 115: 779–788.

Sasson, T. (1995a). African American conspiracy theories and the social construction of crime. *Sociological Inquiry* 65: 265–285.

Sasson, T. (1995b). *Crime talk: How citizens construct a social problem.* Hawthorne, NY: Aldine de Gruyter.

Schneider, A. L., & Ingram, H. M. (1993). Social constructions of target populations: Implications for politics and policy. *American Political Science Review* 87: 334–347.

Schneider, A. L., & Ingram, H. M. (Eds.). (2005). *Deserving and entitled: Social constructions and public policy.* Albany: State University of New York Press.

Schudson, M. (1981). *Discovering the news: A social history of American newspapers.* New York: Basic Books.

Schudson, M. (2011). *The sociology of news* (2nd ed.). New York: W. W. Norton.

Schwartz, H. (2011). *Making noise: From Babel to the Big Bang and beyond.* Cambridge: MIT Press.

Seeley, J. L. (2019). "A give grief kind of guy": Help-seeking, status, and the experience of helpers at a university IT help desk. *Symbolic Interaction* 42: 127–150.

Shibutani, T. (1966). *Improvised news: A sociological study of rumor.* Indianapolis, IN: Bobbs-Merrill.

Shih, K. J-K. (2019). A comparison of the US newspaper coverage of US Uncut and Occupy. *Sociological Quarterly* 60: 94–115.

Silver, I. (2006). *Unequal partnerships: Beyond the rhetoric of philanthropic collaboration.* New York: Routledge.

Silver, I., & Boyle, M-E. (2010). Constructing problems by promoting solutions: Corporate advertisements about US poverty. *Journal of Poverty* 14: 347–367.

Silverman, C., & Alexander, L. (2016, November 3). How teens in the Balkans are duping Trump supporters with fake news. *BuzzFeed News.* Retrieved from https://www.buzzfeednews.com/article/craigsilverman/how-macedonia -became-a-global-hub-for-pro-trump-misinfo.

Slater, T. (2018). The invention of the "sink estate": Consequential categorisation and the UK housing crisis. *Sociological Review Monographs* 66: 877–897.

Sloan, J. J., III, & Fisher, B. (2011). *The dark side of the ivory tower: Campus crime as a social problem.* New York: Cambridge University Press.

Snow, D., & Benford, R. (1988). Ideology, frame resonance, and participant mobilization. *International Social Movement Research* 1: 197–217.

Snow, D., & Benford, R. (1992). Master frames and cycles of protest. In A. D. Morris & C. M. Mueller (Eds.), *Frontiers in social movement theory* (pp. 133–155). New Haven, CT: Yale University Press.

Snow, D. A., Rochford, E. B., Jr., Worden, S. K., & Benford, R. D. (1986). Frame alignment processes, micromobilization, and movement participation. *American Sociological Review* 51: 464–481.

Sobieraj, S. (2011). *Soundbitten: The perils of media-centered political activism*. New York: New York University Press.

Soltero, G. (2016). The Mexican transmission of "Lights Out!" *Journal of Folklore Research* 53: 115–135.

Soyer, M., & Ziyanak, S. (2018). The battle over fracking: The mobilization of local residents. *The Qualitative Report* 23: 2222–2237.

Spector, M., & Kitsuse, J. I. (1977). *Constructing social problems*. Menlo Park, CA: Cummings.

Staller, K. M. (2006). *Runaways: How the sixties counterculture shaped today's policies and practices*. New York: Columbia University Press.

Starr, P. (1982). *The social transformation of American medicine*. New York: Basic Books.

Stein, A. (2018). *Unbound: Transgender men and the remaking of identity*. New York: Pantheon.

Stephens-Davidowitz, S. (2017). *Everybody lies: Big data, new data, and what the Internet can tell us about who we really are*. New York: Dey Street.

Stone, A. L. (2019). Frame variation in child protectionist claims: Constructions of gay men and transgender women as strangers. *Social Forces* 97: 1155–1176.

Stone, D. A. (1989). Causal stories and the formation of policy agendas. *Political Science Quarterly* 104: 281–300.

Strang, D., & Meyer, J. W. (1993). Institutional conditions for diffusion. *Theory and Society* 22: 487–511.

Suarez, E., & Gadalla, T. M. (2010). Stop blaming the victim: A meta-analysis on rape myths. *Journal of Interpersonal Violence* 25: 2010–2035.

Taylor, V. (1989). Social movement continuity: The women's movement in abeyance. *American Sociological Review* 54: 761–775.

Toulmin, S. E. (1958). *The uses of argument*. Cambridge, UK: Cambridge University Press.

Tuchman, G. (1978). *Making news: A study in the construction of reality*. New York: Free Press.

Tufekci, Z. (2017). *Twitter and tear gas: The power and fragility of networked protest*. New Haven, CT: Yale University Press.

Turow, J. (1997). *Breaking up America: Advertisers and the new media world*. Chicago: University of Chicago Press.

Tyson, N. deGrasse. (2009). *The Pluto files: The rise and fall of America's favorite planet*. New York: W. W. Norton.

U.S. Census Bureau. (1975). *Historical statistics of the United States: Colonial times to 1970*. Washington, DC: U.S. Government Printing Office.

Useem, B., & Zald, M. N. (1982). From pressure groups to social movement: Organizational dilemmas of the effort to promote nuclear power. *Social Problems* 30: 144–156.

Vardi, I. (2014). Quantifying accidents: Cars, statistics, and unintended consequences in the construction of social problems over time. *Qualitative Sociology* 37: 345–367.

Vasterman, P. (Ed.). (2018). *From media hype to Twitter storm: News explosions and their impact on issues, crises, and public opinion.* Amsterdam: Amsterdam University Press.

Vosoughi, S., Roy, D., & Aral, S. (2018). The spread of true and false news online. *Science* 359: 1146–1151.

Wagner-Pacifici, R., & Schwartz, B. (1991). The Vietnam Veterans Memorial: Commemorating a difficult past. *American Journal of Sociology* 97: 376–420.

Walker, J. (2014). *The United States of paranoia: A conspiracy theory.* New York: HarperCollins.

Warshaw, R. (1988). *I never called it rape: The Ms. Report of recognizing, fighting, and surviving date and acquaintance rape.* New York: HarperCollins.

Watts, D. J. (2011). *Everything is obvious: Once you know the answer.* New York: Crown Business.

Weinberg, D. (2014). *Contemporary social constructionism: Key themes.* Philadelphia: Temple University Press.

Weinberg, I. (1971). Social problems that are no more. In E. O. Smigel (Ed.), *Handbook on the study of social problems* (pp. 637–672). Chicago: Rand McNally.

Weisner, C., & Room, R. (1984). Financing and ideology in alcohol treatment. *Social Problems* 32: 167–184.

Welch, M. (2000). *Flag burning: Moral panic and the criminalization of protest.* Hawthorne, NY: Aldine de Gruyter.

White, L. (2000). *Speaking of vampires: Rumor and history in colonial Africa.* Berkeley: University of California Press.

Whittier, N. (2009). *The politics of child sexual abuse: Emotions, social movements, and the state.* New York: Oxford University Press.

Wilcox, M. M. (2014). Lgbttsqqiaa . . . *Contexts* 13(1): 12–14.

Wolfson, M. (2001). *The fight against big tobacco: The movement, the state, and the public's health.* Hawthorne, NY: Aldine de Gruyter.

Wong, W. W. Y. (2017). Speculative authorship in the city of fakes. *Current Anthropology* 58: S103–112.

Wylie, S. A. (2018). *Fractivism: Corporate bodies and chemical bonds.* Durham, NC: Duke University Press.

Xu, J. (2018). Legitimization imperative: The production of crime statistics in Guangzhou, China. *British Journal of Criminology* 58: 155–176.

Zegart, A. B. (2004). Blue ribbons, black boxes: Toward a better understanding of presidential commissions. *Presidential Studies Quarterly* 34: 366–393.

Index

Note: Page numbers in *italics* refer to illustrations and examples.

A

AA (Alcoholics Anonymous), 106–7, 245, 256
ABC, 143
abeyance, 88–89
abortion issue
    framing, 85
    movements and countermovements and, 70
    policymaking on, 217
    as position issue, 42
    public opinion polls on attitudes toward, 173–74
    Roe v. Wade, 206
    segmented audience and, 43–44
    use of focus groups on, 181
    warrants of claims regarding access to, 37–38
acoustical attacks, 112
activists as claimsmakers, 20, 67–100
    alliances with experts, 126
    careers as, 82
    case study of, *97–100*

    framing and, 70–77, *78*, 95, *95*, 96
    cultural resources and, 76–77
    diagnostic frames, 71
    disputes within a movement over, 76–77
    feedback and reframing, 75, 76–77
    frame alignment, 73–76
    integrity issues in, 77
    master frame, 85
    motivational frames, 71
    names in classification and, *74*
    prognostic frames, 71
insider claimsmakers, *68*, 68–69, *see also* experts as claimsmakers
opportunity structures and, 83–89
    cultural opportunities, 83–85
    political opportunities, 85–89
outcomes, 286–87
outsider claimsmakers, 67–68, *68*
ownership of a social problem, *see* ownership of a social problem

377

target populations, 225

technological change, decline in social
        problem due to, *294*

teen activists, *84*

television
    changes in news programs, 143–45
    effect of violence, 161–62
    see also media and media coverage

Temporary Assistance for Needy Families
        (TANF), *249*

terminology of constructionist approach,
        15–17

terrorism, *see* September 11, 2001
        terrorist attacks

Texas, *261*

textbook content, 45

theorization, 319

think tanks, 121, *122*, 207

time as basis for comparative research,
        310

Title IX, sexual assault complaints and,
        269

tobacco smoking, 118, *234*, 319

topical joke cycles, 195–96

toxic exposure, mothers managing
        children's, *265*

traffic fatalities, *230*, 234

transformation, frame, 75, 76

transgender
    gender categorization and, 12
    use of term, *147*

transgender bathrooms, *63–66*

transgender rights movement, 65–66

transmitters, *315*, 317, *318–19*

treatment for alcoholism, 106–7

"trending" topics on Internet, 184

troubling conditions, 277, 341
    as basis for comparative research,
        310
    definition of, 16
    persistence of, 273

Trudeau, Justin, *52*

Trump, Donald
    acoustical attacks in Cuba and
        election of, 112
    "fake news" and, 166, 167
    wall between Mexico and United
        States, 305

Trump administration, rules for handling
        campus sexual assault
        complaints, 270–71

twelve-step programs, 107, 245, 256

Twenty-First Amendment, 273

Twitter, 158, 159, *160*, 183

two-spirits, 12

2020 census, *175*

typifying examples, 32, 137–38

U

UFO abductions
    as social construction, 13–14
    as troubling condition, 16

underdogs, stories about, *48*

undocumented immigrants, 223

United States
    sexual harassment in, 312–13
    workplace bullying in, 320

urban legends, *see* contemporary
        legends

urban manure problem, solving, *294*

US Uncut, *80*

V

vaccinations, *72*, 230–31

valence issues, 42, 138, 208

values
    ideological critiques and, 299
    policymaking and, 116
    warrants and, 37

variants of contemporary legends, 188

vegetarianism, 44, 75

veterinarians, euthanasia and, *255*